General Alexandre Dumas

John G. Gallaher

GENERAL ALEXANDRE DUMAS
Soldier of the French Revolution

Southern Illinois University Press
Carbondale and Edwardsville

Library of Congress Cataloging-in-Publication Data
Gallaher, John G.
General Alexandre Dumas : soldier of the French Revolution / John
G. Gallaher
p.   cm.
Includes bibliographical references and index.
1. Dumas, Thomas Alexandre, 1762–1806. 2. Generals—France—
Biography. 3. France. Armée—Biography. 4. France—History,
Military—1789–1815. 5. Dumas family. I. Title.
DC146.D83G35   1997
944.04'092—dc20
[B]   96-25583
ISBN 0-8093-2098-3 (cloth : alk. paper)   CIP

The paper used in this publication meets the minimum requirements of American
National Standard for Information Sciences—Permanence of Paper for Printed Library
Materials, ANSI Z39.48-1984. ∞

Contents

MAPS

PREFACE

Thomas-Alexandre Davy de la Pailleterie, who took the last name of his black slave mother, Marie Dumas, rose from the rank of private in the army of Louis XVI to general of division during the French Revolution. His father was Alexandre-Antoine Davy, a lesser French nobleman who spent more than twenty-five years in Saint Domingue. An illegitimate mulatto, born in a French colony (1762), Thomas-Alexandre's future was not promising. But when the French Revolution opened all ranks in the army to all men, Alexandre Dumas rose rapidly. He commanded the Army of the Alps in 1794 and served under General Bonaparte in Italy (1796–1797) and Egypt (1798–1799). His bad relationship with Bonaparte brought an early end to his military career, and two years in an Italian prison destroyed his health and brought an early end to his life (1806).

General Dumas is best known for having fathered the author of *The Three Musketeers* and *The Count of Monte Cristo*. However, his life provides an excellent study of the revolutionary principles of liberty and equality as they applied to a "man of color" who had neither a powerful family to support him nor political or social connections. His life also provides a look into the relationship between the army and the government in Paris during the Reign of Terror. Finally, his relationship with Napoleon Bonaparte provides a very interesting window to view a side of the Emperor of the French that is not always manifested in studies of Napoleon.

My interest in General Dumas came by way of my studies of foreign soldiers in the armies of the French Revolution and the empire. Among the documents at the Château de Vincennes (Service Historique de l'Etat-Major de Armée) dealing with the Légion franche des Américains (X^k 9), an all black corps, I found Alexandre Dumas. The printed information of General Dumas comes primarily from the first volume of his son's *Mémoires*. However, Alexandre Dumas (*père*) idolized his father, hated Napoleon, and made little effort to hide his feelings. As a result, he is selective as to what he includes and excludes with respect to the life of his father. Nevertheless, one must begin any study of the general with the son's *Mémoires*. But Dumas (*père*) must be carefully checked against the archival material whenever that is possible. Other biographers have relied heavily on Dumas (*père*). I have relied primarily on the archival correspondence, reports, and other documents to provide what I hope is a more objective and balanced study of this unusual man.

In writing this book, I made extensive use of the War Archives at Vincennes, and I wish to thank its staff for their help and cooperation. At the Dumas Museum in Villers-Cotterêts, Monsieur René and Madame Josette Doyelle were most gracious and helpful, and I extend to them my deepest gratitude. At Southern Illinois University at Edwardsville, the Graduate School provided financial support for me to work in French archives, and the School of Social Science helped by providing the time. For this support I am thankful, as without it my task would have been much more difficult. I wish further to express my gratitude to Diane Clements who produced the excellent maps for this study. I would also like to thank Carol Burns and Julie Bush for carefully reading and correcting my manuscript; however, I alone am responsible for any mistakes or errors. Finally, I would like to express my gratitude to my wife, Maia, for her patience and understanding during the years I have worked on this book.

GENERAL ALEXANDRE DUMAS

1

THE EARLY YEARS

Alexandre Dumas, born Thomas-Alexandre Davy de la Pailleterie, was the son of a lesser French nobleman and an African slave. Being half black and half white, he fell into something of a middle category of French society. Because he was half black, the white population, whether aristocratic or common, clearly considered themselves to be superior by virtue of color. By the same token, the fact that he was half white gave him a position in society clearly above the free blacks and slaves. This was particularly true on the island of Saint Domingue, where he was born and lived his early years, but it was also true, although to a lesser extent, in France during his teen years and early twenties. Had Dumas's mother been white, his life and career would surely have been quite different. He would have inherited his father's title and noble status, and if he had chosen to enter the army, it would have been with a commission. How such a young nobleman would have fared during the French Revolution would be pure speculation. However, being a mulatto, and an illegitimate child with a very dubious and uncertain future, he chose to enter the army as a private using his mother's name.

Racial issues during the revolutionary period in France have been studied in general—constitutionally, socially, ethnically, and so on—but the life of Alexandre Dumas provides an excellent opportunity to view the issues of race relations during this period in an individual case study. Being half black—a "man of color"—was a hindrance before the Revolution but a benefit at a crucial point of his career in the middle of the Revolution (1793), and his color had a neutral effect or no effect at all on his later years. In particular, his rapid promotion to lieutenant colonel was because he was black, but his promotion to general of division had nothing to do with color; rather, it was because he was a republican.

Dumas's military career spanned the decade of the French Revolution and provides great insight into the relationship between the army and the government of France during the most turbulent years of the Revolution. He was a sincere republican, but neither a radical nor a Jacobin. He was a successful army commander in 1794 and proved himself a good organizer in Italy (1797) and Egypt (1798). Few could equal him at the head of cavalry troops. He was brave to a fault and quick to anger, and his strength became legendary. His

1

military career was exemplary. However, he was unable and unwilling to maintain a good relationship with Napoleon Bonaparte, and this, coupled with poor health, brought about an early end to his military career.

Over the past two centuries, General Dumas has been rather vaguely known to French military historians who studied the armies of the French Revolution and the Napoleonic period, and in literary circles, he is known as the father of Alexandre Dumas (*père*), author of *The Three Musketeers* and *The Count of Monte Cristo*. One might also add that he was the grandfather of the dramatist and novelist Alexandre Dumas (*fils*). Yet, in his own right, he has generally been ignored. Nevertheless, a close study of the life and times of General Dumas yields important information.

Indeed, his military career is a textbook example of the rise of a private in the army of Louis XVI to the rank of general of division in the revolutionary army. Dumas is proof, if any is really needed, that the Revolution opened the ranks of the officer corps to men of talent, ability, merit, and ambition, rather than of simply class, as was the case under the Old Regime. To be sure, Dumas may not have been a brilliant strategist or tactician, as was Napoleon Bonaparte, but he was capable, intelligent, energetic, and ambitious. Had it not been for the Revolution, he probably would have ended his military career a sergeant rather than a general. But the Revolution provided the opportunity for him to march into the annals of history.

Dumas's command of the Army of the Alps (1794) provides an in-depth look into the relationship between the military and the revolutionary government, both locally and in Paris. The heavy hand of the Committee of Public Safety was felt in every aspect of military operations, and the shadow of the guillotine was always before Dumas as he walked that fine line between the authority of the central government, the local Jacobins, and the commander of a French army in the field.

The relationship between Dumas and Napoleon not only provides a deeper understanding of Dumas but also gives a unique insight into the personality of the future emperor of the French. What is curious are the offenses, injuries, injustices, and slights that Napoleon was able to overlook, forgive, or at least put aside at the time, and those that were "unforgivable." Mistakes on the battlefield, harsh words spoken in time of stress or anger, misunderstandings, even the failure to carry out orders could be overlooked and forgiven. But the failure to attach oneself to Napoleon and his rising career was neither acceptable nor forgivable. In Dumas's case, it was his "desertion" of General Bonaparte—that is, his leaving Egypt early in 1799 when the general wanted him to remain with the army—that was unpardonable, and Napoleon even continued to punish his wife and children after his death. Dumas's life was both a triumph and a tragedy. The illegitimate son of a slave, he rose to the highest rank in the French army, only to die in semi-disgrace at an early age.

The town of Jérémie is located in the extreme western part of the peninsula that forms the Southern Province of Haiti. In the mid-eighteenth century, this French colony known as Saint Domingue comprised the western two-fifths of the island while Spain struggled to control the remaining three-fifths. The long peninsula on which the town was situated was mountainous, making overland communication with Les Cayes, the provincial capital on the southern coast, and Port-au-Prince to the east extremely difficult except by sea. The semi-isolation of the parish of Jérémie made it one of the most rural and backward regions of a rural and backward colony. Just outside this small remote town, more than three thousand miles from France, Thomas-Alexandre Davy, to be known to history as Alexandre Dumas, was born on March 25, 1762.

Saint Domingue became the most valuable French colonial possession following the loss of Canada and the Louisiana Territory at the end of the Seven Years' War (1756–1763). Sugar was rapidly becoming the principal money crop, replacing coffee and indigo. As growing sugar was very labor-intensive, the demand for black slaves increased, which in turn stimulated the African slave trade in the fifty years preceding the French Revolution. However, the mountainous terrain of the long, narrow peninsula of the Southern Province made the region about Jérémie poorly suited for sugar. Coffee remained the number one cash crop and slaves the source of labor.

The parish of Jérémie had a population of only four hundred whites but more than two thousand black slaves. Dumas's father, Alexandre-Antoine Davy, the Marquis de la Pailleterie, was one of the whites while his mother, Marie-Cessette Dumas, was one of the slaves. Virtually nothing is known of Marie Dumas, but there is a great deal of information on Alexandre-Antoine and the Davy family.

The earliest record of the family dates back to the first part of the fifteenth century when one Isembart Davy purchased a parcel of land at Bielleville, in Normandy.[1] During the course of the fifteenth century, the Davys acquired additional lands and questionable noble status. The family bought the fief of Renneville, also in Normandy, and assumed the life-style of the nobility without a patent or acknowledgment from the king. They maintained that life-style for a prolonged period of time, and after three or more generations, according to local custom, they were accepted in the Second Estate (the nobility) of Normandy. It was not unusual to achieve noble status in this manner during the last half of the Hundred Years' War and the decades of confusion and weak monarchy that followed. The Davy family thus became a part of that social class referred to as the *noblesse d'agrégation*, that is to say, those who had neither a royal letter of ennoblement nor a royal position that was accompanied by ennoblement. Thus, there remained a gray cloud hovering over the noble origins of the family.

The sixteenth century saw the consolidation of the Davy family in Normand noble society. Good management, the acquisition of land and title, and advantageous marriages all enhanced the family's status. In this century, Pierre Davy inherited the Pailleterie estate and added the title to his name, thus becoming Davy de la Pailleterie. The family continued to improve its social and economic status in the first three-quarters of the seventeenth century. Charles Davy de la Pailleterie married Marthe de Bréville of an influential family well above his own position. One of their children, Charles, inherited an estate in Champagne from his maternal grandfather. This cadet branch of the Davy family gave rise to the mistaken belief that the ancestors of the author Alexandre Dumas (*père*) came from Champagne rather than Normandy.

Whether from generally difficult times in Normandy in the last quarter of the seventeenth century or simply from poor management, the value of the estates owned by Charles's older brother, François, declined by 50 percent during his lifetime. François married Jeanne-Françoise-Paultre (or Pautre) de Dominon, of good Orleans nobility but of little more wealth than his own. From this union were born three sons. Alexandre-Antoine, the oldest, born February 26, 1714, was the father of General Dumas. He inherited the family title and land but with an income that placed him in the ranks of the lesser nobility. His two younger brothers were Charles-Anne-Edouard, born in 1716, and Louis-François-Thérèse, born in 1718. François's sons would have to make their own way in the world with little help from the family.

With the financial condition of the family having improved very little by the 1730s, all three of the brothers initially sought their fame and fortune in the service of the king. However, only the youngest of the three made a career of the military. At the age of sixteen, Louis-François was given a commission in an artillery regiment. In his thirty-nine-year career, he rose to the rank of colonel. During his honorable years of service, he made the campaigns of the wars of the Polish Succession and the Austrian Succession. He was first wounded in the Polish war and again at the siege of Prague. He also fought at the impressive French victory of Fontenoy. In recognition of his service and wounds, he was given the Cross of Saint Louis along with a small annual gift of three hundred livres a year. When the Seven Years' War broke out in 1756, Louis-François's old wounds kept him from campaigning, but he commanded coastal artillery in his native Normandy. He had married Anne-Françoise du Caestre in 1748, but they had no children. The colonel retired in October 1773. He enjoyed his pension of three thousand livres only three months, as he died in January of the following year. Although Alexandre Dumas never met his uncle Louis-François—the colonel had died several years before Dumas arrived in France from Saint Domingue—he knew of his uncle's proud military record. But one colonel does not establish a family tradition, and there is no documentary evidence that his soldier-uncle had any effect upon Dumas's decision to embark upon a military career of his own.

The example of his very successful uncle Charles might have been expected to have had some effect on young Dumas. Indeed, it was Charles who enticed and then introduced Dumas's father to the Antilles. This second son of Alexandre Davy was born at Bielleville on July 26, 1716. At the age of sixteen he enlisted in an army unit that was shipping out to Saint Domingue. Charles had decided to seek his fortune (he seemed to care little for fame) in the West Indies. However, being without financial backing, he determined to use the army as a means of reaching the West Indies and gaining knowledge of the economic conditions without financial risk. Robert Landru, who has written the definitive study of the ancestry of the Dumas family, says that Saint Domingue was the French El Dorado of that period and that Charles was "of his time: of that nobility which had been encouraged by the edits of Louis XIV, inspired in the beginning by Colbert, to abandon the tradition that only a career in the army . . . was suitable for their class."[2]

The economic conditions were favorable on Saint Domingue, and there were fortunes to be made. Charles served out his time in the army and took his discharge. On February 17, 1738, he married Marie-Anne Tuffé at Fort Dauphin. She was the daughter of François Tuffé and Marie Guitton, wealthy plantation owners who provided a most generous dowry to go with Marie-Anne. This dowry, a sugar plantation complete with a house, refinery, stables, and slaves, made Charles a wealthy man overnight and was the foundation for the fortune he would amass. He acquired additional lands from the Guitton family, and through hard work and wise management Charles prospered. His land holdings were on the north coast of Saint Domingue near the Spanish frontier and included a wharf that bore the name of Monte Christo. By 1753, Charles had been in Saint Domingue for twenty-one years and was worn out and in poor health. In July of that year, he returned to France to recuperate and enjoy the fruits of his labor. He purchased estates in Normandy and Artois and engaged in numerous business undertakings with mixed results. The Seven Years' War virtually destroyed the export industry in Saint Domingue, which deprived Charles of most of his income and caused him to go into debt in the 1760s. He returned to the island without his wife in 1771 to once again take personal charge of his plantations, which had not been managed in his absences with the greatest care or productivity. He died two years later, leaving behind him a wife, a daughter (Marie-Anne Charlotte Achille, who married Louis-Léon Eugène, Count de Maulde, Marquis de la Buissière), and an estate valued at one and a half million livres in Saint Domingue and at more than a million livres in France.[3]

The father of the future general and the oldest of the three brothers was Alexandre-Antoine. He may have set the example for his two brothers by enlisting in an artillery regiment at the age of sixteen. He received his training as a second lieutenant and served in the War of the Polish Succession as a lieutenant, notably at the siege of Philipsbourg (1734). When the Peace of Vienna brought the war to an end in 1738, the twenty-four-year-old Lieutenant Davy resigned his commission to follow the example of his brother Charles. Charles had already established himself on the north coast of Saint Domingue through his marriage and made it known that he was willing to help his older brother get a start in the new world.

Alexandre-Antoine sailed to Saint Domingue in 1738 and remained on the island for thirty-seven years. There is a conspicuous lack of information about him during those years. Perhaps this is because he neither married into

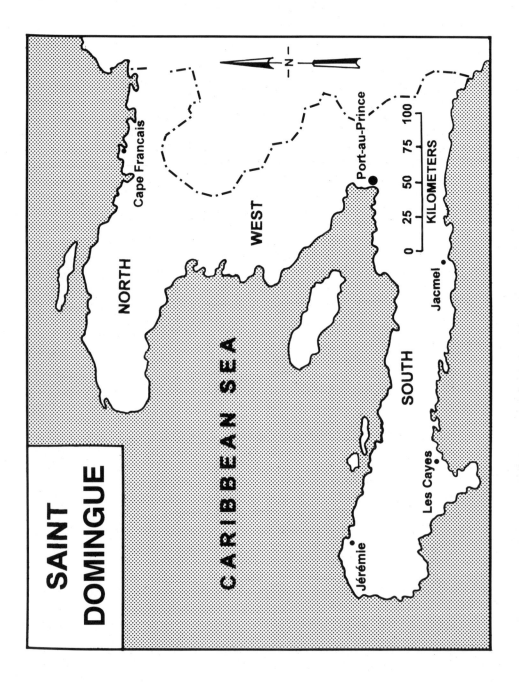

wealth, as did his brother, nor did he become wealthy on his own. He lived with Charles for the first ten years and presumably worked for his brother in that period. But then problems arose between the two men, most likely the result of the fact that Charles was becoming wealthier with each passing year while Alexandre-Antoine's fortunes changed little. In any event, the older brother—who at some point, perhaps at this time, took the name Antoine Delisle ("of the island")—departed without telling Charles where he was going. With the money that he had accumulated, he bought land just out of Jérémie. It is not clear whether this purchase, which was probably the cheapest land available, was already a modest tobacco plantation or if Alexandre made it into a plantation. Whichever was the case, for the next twenty-seven years he lived and worked on this land in one of the most remote parts of Saint Domingue.

Conditions on the island were, at their best, primitive in the mid-eighteenth century. The original native population had died of the new diseases brought by the Europeans or were killed off by the Spanish and the French, and few towns could boast of a white population of more than a few hundred. Cape Français on the north coast was the principal town and the seat of the governor. In the south, Port-au-Prince, Jacmel, and Les Cayes Saint Louis served as ports for imports and exports. The French population was a mixture of adventurers and outcasts. France had already begun the practice of "dumping" the undesirables of the mother country—vagabonds, petty thieves, and in general those who were "judged unable to be assimilated in the metropolitan population" in the colonies.[4] The latter group was not inclined to engage in hard work, and the vagabonds and thieves had come to get rich, not to work. Furthermore, the climate of the island was tropical, making it difficult for those Frenchmen who were willing to work. Only the most healthy survived the conditions on the island, and many Europeans died within a year of their arrival. It is not surprising that the French colonists, like the Spanish and English, turned to slave labor.

The slave trade with the West Indies was well established by 1700, and it flourished in the eighteenth century. The French government tried, in vain, to create a monopoly of the slave trade with its colonies, particularly Saint Domingue, Martinique, and Guadeloupe. But with each war with England, and in particular the Seven Years' War, this trade was virtually stopped. The slaves came from Africa's west coast.[5] The slave population of Saint Domingue far outnumbered the French in the mid-eighteenth century, by which time sugar had become the dominant cash crop. Because the clearing of land and the production of sugar was very labor-intensive, the demand for slaves increased steadily, as did their value, in the century preceding the French Revolution.

Alexandre Antoine owned slaves who worked on his tobacco and coffee plantation. One of his slaves, Marie-Cessette Dumas, served as both his housekeeper and his mistress. She gave birth on March 25, 1762, to a son named Thomas-Alexandre. There is little information about Marie-Cessette. Who were her parents? Was she born in Saint Domingue or in Africa? How old was she when she died in 1772? What was the cause of her death at what one may presume to have been an early age? There simply are no answers to these questions. Furthermore, when her grandson Alexandre Dumas (*père*) wrote his memoirs in the late 1840s, he spoke with pride of his paternal grandfather and the Davy de la Pailleterie family but referred to his paternal grandmother, Marie-Cessette Dumas, not by name but as the "wife" of Alexandre-Antoine. There is not even a hint of the fact that she was a black slave.[6] Fifty years later, in 1897, Ernest d'Hauterive (a relative by marriage), in his study of General Dumas, states only: "Shortly after he [Alexandre-Antoine] arrived in America, he married Marie-Cessette Dumas."[7] Again, there is no mention that she was a black slave. Both authors deliberately misled their readers to think that Marie Dumas was a white French colonist.

On the issue of marriage, and thus legitimacy, there is another problem. Both Dumas (*père*) and d'Hauterive state that Alexandre-Antoine was married to Marie-Cessette. However, there is no record of such a marriage. Furthermore, while there are records of marriages between French colonists and black slaves, such marriages were rare. The common practice on the part of the French was to take a slave as a mistress with the understanding that upon the departure of the colonist, whether by death or his return to France, the mistress would be granted her freedom.[8] In the case of Alexandre-Antoine, there is no evidence that he married Marie-Cessette; at the same time, there is no evidence that they were not married. One is thus left only with the customs of time and place, and that would suggest that Thomas-Alexandre was illegitimate.

The world into which the future General Dumas was born seemed to promise him little in the way of comfort or opportunity. As a mulatto, he was considered to be one of "color," translated in the colonies as a black man, for in the color-conscious islands of the West Indies, one with any hint of black ancestry, dating back even to the great-great-great-grandparents, carried the stigma of "colored." With "the least trace of negro blood, law and opinion joined in imposing a legal and social ostracism which made of him [the mulatto] a veritable outcast. He could hold no public office, no position of trust or confidence."[9] The mulatto was "further forbidden to engage in the learned professions" and was "declared incapable of acquiring a patent of nobility or receive the higher decorations, such as the Cross of Saint-Louis."[10]

Thomas-Alexandre spent the first ten years of his life in the care of his black mother on his father's modest plantation on the side of a mountain on a tropical island. His education must have been typical of a mulatto boy on a rural plantation, that is, of a basic and crude nature. His father, who had entered the army at sixteen, was not well educated, and there is no information to indicate that his slave mother could even read or write. Some of the wealthiest planters sent their white children to France to be educated. In the case of Thomas-Alexandre, it must be assumed that whatever formal learning took place occurred on the plantation at the hands of his parents.

There apparently was one other child, a daughter, from the relationship between Alexandre-Antoine and Marie-Cessette, but Dumas (*père*) does not acknowledge the existence of Rose, and there is no information about her other than she remained in Saint Domingue after the departure of her father and brother. In the same way, neither the cause nor any of the circumstances leading to or surrounding the death of Marie-Cessette are known, nor is there any indication of the effect that this sad event had upon her son.

For fourteen years, Thomas-Alexandre lived in this rural, isolated, and backward setting. His son, Dumas (*père*), tends to glorify the free and uninhibited existence on a beautiful tropical island,[11] but in fact, Thomas-Alexandre took the first opportunity he had to leave Saint Domingue. His father sailed for France in 1775, leaving both of his children behind. Alexandre-Antoine, then in his mid-sixties, was ready to retire and to enjoy the fruits of his many years in the colony. The loss of Marie-Cessette made his life lonely, and a hurricane in 1772 had caused great damage on the island that discouraged many planters. Undoubtedly, a combination of reasons, conditions, and events led to his decision to sell his holdings in Saint Domingue and return to France. His departure from the island is perfectly understandable; what is puzzling is that he had remained in Saint Domingue as long as he did. He left behind his pseudonym, Antoine Delisle, and sought to reestablish his life in French aristocratic society.

The Marquis de la Pailleterie, Alexandre-Antoine's father, had died in 1758. Therefore, Charles, the second son, who fully believed that his older brother was dead because no one had heard from him since he had disappeared and changed his name, had taken the title of Marquis de la Pailleterie and possession of the family estates in Normandy. Upon his death in 1773, the estates passed to his daughter Anne-Charlotte Davy, who was married to the Count of Maulde. The return of Alexandre-Antoine, as it were from the dead, to claim his inheritance caused considerable embarrassment and confusion. However, he established his identity, and his niece was cooperative. He was confirmed in his title of Marquis de la Pailleterie and reestablished his financial position in a comfortable manner.[12]

The following year, 1776, Thomas Alexandre arrived in France and joined his father in Normandy.[13] Although Normandy was rural and provincial, it must have been a cultural shock for the fourteen-year-old from Jérémie. Moving from life on a small, rural plantation on Saint Domingue to that of French nobility was surely a pleasant surprise for the boy. Within a year, Alexandre-Antoine had resolved his financial affairs in Normandy and with his son settled on the rue de l'Aigle d'Or in Saint-Germain-en-Laye. That he could afford to live in this fashionable town just west of Paris would indicate that the marquis had acquired a comfortable income from his lands in Normandy. The two Davys lived together with a housekeeper by the name of Marie-Françoise-Elisabeth Retou until the younger man was in his early twenties. As Thomas-Alexandre grew into manhood, he was very active socially. He had a circle of friends who accepted him, a mulatto, as an equal. He was, after all, the acknowledged son of a marquis. Furthermore, he was handsome with a fine physical build and seemed dedicated to the pleasures of life. In fact, his father came to disapprove of his fast, loose, and useless life-style. The relationship between his father and Marie-Françoise gradually progressed beyond that of employer and employee, and the younger Davy, with his father's blessing and financial support, went to live in Paris. While the exact year is uncertain (albeit before September 1784), it is known that he had rooms in the rue Etienne, which were later destroyed when the rue de Rivoli was constructed.

Paris in the 1780s was the center of the universe for a young, single man of Thomas-Alexandre's status. He had no introduction to the court of Louis XVI, so life at Versailles was out of the question. But Paris was an ideal place for young Davy, who had a sufficient allowance from his father to partake of its many pleasures and distractions.

The difference between the life-styles of the young Davy and his father and uncles when they were young is striking. Alexandre-Antoine and both of his brothers had entered the military at the age of sixteen, and Alexandre-Antoine was in battle before he was twenty years of age. In contrast, Thomas-Alexandre spent his time dining with friends, going to the theater, and escorting young ladies to the fashionable places in Paris. Without a care in the world, he enjoyed life to its fullest.

But being a "man of color" was an inescapable part of his life at this time. There was always the question of legitimacy and inheritance that lurked in the back of young Davy's mind. It was certainly questionable as to whether or not he would become the Marquis de la Pailleterie upon the death of his father. But pre-revolutionary France was becoming increasingly race-conscious. The ideas of equality, in the broadest sense, that were so basic to the Enlightenment were taking hold among the bourgeoisie and the liberal nobility. This was to the distress of the more conservative aristocracy, the merchant class of the seaports (who were thriving on the slave trade), and wealthy absentee plantation owners. The Society of the Friends of the Blacks was not founded until 1789, but the men who formed the society were at work in the decade before the Revolution, and the concept, not the fact, of total equality for blacks was well established before 1780.[14]

Conditions in France for a mulatto on the eve of the French Revolution were infinitely better than they were in Saint Domingue. Thomas-Alexandre moved in the white society of Paris in a way that would never have been accepted in the colonies. Yet there is evidence that he had problems because of his color. On September 14, 1784, the twenty-two-year-old Davy attended a performance at the Théâtre des Grands Danseurs du Roi, commonly known as the Nicolet Theater, and became involved in an unpleasant episode that involved his color. In the police report that he filed the day after the affair, he wrote the following account of what had taken place:

Yesterday, being at the Nicolet [Theater] with a young lady, a man [Major Titon de Saint Lamain] approached us. He said to the lady: "Madame, you are very lovely, and have a nice figure and lovely bosom. I would be very pleased to have your address. . . . Is Madame from out of town; would she like me to show her around Versailles?" He asked her if she liked Americans [persons of color from the colonies of the Antilles]. The lady having answered yes, he congratulated her, and began to mock me. With this, I said to him: "Madame is courteous; I pray you to leave us alone." Monsieur left with a great laugh while saying: "I believe that he wanted to speak to me. Madame, I thought that you were with one of your servants. . . . We know that this is a mulatto. In your country [he said to Thomas-Alexandre] they would put your hands and feet in irons. If you say one word I will have you arrested by the guard and sent to prison. . . ." I answered him that I had only contempt for his remarks, and that I knew that he was a commissioner of the War Office. . . . Then he lost his temper and one of his friends raised his cane at me and said: arrest him. I wanted to leave with the young lady to avoid any further trouble. But monsieur blocked my passage and had me arrested by the guard. Taking me by the hand, he [the guard] said to me that I must kneel before him and demand his pardon before the lady. The young lady left alone and I returned to my lodgings. Then Monsieur came and said to me in a loud insulting voice: You are free. I have obtained your request for pardon. . . . Signed Dumas Davy[15]

Alexandre Dumas (*père*) provides a more lively version of this affair in his *Mémoires*. The author of *The Three Mousquetaires* could not tell this story without adding a duel between his father and the "mousquetaire" Titon in which the young Davy wounded his swaggering opponent in the garden of the duc de Richelieu.[16] Dumas (*père*), always the romantic, could not allow the facts to interfere with a wonderful story. While it is true that he had the advantage of knowing and speaking with many friends and acquaintances of his father, one must bear in mind when reading his *Mémoires* that his life was dedicated to telling a good story, not to the accurate relating of past events. This is not to say the *Mémoires* should be put aside and discounted, only that they must be used carefully and cross-checked whenever possible.

Being black in an all-white society, a society that recognized slavery as the law of the kingdom, clearly had a profound effect in the shaping of the personality and character of the future General Dumas. He became quick to anger and to demand just recognition. The least slight became cause for a duel. During his teenage years at Saint-Germain-en-Laye, he took very seriously his fencing instruction and became an excellent swordsman. In this manner he would be able to demand satisfaction, with sword in hand, from those who would tread, no matter how lightly, upon his toes. As a black man, the Old Regime was not his friend, and although he was not legally discriminated against, he was always a mulatto, a free man of color, the illegitimate son of a lesser nobleman. It is entirely understandable that he would wholeheartedly embrace the Revolution in 1789, with its ideals of liberty and equality, and the Republic in 1792, which promised to put into practice those ideals. However, before the Revolution, young Davy would have problems of a different nature.

The decision of Alexandre-Antoine, nearly seventy-two, to marry his housekeeper, Marie Retou, brought a sudden change in the life of Thomas-Alexandre. Marie, thirty-eight years younger than her husband, came from Carrières-sous-Poissy where her family cultivated grapes and the land. The young, carefree Davy did not get along with his new stepmother, and it is very likely that there had been friction between the two that figured into his leaving Saint-Germain-en-Laye several years earlier. Coming from a lesser bourgeois, hardworking background, Marie undoubtedly disapproved of the self-indulgent, parasitic life of Thomas-Alexandre. The senior Davy lived comfortably, but he was not wealthy. The expense of supporting his own household and that of his twenty-three-year-old son in Paris put a strain on his income. Shortly after his marriage on February 14, 1786, he informed his son that he would no longer support him. Thomas-Alexandre quickly came to the realization that living in Paris without money was not only not enjoyable but also quite impossible. He had no professional training or marketable skills. His family had no influence in France, as his father had lived the better part of his life in Saint Domingue and his uncles, Charles and François, who might have been of help, were dead. He therefore decided to join the army.

A military career was a likely choice for one in his situation. However, that he entered the army as a private is another matter. Free black men could not be officers in the king's service. But young Davy was more than a free black man; he was a mulatto and the acknowledged son of the Marquis de la Pailleterie, who held the honorary title of colonel. His uncle Louis-François, who had made the army his career, had been a colonel at the time of his retirement. One would have thought that in a system of privileges, exceptions, and favors, a commission could have been found for the young man. Perhaps the story related by Dumas (*père*), if doubtful in its preciseness, captures the spirit of the relationship between father and son at that moment. Without a means of support, the author writes, Thomas-Alexandre went to his father to inform him that he had made a decision upon a career:

> "What may that be?" asked the marquis.
> "To enter the service."
> "As what?"
> "As a private."
> "And where?"
> "In the first regiment that comes."
> "Wonderful!" replied my grandfather; "but as I happen to be called the Marquis de la Pailleterie, and as I am Colonel and Commissary-General of Artillery, I do not mean you to drag my name through the lowest ranks of the army."

"Then you object to my enlisting?"

"No: but you must enlist under an assumed name."

"That's fair enough," said my father; "I will enlist under the name of Dumas."

"Very good."

And the Marquis, who in other ways had never been a very affectionate father, turned his back on his son, leaving him to follow his own devices.[17]

The young Davy, then twenty-four, enlisted in the Queen's Dragoons, the 60th Regiment, on June 2, 1786. He dropped Thomas and took his mother's last name, enlisting as Alexandre Dumas.

The cavalry was the glamour branch of the army. The uniforms were more colorful and decorative; the men were more impressive on horseback; they walked with more of a swagger in their step; they bragged in a louder voice in the inns; and in every respect they considered themselves the pride of the king's army. And indeed the ladies did turn their heads when they passed by. Young Dumas adjusted easily and quickly to his new life, despite the drastic change it was from his playboy days in Paris.

Dumas lived on his private's pay, for although Alexandre-Antoine died just three weeks after Dumas had entered the army, he was not mentioned in his father's will. The marquis left his entire estate to his widow. Without money, without family, without a past, and with a new name, Alexandre Dumas began life anew in the lowest rank of the French army. At the time of his enlistment, Dumas was described as "a native of Jérémie on Martinique [*sic*], age 24, height 5 feet 8 inches. Black frizzy hair and eyebrows, black eyes, round and plain face, brown, small mouth, thick lips, a small wart on the right cheek, a larger one on the right side of the forehead."[18]

The French army had been the finest in Europe during the reign of Louis XIV, but the first half of the eighteenth century saw a decline in its effectiveness. At the same time, the Prussian army was becoming an extremely fine-tuned war machine. In the Seven Years' War, the Prussian army under Frederick the Great defeated in turn the French, Austrian, and Russian armies, showing to the world that indeed it had no equal. After the humiliating defeat at Rosebach, at the hands of Frederick's army, the French were forced to acknowledge, at least to themselves, that reform was necessary. Under the very capable direction and influence of men like Jacques-A.-H. de Guibert, Pierre de Bourcet, and the Chevalier Jean Du Teil, the French army embarked upon a series of reforms designed to reestablish it as the dominant military force in Europe. Some changes were taken directly from the Prussian model; others were new innovations or theories that had their origins with the French army. Collectively, they laid the foundation for the armies of the Revolution and ultimately the armies of the Napoleonic era. By the time Alexandre Dumas joined this army in 1786, it was a well-trained and well-disciplined military force. If there was a weak link in the French army, it was the upper ranks of the officer corps. These men were still political appointees, or they had purchased or inherited their command.[19]

Alexandre Dumas spent six rather uneventful years in the royal army of Louis XVI. When he joined the Queen's Dragoons, it was stationed in the Alsace, and it was there that he was introduced to army life. In March 1788, the regiment moved to Laon where it was under the command of the duc de Guiche. Dumas undoubtedly underwent the customary hazing of all new recruits, but the big, strong mulatto, who was already a skilled swordsman, quickly earned a reputation that brought him the respect and admiration of his comrades in arms. Legend has grown up to exemplify his strength, swordsmanship, and quick temper. He is alleged to have fought three duels in one day, in one of which he was wounded in the head.[20] While such stories may be exaggerations, there is no question but that he was, in fact, both unusually strong and skilled with a sword.

Life was calm and quiet, and probably dull, for a young man who had been accustomed to living well in Paris. Garrison duty in a provincial town like Laon could provide only minimum diversions and recreation for the troops during their free time. Laon was a walled city about one mile long and less than a quarter-mile wide at points; it crowned a long, narrow hill that rose above the plains in the northeast part of the province of the Isle de France between Saint-Quentin and Reins. With its medieval cathedral, it had been a principal military feature of the defense of France's northern frontier for centuries.

On August 15, 1789, Dumas, with a small detachment of dragoons, was sent to the village of Villers-Cotterêts, on the road from Laon to Paris. The town fathers had requested a platoon of soldiers to back up the town's militia as a result of the bloodshed in Paris and disturbances throughout the countryside. The troops were quartered in the homes of the citizens. Dumas was assigned to the house of Claude Labouret. It was at this time that he met Labouret's daughter, Marie-Louise-Elisabeth, who would become his wife in 1792.

2

THE REPUBLICAN GENERAL

The French Revolution broke out over Paris and the provinces of France in the summer of 1789 with a fury not known since the Wars of Religion some two hundred years earlier. The conflict between the king and the Parliament of Paris over the question of taxation and basic economic reform culminated in the calling of the Estates General. But it was the aggressiveness of the Third Estate in the summer and fall of 1789 that introduced major changes in the political, social, and religious fibers of France. Violence broke out in Paris on July 14 when the people attacked the Bastille and first blood was shed. A great fear swept over rural France, and in some provinces the châteaux of aristocrats were burned. The Estates General had been reorganized into the National Assembly at the end of June, and early in August its members abolished, at least on paper, the remains of the feudal system. The government moved from Versailles to Paris in October of the same year, where it came under the ever-increasing influence of the people. The lands of the Catholic church were confiscated by the government to be sold in order to reduce the national debt. Next, the power and privileges of the church were first curbed and eventually abolished. The National Assembly then set about writing a constitution for France that would greatly curtail the powers of the king to the advantage of an elected legislative assembly. In the fall of 1791, France officially became a constitutional monarchy. Almost every aspect of French life was affected by this great upheaval. It is thus not at all surprising that the army underwent change and internal conflict at the same time as the rest of France.

The pre-revolutionary army had been totally controlled and dominated by the aristocracy. Ninety percent of the officer corps was of noble birth, and the 10 percent who came primarily from the bourgeois class, the so-called officers of fortune, tended to be restricted to the lower ranks of lieutenant and captain. In 1758, the minister of war had issued an order declaring that no one should be given a commission unless they could produce a certificate of nobility. Because some commoners still managed to become officers, in 1781 an order was published by the minister requiring "any future officer (unless rising from the ranks) to present original documents attesting to his nobility."[1] In this pre-revolutionary army, Alexandre Dumas could hope, at

15

best, to rise to the rank of sergeant-major. Only under the most unusual circumstances might he have become an officer, and even then the rank of captain would have been the highest rank possible. Thus it was to the Revolution, which would open the upper ranks of the army to all citizens, that Dumas owed the opportunity that enabled him to achieve the rank of general of division, the highest rank in the Revolutionary army.

These changes actually began in 1788–1789 when the aristocratic officers made common cause with the officers of fortune and the noncommissioned officers to push through reforms that had been proposed in the wake of the army's defeats in the Seven Years' War. Commissions would be granted on the basis of ability and merit, not on birth. This was intended to improve the quality of the officer corps. But before this reform had any effect, the Revolution threw France and the army into great confusion. The creation of the constitutional monarchy, which required all officers to take an oath of allegiance not only to the king but also to the National Assembly (and in 1791 to the newly elected Legislature), coupled with mutinies in some of the regiments and the general hostility toward aristocrats, caused many officers to resign their commission. By the end of 1791, six thousand out of nine thousand officers of the Old Regime had left the army.[2]

In 1791 the bourgeoisie, which controlled the National Assembly, considering the royal army to be an instrument of the king and the aristocracy, created what might be called a "bourgeois army" to exist side-by-side with the royal army. This new army was made up of the volunteer battalions and free-lance corps (or legions) raised throughout the country. Its officers and men came primarily from the ranks of the national guard units that had been created in 1789. In theory it was to be a citizen army whose officers and men owed allegiance to the nation rather than to the monarchy. It is true that there were some aristocrats in its officer corps, such as the young Louis-N. Davout, the future marshal of the empire, but they, like Davout, had already broken with the aristocratic officer corps of the Old Regime and embraced the principles of the Revolution. It was in one of the new revolutionary corps that Alexandre Dumas would rise virtually overnight to the rank of lieutenant colonel and begin the significant phase of his military career.

Private Dumas was on garrison duty at Laon during the summer of 1789. Except for the four months that he was posted at Villers-Cotterêts (August 15–December 19, 1789), he remained for the next two years some hundred miles northeast of Paris at Laon. Neither he nor his regiment played any meaningful role in the events of the Revolution during those first critical years. However, Dumas was attracted to the principles and ideas of the French Revolution from its beginning. Alexandre, who had been introduced to prejudice and inequality from his earliest recollections, thought the ideas of the Revolution, which were derived from the basic concepts of the Enlightenment, offered true equality, as well as fraternity and liberty hitherto unknown in France or her colonies. The Friends of the Blacks, with men like the Abbé Henri-Baptiste Grégory and Marie-Jean-Antoine-Nicolas Caritat, the Marquis de Condorcet, was working for the abolition of slavery throughout the French empire. The Third Estate of the Estates General, which became the controlling power of the National Assembly, endeavored to curb the power of the king and the aristocracy. The Jacobins on the political left were agitating for the creation of a republic. Dumas, who had benefited from his father's money and noble status, had separated himself from the privileged class when he changed his name and joined the army as a private. With nothing to gain from the Old Regime and everything to gain from the new, he supported virtually all that the Revolution embraced. He became an enthusiastic republican at an early point in the Revolution, because a republic seemed to be the political and social embodiment of the new and free order. In fact, when others, to maintain or further their careers, supported Napoleon Bonaparte and became monarchists (after 1804), Dumas remained a republican.

The reforms within the army that were brought about by the Revolution were yet another reason why it had Dumas's support. He did not personally benefit during the early years except in general ways (for example, from the removal of humiliating forms of punishment). But on April 20, 1792, France declared war on Austria, and shortly thereafter on Prussia. While the war was almost a disaster for France in 1792 and 1793, it catapulted Corporal Dumas to General Dumas.

With the approach of war in 1792, Alexandre had been promoted, after six years of service, to corporal on February 16. In an effort to play down the esprit de corps and the uniqueness of the regiments of the royal army and to turn it into a national army, the new Legislature, which had been elected under the new constitution in the fall of 1791, had decreed that all regimental names or titles be dropped. The old names would be replaced by giving every regiment a number. Thus, the Queen's Dragoons became the 6th Dragoons, and in the spring of 1792 it was sent to become a part of the newly formed Army of the North. This army was commanded by Marshal Jean-Baptiste-Donatien de Vimeur, Comte de Rochambeau, who as commander of the French expeditionary force in North America during the American War of Independence had shared with General George Washington the victory over Lord Charles Cornwallis at Yorktown in 1781.

In Paris, General Charles-François du Périer Dumouriez, as minister of foreign affairs, was the dominant influence upon the government for military matters. He believed that an invasion of the Austrian Netherlands would bring about a popular uprising of the French-speaking (Belgian) population, the expulsion of the Austrians, and the annexation of the territory south of the Rhine. To this end, Rochambeau was ordered to march his Army of the North into the Low Countries. But the old marshal, who knew that his army, a mixture of regular troops and volunteer battalions, lacked the training, discipline, and experience to successfully carry out the campaign, tried to stall for time. With direct orders from Paris to march immediately, Rochambeau cooperated by sending three columns into Belgium. Two of them accomplished nothing; however, the third, commanded by General Armand-Louis de Gontaut, duc de Biron, fought a successful engagement with the Austrians at Quiévrain on April 28 and then continued its advance. The 6th Dragoons, with Corporal Dumas, made up part of Biron's force of thirteen thousand men. Although the "battle" of Quiévrain was little more than a large successful skirmish, it was a success. There is no indication that Dumas personally engaged the enemy. However, before reaching Mons, Biron decided that his force was not sizable enough to continue his advance any deeper into enemy territory, and he began a general withdrawal. On April 30, as his troops again reached Quiévrain, this time marching in the opposite direction, panic broke out in the ranks, and the entire force fled in disarray back to Valenciennes from whence it had begun the campaign.[3]

Dumas's first experience of war—a "campaign" that lasted less then a week—was a disaster. The first engagement at Quiévrain was insignificant, but the panic of the 30th must have made an impression on that brave soldier. The cry had gone up that the army had been betrayed. Treason was on everyone's lips. After all, they were retreating without having been defeated. In fact, there had not even been a serious battle. When panic broke out among the troops on April 30, the enemy army was not even in the vicinity of Quiévrain. The Austrians had no hand at all in sending Biron's army fleeing back to Valenciennes.

Dumas was not the only future general or important dignitary to experience this humiliation. Two future marshals of the empire were with Biron's army, Colonel Alexandre Berthier (on the general's staff) and Captain Adolphe-Edouard Mortier. Alexandre Beauharnais, the first husband of Josephine (Marie-Joseph-Rose Tascher de la Pagerie), was also a staff officer, as was the duc de Chartres, the future King Louis Philippe (1830–1848). It should finally be noted that General Biron fared much better than did General Théobald Dillon. This unfortunate Irishman commanded a small army (twenty-five hundred men) that advanced on Biron's left from Lille toward Tournai. When he met an Austrian force on April 29, he decided to withdraw as he believed that his troops could not be relied upon in an engagement with the enemy. Cries of treason and betrayal went up from his men, and they fled in panic back to Lille. Upon reaching that city, they seized their general, murdered him, and hung his mutilated body in the town square.[4]

It is perhaps an understatement to say that the war did not go well for France in the summer of 1792. The dismal showing of the Army of the North led to the replacement of Rochambeau by General Dumouriez. Biron was first offered the command, but he is quoted as saying that he would rather die as a common soldier than be hanged as a general.[5] (Perhaps he was thinking of the unfortunate Théobald Dillon.) In any event, there was little activity on the northern front where Dumas and the 6th Dragoons remained. A portion of the Army of the North marched to the aid of General François-Etienne-Christoph Kellermann, who faced the invading Prussian army. But Dumas remained at the fortified camp of Maulde and took no part in the battle of Valmy on September 20–21 that stopped the Prussian advance on Paris.

The 6th Dragoons manned the outposts of the camp at Maulde and carried out probing reconnaissance missions to gain knowledge of the enemy's strength and movements. On one occasion, Corporal Dumas, at the head of four troopers, surprised an Austrian patrol, and before the enemy soldiers could regain their composure, Dumas, virtually single-handedly, made prisoners of them all.[6] As few enemy soldiers had been taken prisoner by the Army of the North, Dumas's exploit was met with great fanfare. He was mentioned by name in an order of the day, which greatly enhanced his reputation and made him a prime candidate for promotion. However, events in Paris led more directly to his good fortune.

On August 10, 1792, the people of Paris invaded the Tuileries and Louis XVI took refuge with the Legislative Assembly. The king was relieved of his duties, and a legislative directory, dominated by Georges-Jacques Danton, was put in place to govern until an election could be held for a new assembly. On September 21, the newly elected Constituent Assembly abolished the monarchy and France was proclaimed a republic. September 22 was the first day of the first year of the French Republic. In the six-week interim between the removal of the king and the beginning of the Republic, the provisional government, desperate to improve the bleak military situation, authorized the formation of what might be called free-lance military corps. The initiative was taken by individuals, and "legions" began to take form in a haphazard manner with little supervision from the government or the army, both of which were in somewhat of a state of disarray. A number of legions came into existence with names such as "Légion du Nord," "Légion de la Moselle," which was also referred to as the "Légion de Kellermann," and "Légion du Centre."[7] It was in this state of affairs that the "Légion franche des Américains et du Midi" was created.

On September 7, 1792, a number of free blacks went to the Legislative Assembly. One of them, Raimond, speaking on behalf of the group, declared that they wished to take part in the defense of France against its enemies. The Legislature accepted the offer and authorized the formation of a legion.[8] The legion was made up predominantly of free black men, the great majority of whom were from the French West Indian colonies; the term "American" referred to the French Antilles, not North or South America. This corps was more commonly referred to as the "Black Legion" or the "American Legion." It was to be made up of "four squadrons of two companies each on the model of a regiment of chasseurs."[9]

The man who founded it was Joseph Boulogne, Chevalier de Saint Georges, a mulatto like Dumas who had been born in the Antilles on the island of Guadeloupe on December 25, 1745. His father, Jean-Nicolas de Boulogne, of a "good" and moderately placed French noble family, was an official on the island, while his mother was a black slave. He received a fine education in France, taking an interest in and excelling in the fine arts. At the age of thirteen, his father placed him with a fencing master, and for the next four years he excelled in both the arts and in fencing. He entered the king's musketeers and gained the reputation as one of the finest swordsmen in France. He also made a name for himself as a musician and a composer in the years before the Revolution. At one point in his career, he attached himself to Philippe, duc d'Orleans, and traveled to England with the duke. While there he engaged in a fencing match with the Chevalier d'Edon for the pleasure of the court of St. James, because the English wished to see the two most famous swordsmen of their times.

Saint Georges embraced the ideas of the Revolution and became a devout republican. He served two years in the national guard with the rank of captain. But at the age of forty-seven, Saint Georges was more interested in politics than in military affairs. His formation of a legion was an act of patriotism that endeared him to the republicans who after September 1792 dominated the government.[10]

Saint Georges had actually begun to recruit officers for the legion before the government had authorized its creation. He knew of Corporal Dumas and of his reputation as a brave soldier, an exceptional swordsman, and a sincere republican. A fellow mulatto who had similar origins and a military background, Dumas was a perfect choice to be an officer in the new legion. Saint Georges offered the thirty-year-old corporal a commission as second lieutenant in the Black Legion. However, it so happened that Colonel Joseph Boyer was also forming a legion under the name "Hussards of Liberty and Equality," and he too had heard of Dumas's reputation and had extended to the corporal the rank of lieutenant. As Boyer offered the higher rank, Dumas accepted it and was commissioned a lieutenant on September 2, 1792. When Saint Georges was informed of these events, he was furious. In no mood to enter into a bidding war for the services of Dumas, Saint Georges offered him the rank of lieutenant colonel and second in command of "his" legion. Boyer could not improve on such an offer. Dumas accepted the position, and his commission as lieutenant colonel was dated September 15. He left behind the 6th Dragoons and moved into the pages of history of the French Revolution.[11]

Dumas joined the Black Legion at Laon where its newly recruited men were mustering. Colonel Saint Georges spent most of his time in Paris inducting officers and men, leaving his second in command to organize and train the troops. There were actually two lieutenant colonels in the legion in its early months; Saint Georges had recruited François-Jacque La Roche with that same rank. This was highly unusual and most likely not permissible. But Saint Georges did as he pleased in those confusing years, and no one called him to account. However, La Roche does not seem to have been active in the affairs of the legion, and Dumas acted as the functioning second in command.[12]

The transition for Dumas must have been a shock. Almost overnight he was catapulted from a corporal leading patrols of five or six men on reconnaissance missions to commanding a legion that quickly reached battalion strength. It was "on-the-job training" for the relatively young and very inexperienced officer with virtually no help from Saint Georges, who himself was a new and inexperienced colonel. But Dumas was not lacking in confidence,

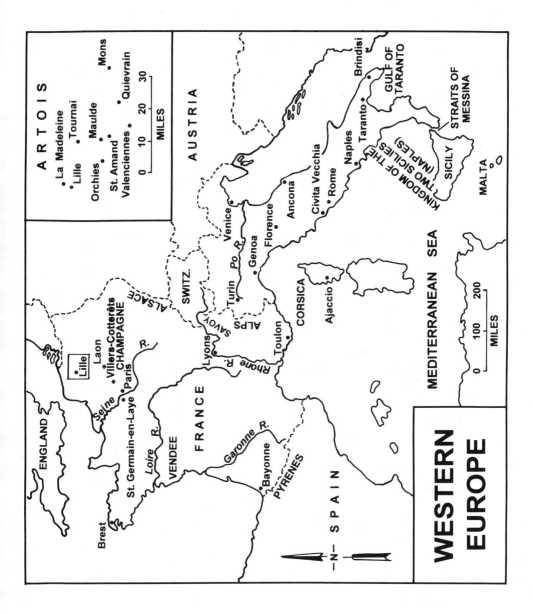

WESTERN EUROPE

nor was he afraid of hard work. He undertook his new duties with vigor and determination, and despite shortages of uniforms, equipment, and money, he gradually shaped up a legion of more than a thousand men.

In November 1792, when the Constituent Assembly was preparing to place Louis Bourbon (titles had been abolished) on trial for treason, Dumas married Marie-Louise-Elisabeth Labouret. In 1789, he had been quartered in the home of Claude and Marie-Joseph (Prévot) Labouret where he met and fell in love with their daughter. But as a corporal in the army, he was in no position to assume the responsibilities of a wife. It is said that before he left Villers-Cotterêts, Dumas spoke to young Marie's father about marriage and was told that when he had been promoted to the rank of sergeant, he might have the hand of his daughter.[13] Thus when his troop was recalled to Laon, Dumas bid farewell to Marie-Louise but vowed not to forget her. Two years later, Lieutenant Colonel Dumas returned to Villers-Cotterêts to renew the relationship and—if she was willing and her father did not object—to make her his wife.

The Labouret family was of very modest wealth. Claude and Marie-Joseph owned and operated the hotel l'Ecu on the main square of Villers-Cotterêts, which provided an adequate income for the family. The hotel provided overnight accommodations and meals for travelers on the stagecoach line from Paris to Soissons, Laon, and points north. Claude was also the commander of the local national guard.[14] To marry their daughter to a lieutenant colonel in the army who was only thirty years of age and who could be expected to continue to rise in the ranks was indeed an advantageous alliance. There did not seem to be any problem at all with the fact that Dumas was a mulatto. The couple was married on November 28, 1792. The wedding, a civil service, took place in the Hôtel de Ville of Villers-Cotterêts as Saint Nicolas, the only church in the town, had been closed as a place of Catholic worship and was being used by the local Jacobin club as a meeting hall.[15] On the marriage certificate, Dumas gave his mother's name as Marie-Cessette Dumas and his father's as Alexandre-Antoine Davy.[16] It is most likely that the Dumas were later married in a Catholic ceremony, because Marie-Louise was Catholic and their son, Alexandre Dumas (*père*), was baptized in the church of Saint Nicolas in 1802.[17]

As is the case when soldiers marry in time of war, the honeymoon was brief. On December 15, Dumas rejoined his command, which was still recruiting and training. He carried with him a letter signed by the members of the administrative consul of Villers-Cotterêts testifying to the fact that Lieutenant Colonel Alexandre Dumas had made his residence in that town and that he was a good and patriotic citizen.[18]

On December 6, while Dumas was on leave of absence, the legion had been given the organizational structure of a light cavalry regiment. At that time it had only two companies.[19] With the reorganization of the Army of the North in February 1793, the Black Legion became a part of the command of General François-Raymond Duval. Its name was changed to the 13th Chasseurs (regiment), and it was posted to Lille, where it arrived on February 23. Shortly after its arrival, General Nicolas-Joseph Bécourt, the commander of Lille, reviewed the new regiment and wrote the following to the War Office in Paris:

> The 13th Regiment of Chasseurs, referred to as St. Georges, arrived the day before yesterday. It is in very poor condition . . . ; there are only fourteen officers present with this corps while thirteen are missing. They are amusing themselves in Paris. Citizen [Captain Pierre] Aveneaux, Quarter Master [and treasurer] has been absent for two months and he gives no sign of life, according to a report by Lieutenant Colonel Dumas.[20]

Dumas was the only senior officer with the fledgling regiment as Saint Georges was "recruiting" in Paris.

The 13th Chasseurs was less than battalion strength, and its training was not completed. Thus, it remained a part of the garrison of Lille when Dumouriez led the Army of the North into Belgium and Holland in the spring of 1793. Nor did its condition improve in the months that followed. When General Simon-Camille Dufresse, the new commanding officer of Lille, inspected the regiment on April 4, he found it still in poor condition and wrote to the minister of war that "it is most essential to reorganize the 13th Chasseurs without delay so as to appoint patriotic officers who will be able to change the bad spirit that prevails here. Every day there are chasseurs who desert to the enemy."[21]

The Black Legion had been created by Saint Georges more for political and personal reasons than for military reasons. The officer corps was, with some exception, inexperienced and incompetent. What experience they did have tended to be with colonial units in the West Indies or as volunteers in national guard battalions. There is no indication that any of them had ever held the rank of officer before joining the legion, and few had ever served in a regular army regiment. In fact, while Dumas had served in the king's army as a private, Saint Georges had served only in the national guard. The officers were mostly older men, some of them brought out of retirement with the lure of a commission. The commanding generals under whom they served recognized their inadequacies and wisely kept them out of serious combat through the spring and summer of 1793.[22] By the fall, the regiment was completely reorganized; however, by that time Dumas had been promoted and reassigned.

General Dumouriez was defeated at Neerwinden by the Austrian army under the prince of Coburg on March 18, 1793. Whereas the military picture had been rather bright through the winter of 1792–1793, gloom set in along the northern front after Neerwinden. Dumouriez, who had become frustrated by the increasing influence of the political left (the Jacobins), decided to march on Paris with the Army of the North and to consolidate the power of the Girondin (the moderate republicans), or perhaps, as some said, to restore the Constitution of 1791, which provided for a constitutional monarchy. However, it all became academic when, lacking the full support of the army, he went over to the enemy, taking with him the future king of France—Louis Philippe of the house of Orleans. Dumas was involved in the rather theatrical series of events that led to the failure of Dumouriez's plans and his rapid exit from the stage.

Following the defeat at Neerwinden, there were rumors in Paris that the government was in danger. A delegation of four members of the Constituent Assembly and the minister of war (General Pierre de Riel, Marquis de Beurnonville) were sent to the Army of the North to remove General Dumouriez from his command and bring him back to Paris to answer charges of treason. When the representatives of the government reached Lille, they requested a military escort. One hundred men of the 13th Chasseurs were assigned to accompany them to Dumouriez's headquarters at Saint Amand. Both Colonel Saint Georges and Lieutenant Colonel Dumas volunteered to head the escort, and the services of both men were accepted. The representatives were pressed for time, so the column moved at a rapid pace across the flat countryside. By the time it reached Orchies, the horses were spent. The representatives acquired fresh horses, but the chasseurs escort had to be changed, and the men of the 13th remained at Orchies while a new troop was provided by the garrison of that town to complete the journey. The delegation from Paris reached Dumouriez's headquarters on April 1, but they did not remove the general; rather, he arrested the representatives of the people and the minister of war and turned them over to the enemy as prisoners.

Dumouriez had crossed the Rubicon. The plotting, planning, and scheming had come to an end, and the hour for action was at hand. He sent word to Orchies for General Joseph Miaczynski, who commanded the garrison of the town, to march on Lille and secure that major city and its garrison in preparation for his march to Paris. Saint Georges and Dumas were with Miaczynski when he received these orders, and the general invited them to accompany him to Lille in support of Dumouriez. Both refused, and as they were not under his orders, they immediately mounted and with their chasseurs retraced their earlier march to Lille. They reported to General Duval what they had learned, and the general, with the support of the city authorities, prepared at once to defend Lille. When Miaczynski arrived, he found Lille prepared for an attack and determined to remain loyal to the government in Paris. As he did not have sufficient strength to take the city by force of arms, he withdrew, leaving Dumouriez's path by way of Lille blocked. Had Saint Georges and Dumas gone over to Dumouriez and not returned to Lille and warned the garrison, the city, in an unprepared state, could have been taken by Miaczynski, who had enough men to capture it with the element of surprise on his side. Nor was the garrison at Lille the only army unit to oppose General Dumouriez. Other units, in particular the volunteer battalions, remained loyal to the government. Colonel Louis-N. Davout, at the head of his 3rd Battalion of Volunteers from Yonne, not only remained loyal to the government but also chased and almost captured Dumouriez before he was able to reach Austrian lines.[23]

Following the Dumouriez affair, the northern front was quiet and the 13th Chasseurs moved into the fortified camp of the Madeleine. However, Saint Georges, after turning over command of the regiment to Lieutenant Colonel Dumas, remained at Lille.[24] Left on his own at the Madeleine, Dumas continued the training and equipping of the regiment. At the end of April 1793, a company of seventy-three men was detached from the regiment and ordered to Brest. It was the intention of the government to send these black soldiers to Saint Domingue to serve as national police. But when the men learned of their destination, they sent a delegation to Paris to request that they be employed in one of the armies in France. Their request was honored, and the company became a part of the the Army of the West and served in the Vendée, where the government was putting down an insurrection.[25]

In the late spring of 1793, Saint Georges engaged in illegal dealings from which he made a considerable amount of money, to the detriment of the regiment. He purchased horses of high quality with government money, sold them, and then purchased more horses of poor quality. The poorer mounts were then sent to the regiment, and he kept the profit that was generated. His illegal transactions were brought to the attention of the minister of war, and the colonel was called to Paris to explain his actions. In the capital, he attempted to exonerate himself by throwing the blame on his second in command. It was Dumas, he said, who was in command of the regiment at Madeleine and responsible for the mounting of the chasseurs. But when Dumas was confronted in writing by the minister, he was able to prove beyond any doubt that he had purchased no horses. His name was cleared; however, the friendship between himself and Saint Georges was permanently altered. There was a reconciliation in Paris in the summer of 1793, but the two men parted in September. There is no indication that their paths ever again crossed.[26]

Saint Georges was not officially removed from his command of the 13th Chasseurs until September 1793, but he did not return to the regiment. Dumas was not promoted to the rank of colonel, although he was acting commander during the summer of that year. He was involved in limited patrol duties, and while his son tells stories of his exploits at this time, there does not seem to have been any serious activity involving the regiment.[27] Then on July 30, Dumas was promoted to general of brigade in the Army of the North. There is no indication of what new command he received with this rank. If he was given a command, it was of little consequence, for five weeks later, on September 3, he was named general of division.[28]

The rise of Alexandre Dumas from private in February 1792 to general of division in September 1793—from the lowest rank in the army to the highest—was nothing less than spectacular. Only under the unusual circumstances of the French Revolution could this have happened. That he was black actually worked in his favor in 1792 when he rose to lieutenant colonel; however, his color had nothing to do with his promotion from lieutenant colonel to general of division. There are other examples of men who had risen quickly through the ranks. Twenty-one-year-old Louis-N. Davout had advanced from lieutenant to lieutenant colonel overnight in his battalion of volunteers, and Napoleon Bonaparte was a general of division at the age of twenty-six. But these men had graduated from the Ecole Militaire in Paris and had been officers before the Revolution.

Dumas's promotions were not based on experience, years in rank, or even ability. Not only had he never commanded in a major battle, he had not even fought in a major battle, nor had he taken part in a serious campaign. On the other hand, he was known to be brave and fearless in the face of the enemy. But his principal qualification to be a general and to command an army was that he was also known to be a sincere and dedicated republican. In the France of 1793, at war with Austria, Prussia, England, Spain, and many of the lesser states of Europe, with insurrection in the Vendée and in the south of the country, and with generals like Dumouriez and the Marquis de Lafayette threatening to overthrow the government and then deserting to the enemy, the government in Paris required first that its generals be republicans loyal to the regime in Paris. Second, it was desirable that they be able to command an army and wage war. Dumas clearly met the first priority, but only time would tell whether or not he would meet the second. He was then a political appointee, one who could be trusted with the command of an army. If he was not a strategist or tactician, he would learn on the job with the assistance of representatives from the government. In any event, the grand strategy would be drawn up in Paris. The general would only have to lead his men against the enemy. A brave soldier such as Dumas could surely do that and at the same time remain loyal to the Revolution.

Five days after his promotion to general of division Dumas was named commander in chief of the Army of the West Pyrenees.[29] On September 15 he wrote from Lille to the minister of war, "I will leave for Paris tomorrow and from there I will go to the post that you have conferred upon me."[30] In the same letter, he requested that General Dufresse be named his chief of staff, declaring that the latter was a good man with whom he could work well. Putting his affairs in order in the north, the new general of division set out for Bayonne to assume his first command of an army. However, when he arrived, all was not in order.

The organization of the government in Paris and in turn its working relationship with the army had been in a constant state of upheaval since the creation of the Republic. The army was no longer the "king's army" but had become the "people's army." Many of the high-ranking officers were royalists or were believed to have royalist or anti-Jacobin sentiments. The Committee of Public Safety had been created in the spring of 1793 by the Girondins, who were able, at that time, to exert a dominant influence in the National Convention. But the defection of Dumouriez and the trial and acquittal of Jean-Paul Marat, a leading Jacobin attacked by the Girondins, had brought about the decline of that moderate wing of republicans. On June 2, the twenty-nine leading Girondins of the Convention were arrested, and control of the government passed into the hands of the Jacobins (the Mountain, or the leftwing of the Jacobins). By the second week of September, the Jacobins dominated the Committee of Public Safety, which began to function as a twelve-man executive. Maximilien-François Robespierre, seconded by Louis-Antoine Saint-Just and George-Auguste Couthon, was becoming the dominant figure in the committee and thus the most influential single man in the government. Lazare-Nicolas Carnot, an army engineer and member of the Convention elected to the committee on August 11, became the committee's principal military advisor (seconded by Prieur de la Côte d'Or) and as such more important than the minister of war in military matters. For his direction of the war in 1793–1794, he would be remembered as the "Organizer of Victory."

Although the primary direction for military affairs came from Paris, the Convention adopted the practice of sending its members into the provinces and to the various armies on the frontiers. The representatives were to assure loyalty to the government and that the orders and directives from the Committee of Public Safety were carried out promptly and correctly. These "representatives on mission" were given extraordinary powers to fulfill the wishes of the government. They had the authority to overrule local civil officials and generals of armies and even to arrest them and send them to Paris to explain their actions to the government. The authority of representatives on mission was virtually unlimited. They answered only to the Convention, of which they were members and from whence came their power. The Reign of Terror, which is generally dated from the summer of 1793 to the summer of 1794, moved into high gear when, upon the recommendation of Saint-Just in October 1793, the Convention decided that it would take on "the central direction of the entire state apparatus, subject only to the oversight of the Convention" itself.[31] With the passage of the Law of Suspect on September 17 and the General Maximum Law on September 29, the machinery of the Reign of Terror was in place; and during the nine months preceding the fall of the Jacobins on the 9th of Thermidor (the eleventh month of the revolutionary calendar; July 27, 1794), some sixteen thousand French men and women lost their lives to the guillotine.[32] Every army commander and general lived in the shadow of the guillotine. For a general to incur the displeasure of the government or its representatives was a braver act than to lead his men against the enemy. It was in this threatening political atmosphere that Dumas arrived in the south of France with orders to assume command of the Army of the West Pyrenees.

The new commander reached Bayonne, secured lodgings, and presented himself to the authorities on October 29. One might imagine his surprise when he was informed that command of the army already had been given to General Jacques-Léonard Muller. The representatives on mission at Bayonne, who had been sent to oversee the Army of the West Pyrenees, had not waited for Paris to replace General Pierre-Joseph d'Elbhecq (or Delbecq), who had died on September 1. Upon the death of General d'Elbhecq, the local executive council, composed primarily of the representatives on mission, had appointed the senior general of division with the army, Jean-Etienne-P. De Prez de Crassier, as provisional commander. However, De Prez de Crassier's loyalty to the government and the cause of the Revolution quickly became suspect, and he was relieved of his command on September 30 and placed under arrest on October 4. At the same time, Muller, who had been chief of staff of the army, was promoted to the rank of general of division and given command of the Army of the West Pyrenees. There was nothing that Dumas could do about his embarrassing position except write to Paris explaining what had taken place and then sit and wait for a reply.[33]

Dumas (*père*) relates the following account of his father while he was in Bayonne. General Dumas had acquired lodging for himself and his aides-de-camp overlooking the main square in which executions were carried out. Shortly after he had arrived, several people were brought to the square to be executed. A large crowd gathered; spectators were at the windows and balconies overlooking the ghastly events. But Dumas, to show his disapproval, closed his windows, lowered his blinds, and drew his curtains. The crowd below called upon him to show himself and witness the executions. He refused. Amid jeers and threats, the general and his staff sat in his room with pistols in hand and swords by their side until the crowd had dispersed. During this incident, he was chided as "Monsieur de l'Humanité" and, according to his son, became known for his humanity.[34]

In reply to Dumas's letter, the Committee of Public Safety created a new command for the general. Not wishing to overrule the representatives on mission and thereby undermine their authority—and undoubtedly as a face-saving measure for everyone involved—it ordered that ten thousand men from the Army of the West Pyrenees should be sent to the Vendée to join the Army of the West. General Dumas was given command of the newly created division.[35] The general and his small army set out at the end of November for the Vendée. The government had launched a fall campaign against the rebels and wanted to increase the strength of the Army of the West.

The Department of the Vendée was situated in west-central France; its western boundary was the Atlantic Ocean and its northern boundary the Loire River. However, the term "Vendée" was used in a much larger sense to include all of the western departments that raised the standard of the rebellion against the government in Paris in 1793. The West was strongly Roman Catholic and royalist. The creation of the Republic in 1792, the execution of the king on January 21, 1793, and the anti-church policies (the de-Christianization movement) begun by the Jacobin regime in 1793 had all contributed to bringing about the insurrection. The government in Paris had reacted by creating an Army of the West and giving it the task of crushing the rebellion. However, as the government had its hands full with the war in the Netherlands, Germany, the Alps, and the Pyrenees, and with rebellion spreading throughout central and southern France, it could spare little in the way of troops or material to fight in the West. Generally, the troops in the Vendée were of poorer quality than any of the other French armies. They were also poorly supplied and typically poorly led. To be sent to the Army of the West was not an honor for a French officer. General Napoleon Bonaparte would refuse to go to the Vendée in 1794, citing poor health as his reason, when in fact he saw no glory, honor, or advancement in killing Frenchmen in a civil war.

General Dumas arrived in the Vendée in mid-December 1793 and turned over the division of troops from the south to the Army of the West. He was not, however, given a command with that army. On December 22, he was ordered by the Committee of Public Safety to proceed immediately to the southeast of France and there to assume command of the Army of the Alps.[36] The general set out at once, accompanied by his staff. Perhaps this time, he anticipated, he would actually command his own army.

3

COMMANDER OF THE ARMY OF THE ALPS

By the beginning of the year 1794, the Committee of Public Safety was functioning as an executive for the National Convention. Although each member was but one of twelve equals on the committee, in point of fact, some were more "equal" than others, and Robespierre was the most "equal" of them all. As early as the spring of 1793, the Jacobins had begun to quarrel amongst themselves. The Girondin faction, sometimes incorrectly referred to as a "party," was eliminated as a serious opposition to the Jacobins in the summer and fall of 1793. In March 1794, while Dumas commanded the Army of the Alps, Jacques-René Hébert and his close supporters were purged from the Jacobins, and in April Georges Danton and his supporters were also eliminated. The leaders of these two factions of the Jacobins were executed and their followers silenced.

To oppose the leadership of the government during the Reign of Terror was to oppose the people, and as the people represented "goodness" in the tradition of Jean-Jacques Rousseau's "General Will," no one had the right of opposition. Any act against or criticism of the government or of its elected representatives was interpreted as a blow against the people. The government had an obligation to protect the people from such enemies who, attacking goodness, must themselves be evil. Drawing upon this logic, the elected representatives of the people tended to equate themselves with the people and with goodness itself. There was no appeal above the National Convention, and its representatives with the various armies on the frontiers exercised an authority that was answerable only to the Convention.

Robespierre, Saint-Just, Couthon, and company were primarily interested in the political affairs of the government in Paris. Lazare Carnot was left the sometimes thankless task of managing military affairs. He worked closely with the minister of war, who did nothing of a serious nature without consulting him. Correspondence coming from the Committee of Public Safety dealing with military matters was virtually always signed by Carnot, seldom by Robespierre. More than any other single individual, Carnot directed the military affairs of France. His praise was sought by Dumas, while his criticism could mean the end of a military career or even a life.

The military situation of France at the beginning of 1794 was not particularly bright. The armies fighting in the north and on the Rhine were more or less holding their own against the Austrians and Prussians. Fortunately for France, at this time both Austria and Prussia were much more concerned with Poland than they were with western Europe. There had already been two partitions of the kingdom of Poland, and Russia, Prussia, and Austria were poised for the final partition. Austria and Prussia feared that Russia would take all of what remained of Poland while they were occupied fighting France. Thus, they kept major portions of their military strength in north-central Europe to be sure that they would get their share of the spoils when Poland would be finally divided. While the Spanish army on the Pyrenees was less of a threat than the Prussians or the Austrians, it did require French troops to prevent an invasion. In Italy, the Austrians provided the major part of the fighting forces while the Kingdom of Sardinia, also at war with France, provided the troops that faced the French Army of the Alps. To the south of the Army of the Alps, in the maritime province, was the Army of Italy, which operated mainly along the Mediterranean. This latter army faced the Austrians in the republic of Genoa. What undoubtedly saved France in these early years of the war was that both Prussia and Austria were so distracted over the Polish question that they never brought their full strength to bear on the shaky armies of the French Republic. It was under these circumstances that Alexandre Dumas took command of the Army of the Alps.

General Dumas arrived at Grenoble to take up his new command on the night of January 21, 1794.[1] One might have expected that the pride and enthusiasm that is felt by a soldier upon assuming command of his first army might have been dampened after reviewing the troops and the mountainous terrain in which he was being asked to fight. But the inexperienced Dumas was filled with self-confidence, and he accepted the challenges before him, both known and unknown, with the determination of a military commander who was unfamiliar with the frustrations of command under the new Republic.

The longevity and the fate of the commanding officers of the Army of the Alps and its sister Army of Italy should have been enough in themselves to inject gloom, if not actual fear, in the heart of the new commander. General François-Etienne-Christoph Kellermann, who had stopped the Prussian advance on Paris at Valmy in September 1792, had been at the head of the Army of the Alps from December 1792 to mid-October 1793. During those ten months, this capable soldier had been constantly harassed, condemned, criticized, and spied upon by the local Jacobin club and the representatives of the people on mission, who had been sent to the army by the National Convention in Paris. He was even forced to withdraw the bulk of his army from the frontier, where it was opposed by a foreign enemy, to lay siege to the city of Lyon (August–September 1793). This enabled the enemy to advance into French territory. But it was more important to the political leaders of France to put down an insurrection than to prevent a foreign invasion and the loss of French territory. Kellermann had to work with such representatives as Pierre

Chépy, who held all generals in contempt and believed that they were suspect. In order to improve conditions in the armies of the Republic, Chépy proposed

> that every general condemned to death . . . shall be executed in the midst of the army he may have betrayed, that his body should be hanged by its heels on the territory of the enemy, with the inscription, "This monster sold himself to the enemies of the country. The vengeance of the French people, which has taken his head, abandons his remains to birds of prey and to tyrants."[2]

Kellermann was watched closely by the representatives of the people, who in turn were being denounced by the local Jacobin club for not denouncing the general. To justify themselves, the representatives wrote to Paris: "No mother watches her daughter more strictly [than we watch Kellermann]; if he trips, we are there."[3] The local Jacobin club at last had its way and Kellermann, an aristocrat by birth, was recalled to Paris in the early fall of 1793 to answer treasonous charges brought against him. When he had satisfied the Committee of Public Safety that he was a loyal and true republican, he was sent back to his army. Needless to say, he remained under the strictest supervision by the local Jacobins. Kellermann's enemies soon gained the upper hand, and he was removed from his command on October 16. He spent the remaining months of the Terror in prison and was saved from the guillotine, it is generally believed, only because of his victory at Valmy. Tried on November 9, 1794, he was acquitted and restored to his rank in the army. In the spring of 1795 he was found back at the head of the Army of the Alps, and Dumas would serve under his command.

If the hero of Valmy, who had saved his country from the invading Prussian army, could be subjected to such treatment, what hope did lesser men have in coping with the extremists who controlled France in 1793–1794? General François-Amédée Doppet replaced Kellermann, but he lasted only weeks. On November 6, 1793, General Jean-François Carteaux was given command of the Army of the Alps, but he was removed on December 6, charged with "the abuses of power," and imprisoned in the Conciergerie in Paris. Next, General Jean-Louis Pellapra was named temporary commander of the army, but he pleaded old age (he was forty) and poor health and removed himself from harm's way—not of the enemy, but of his own government. Thus it was that General Alexandre Dumas was the fourth commanding officer of the Army of the Alps in a matter of a few months. Two of his predecessors languished in prisons in Paris, and, it might be added, two of the recent commanders of the Army of Italy on his right flank (Generals Camillo Rossi and Gaspard-Jean-Baptiste Brunet) had been executed in November and December.[4]

Dumas either knew or quickly learned of the chaos that characterized the high command in the armies of southeast France and of the fate of those who had preceded him. The government at Paris was being tried to the utmost. In the summer and fall of 1793, the war had not gone well on the frontiers, and more than half of France, the west and the south, was in rebellion against the central government. The Reign of Terror was moving into high gear with the executioners working overtime. Taking command of an army at this time was putting one's life at risk from one's own countrymen. General Rossi had been arrested by his own troops and carried off to prison. Under these most adverse conditions, the new commander of the Army of the Alps stepped into the breach. He was not himself a terrorist, but he was as much a republican as any representative sent out by the Convention or any member of the local Jacobin club, and he would not suffer any interference on their part. It was his army and his responsibility, and he would run it his way.

Even before Dumas arrived at his headquarters at Grenoble, he had been warned of his staff. When he stopped at Lyon, which had recently been re-named Ville Affranchie after the insurrection had been put down, the representatives of the people there had told him that they did not have confidence in the staff officers of the Army of the Alps. Dumas assured everyone, including General Jean-Baptiste Bouchotte, the minister of war, that he would watch over his staff and make sure that they did no harm to the nation.[5]

Once in command, Dumas began by making enemies of the local Jacobins. Shortly after his arrival, he entered the village of Saint Maurice on a tour of inspection. The local authorities were making preparations for the execution of four men who had tried to steal the church bell of their village so as to prevent it from being melted down to cast cannons. To prevent the executions, which the general believed to be uncalled-for in light of the crime, he ordered one of his aides-de-camp to destroy the guillotine and to use the wood to build a fire so that he might warm himself. He then set the four condemned men free to flee to the mountains. The local Jacobins at once denounced him to the Committee of Public Safety in Paris.[6]

Once settled in at his new headquarters at Grenoble, Dumas began to take stock. The Sardinian forces he faced were holding all of the passes through the Alps that led into Italy. The Sardinian army was not one of Europe's better military forces, and the troops occupying the passes were not the best of the Sardinian army. Nevertheless, they were dug-in, and it could be a difficult task to dislodge them in midwinter. Furthermore, the Army of the Alps was far from the cream of the French army.

On paper, Dumas's command was put at fifty-five thousand men, but in fact it numbered less than forty-five thousand.[7] Moreover, most of these troops were doing garrison duty in the villages and towns of the numerous valleys on the west side of the Alps. The army had only three battalions of regular army line troops, which Dumas thought too few, and in February he asked that he be sent at least five additional line battalions.[8] The Army of the Alps was made up primarily of voluntary battalions and draftees. These battalions were generally inferior to the regular line units of the traditional standing army. The difference was between that of the professionals and the amateurs. The great majority of the officers and men of the regular line battalions were veterans of the old royal army. They were well-trained, disciplined, and capable soldiers. In contrast, the volunteers of 1791–1792 were still in the process of becoming good soldiers. Many of them were reluctant draftees who still lacked most of the characteristics of military men.[9]

In 1793–1794, the French army was being reorganized. The volunteer battalions, and the even newer draftees, combined with the regular line battalions. Two new (volunteer) battalions were combined with one regular battalion to form a "demi-" or half brigade. The demi-brigade, with three battalions, was the equivalent of a regiment. This amalgamation was resisted at first by the professional soldiers, but as the new battalions performed poorly in combat when they were not directly supported by regular units, it became clear to all that embrigadement was necessary. General Dumas, at the urging of Paris and the representatives of the people with the Army of Alps, undertook the formation of demi-brigades in his army during the months of February and March 1794. However, as he had only a few battalions of regulars, he was able to form only three demi-brigades. These units became the backbone of his command.[10]

On February 1, 1794, instruction from the Committee of Public Safety, over the signature of citizen Carnot, reached Dumas at Grenoble. "The General in Chief of the Army of the Alps will take measures to capture as soon as possible the passes that the enemy holds of the Petit Saint Bernard and the Grand and Petit Mount Cenis."[11] It went on to order Dumas to employ superior forces and to attack at all points simultaneously so that success would be assured. Once the passes were captured, the Army of the Alps was to dig in and defend them at all costs.[12] Dumas immediately acknowledged having received these orders and expressed his complete agreement with the necessity of capturing and holding the Alpine passes.[13]

Within days of his arrival at Grenoble, and even before he had received direct orders to attack the passes, Dumas had been laying the preliminary work for offensive operations. He wrote numerous letters to his field commanders and sent out lengthy orders of the day. He sent officers to every section of his command to gain firsthand, up-to-date information of the conditions of the troops and their equipment as well as the condition of the terrain. He requested the return of troops that had been sent to the Army of the West Pyrenees, the chasseurs of the battalion of the Haute Alps, and gave orders to be on guard against enemy infiltration from Sardinia and against deserters from his own army.[14] He also gave orders for the formation of an elite unit, a company of guides, made up of forty-eight officers and men to be used in the most difficult terrain of the Alps.[15] Then on February 1, the same day he received his orders from Paris to attack the passes as soon as possible, he received discouraging news from General Jean-François Dours.

General Dours had been sent to inspect the passes in the high Alps and to report back to the commander in chief. Upon his return, Dours provided Dumas with what must have been predictable information for late January in the Alps. The Petit Saint Bernard pass and Mount Cenis and its two passes (Grand and Petit Cenis) were covered with snow. High winds had made all of the passes impassable. However, the temperatures had not dropped low enough to freeze the surface of the snow sufficiently to support the weight of a man. Thus, any type of military operation under these difficult conditions would be almost impossible. Dours recommended that all offensive operations be postponed until the weather and the condition of the snow had improved.[16]

Alexandre Dumas had never lived or even traveled in a mountainous region. The first time he had seen real mountains was in 1792 when he was sent to the Army of the West Pyrenees, and at that time he was no closer than the city of Bayonne. It would be a gross understatement to say that he knew nothing of mountain fighting and even less of doing so in midwinter. Thus, he did what any wise army commander would have done under these circumstances: he stalled for time—time for weather and snow conditions to improve; time to become acquainted with the terrain upon which he was being asked to fight; time to know his army and its abilities and shortcomings; and time to prepare his army for what would appear to be a difficult campaign. In point of fact, Dumas did not even have any reliable maps of the country in which he was being asked to campaign. "Send men, maps, and charts," he wrote to the minister of war on January 30. "I cannot even buy any here. . . . We have only foreign maps. . . . I must sit on my hands until they arrive."[17]

On February 3, he again wrote to the minister of war explaining the situation and enclosing a copy of General Dours's report. He reassured the minister that he was completely and enthusiastically committed to the operations as laid out in his orders from the Committee of Public Safety but that it would require some time. It was not possible, at that point, to move against an enemy that was dug-in along the mountain passes. Then Dumas made a rather bold—and naive and rash—suggestion. He proposed that in order to gain the upper Po River valley and capture Turin (the capital of Sardinia), a French army should gain permission from the Swiss to use the Saint Gotthard pass.[18] It is somewhat puzzling why Dumas believed that a French army could cross the Saint Gotthard in midwinter when he could not operate in the Petit Saint Bernard under similar conditions. Furthermore, it is not clear as to whether he thought he would lead his Army of the Alps through Switzerland and over the Saint Gotthard or if such a task should be given to some other army. In any event, the suggestion, along with his letter of February 3, was passed on to Carnot and the Committee of Public Safety by the minister of war on February 7.[19]

The following day, February 8, the minister of war wrote a sharp, critical dispatch to Dumas. "I read with surprise your letter of February 3," wrote General Bouchotte. "The motives that you have alleged for not having executed the orders of the Committee of Public Safety do not justify your inaction. It is your duty," the minister admonished Dumas, to execute the orders he received. Then in response to Dumas's assurance that the government could count upon him to do his duty, Bouchotte, in an uncalled-for reprimand, wrote: "You say that the Republic can count upon you; the Republic can count only on the nation. It looks to all of its citizens to do their duty whatever might be their situation."[20] Dumas wisely held his tongue, or rather his pen, and made no reply to the minister. He could not undertake an offensive, and the reasons were not acceptable in Paris. He could only continue to stall for time. When Bouchotte did not hear from Dumas for more than three weeks, he wrote on February 27:

> I am very perturbed not to have received any news from you about the expedition ordered by the Committee of Public Safety on 6 pluviôse [January 25] which you should have executed by now. . . . The Committee of Public Safety is waiting for you to explain the motives for your conduct.[21]

General Bouchotte was undoubtedly under pressure from Carnot and the Committee of Public Safety. The Reign of Terror was at its height in the winter and spring of 1794. The Hébertists and the Dantonists were about to go to the guillotine. If men of that stature in the ranks of the Jacobins could lose their heads, no man could feel safe or secure in his political office, and the minister of war was a political appointee. Bouchotte needed action, successful action, on the part of his army commanders. The men of the all-powerful Committee of Public Safety were not men who were willing to accept excuses (such as the snow not being frozen hard enough to walk upon) from an army commander for not carrying out orders. Dumas clearly stood in danger of following in the footsteps of the four men who had commanded the Army of the Alps before him. After all, was not General Kellermann—who had been reasonably successful—languishing in a Parisian prison? Feeling this pressure from Paris, Dumas decided to hold a counsel of war at the end of February.

On the 26th of that month, in the city of Chambéry, Dumas convened his counsel of war at the home of citizen Gaston, the most influential of the representatives of the people with the Army of the Alps. Present at this counsel were Dumas, Gaston, and the three ranking generals of the army: Pierre-Emmanuel Rivus, Nicolas Basdelaune (or De Bas de l'Aulne or Bagdelaune), and Henry-Amable-A. Sarret. The purpose of this gathering was to deliberate on the best way to achieve the goals put forward in the orders from the Committee of Public Safety, that is, to capture the three passes occupied by the Sardinian army: Petit Saint Bernard and Grand and Petit Cenis. The officers first agreed that the capture of the passes would be a great advantage to the Republic as it would considerably facilitate the defense of southeast France. They also unanimously agreed that the campaign against the passes should take place while the ground was covered with a snow that would support the weight of a man. The snow would give the Sardinians a false sense of security and thus give the French the element of surprise. Without a hard crust on the snow, no operation could take place with any assurance of success. The generals also agreed that the snow conditions had been unsuitable for an attack on the passes in the weeks since the arrival of the orders from the Committee of Public Safety at the beginning of February. Finally, it was noted that all of the preparations for the expedition against the passes had been made and that the timing depended upon the weather, which changed almost daily. Secrecy was stressed with respect to troop movements so as not to give any indication of a major offensive.[22]

When the general discussion had been completed, the commander in chief gave his officers their assignments. General Basdelaune would command the expedition to Mount Valagun; General Sarret would command the expedition to Mount Cenis, including the troops of the Maurienne; and General Charles-Henri Vaubois would command the troops of the valley of the Barulonnette. Generals Sarret and Basdelaune were then authorized to issue orders over their own signature to acquire whatever foodstuffs and supplies they deemed necessary for their respective army units to undertake the missions assigned to them.[23] By the end of February, Dumas was ready to move against the enemy, but the weather would not cooperate.

On the day following the counsel of war, Dumas wrote to the the representatives of the people who were assigned by the Committee of Public Safety to watch over him. He enclosed a copy of a summary of what had taken place at the counsel and assured the citizens that all was ready for an attack on the passes but that there were still some last-minute details that needed attention. As snow conditions, the real cause of delay, was not an acceptable reason for postponing the attacks, Dumas explained that his army was spread out over five departments and that the troops were quartered in valleys separated by snow-covered mountains. Before an attack could be launched, he would have to review his troops, and that would take some time because they were not concentrated. Finally, he complained that his troops were lacking muskets, uniforms, and every type of equipment that is needed by an army. He also declared that he needed a good fourth general of division. In conclusion, he brought up the problem of the lack of any clear line of division between his army and the Army of Italy on his right flank. He was never sure at what point his jurisdiction ended, and he feared that this could result in a gap in the line of defense between the two armies. He therefore asked the representatives to look into these matters and to provide him with detailed instructions.[24] Although these complaints and questions were primarily a smoke screen to gain time for the weather to turn cold enough to harden the snow in the passes, they also indicated problems on which Dumas would work over the following weeks.

On the last day of February, General Dumas received from Captain Ratel a twenty-page report that confirmed his evaluation of the difficulties that would be encountered in attacking the Sardinian positions in the mountain passes. Ratel, who commanded the elite company of "guides" in the Department of Mount Blanc, had been sent on a reconnaissance mission to actually go to the passes and report back firsthand on the situation. With a handful of men, he had approached the enemy positions as closely as possible and confirmed the fact that an advance upon the Sardinian defenses would be extremely difficult. He went on to say that the possibility of such an expedition successfully capturing those positions was very unlikely until such time as the snow was frozen hard enough to support the weight of the advancing soldiers.[25] Despite this reassurance, and with the support of his senior generals and at least one of the representatives of the people with the army (Gaston), Dumas had some explaining to do to his superiors in Paris.

The Committee of Public Safety had sent Representative Dumas (no relation to the general) from Paris to General Dumas to find out just why there had been no action taken on its orders to capture the Alpine passes. The arrival of this representative in the last week of February, presumably with direct criticism of the lack of action on the part of the Army of Alps, forced General Dumas to write a lengthy letter to explain and justify his inactivity. On March 1 he actually wrote two letters, one to the minister of war and the other to the Committee of Public Safety, detailing his position. He assured both parties that he would indeed attack at the earliest possible time when victory could be guaranteed. Dumas further told the Committee of Public Safety that Representative Dumas and the representatives assigned to the Army of the Alps could verify all that he had written.[26]

It is clear from these two letters that General Dumas was very concerned about the deterioration of his relations with Paris. It was absolutely necessary that he reassure the Committee of Public Safety and the minister of war of his intentions to carry out their orders as soon as possible and for them to understand why he had not taken any offensive action since his arrival at the end of January. Fortunately for Dumas, Representative Gaston also wrote to his colleagues in Paris justifying the general's action, or rather lack of action, and assuring them that Dumas was acting in the best interest of the Republic.

After briefing the Committee of Public Safety on the political situation in the region of the Alps, Gaston addressed the military situation:

> The General in Chief [Dumas] and myself have reconnoitered all of the positions on our frontier. We have climbed on foot through the snow to the base of Mount Cenis and to the Petit Saint Bernard Pass. As of today the snow is not hard and will not support the weight [of a man]. We hope that the snow conditions will soon be as we need them, and we will be able to accomplish our objectives without delay.[27]

Gaston went on to explain that the decision to postpone the expeditions to capture the passes was perfectly justifiable under the present circumstances. He further wrote that Representative Dumas, whom the Committee of Public Safety had sent especially to look into the actions of the commander in chief, was in full agreement with the delay, as were all of the senior generals of the army, and that Representative Dumas would write the committee to that effect.[28]

Exactly what Representative Dumas wrote to the committee (and he must have sent a report) is not known. But Gaston's letter, along with those written by General Dumas, did buy the time that was needed to carry out the expeditions. Neither the minister of war nor the Committee of Public Safety could remove a commanding general who had the full support of the two principal representatives of the National Convention. Thus, Dumas continued to fine-tune his preparations to carry out his instructions.

The months of February and March were frustrating for General Dumas and his army. They were ready to move against the enemy positions, but the weather conditions prevented any serious action. There were minor engagements with the Sardinians, problems with émigrés, near-panic in some villages due to rumor, and desertions, all of which absorbed the time and energy of the commander in chief while he waited.

On March 16, Dumas reported to the Committee of Public Safety that there had been disturbances to the east of Annecy when a band of men, presumed to be émigrés, came down into a valley and raided a small town.[29] The whole question of emigrants in the Savoy was one that plagued Dumas the entire six months that he commanded the Army of the Alps. The French army had driven the Sardinians out of the province of Savoy. This French-speaking district was in a state of limbo by the end of 1793. In the fall of that year, the French had created several "clubs," that is, pro-French political organizations, in the principal cities. Then the Savoy, controlled by those clubs, abolished the Old Regime and requested annexation to France. Finally, on November 27, 1793, the National Convention annexed Savoy and justified its actions on grounds of geography, language, and the common interests they shared.[30] Thus, when Dumas arrived in the east in January 1794, Savoy had been a part of France for only two months.

The annexation to France may have been generally popular with the majority of the people of the Savoy; however, there were powerful and influential factions and parties that were not pleased with the new arrangements. French republicanism became the law of the land. The old nobility lost their titles and privileges; the Catholic church lost its lands and its privileges. Many of the aristocrats fled over the Alps and took refuge in northern Italy, while many priests who remained in Savoy went underground. General Dumas became almost paranoid in his belief that priests and returning emigrants were trying to sabotage the French war effort in Savoy and were spying on the French and providing the enemy with sensitive information on army strength and movements. He clearly feared that his attacks on the enemy's position in the passes would be compromised by information transmitted by those priests and emigrants.[31]

The annexation of Savoy to France also created another problem for Dumas: what was he to do with the deserters from the enemy army who had been born and raised in Savoy? Many of these men had been taken into the army of the king of Sardinia when Savoy was a part of his kingdom. After

Savoy was annexed to France, some of these men wished to leave the Sardinian army and return home. As they found their way into French territory, they were taken into custody by the French. Dumas's dilemma was how to treat these men. Were they simply deserters from the enemy army who should thus be sent to prisoner-of-war camps, or should they be treated as returning French citizens? In the latter case, might they not be taken into the French army? Finally, it was possible that some of them could be spies, returning emigrants sent by the enemy to gain information. Dumas laid out his dilemma to the minister of war and the Committee of Public Safety in several letters in March and April.[32] Then in mid-April, he received instructions from the minister of war that left the decisions with him. There were many reasons why men were deserting from the Sardinian army, wrote General Bouchotte, and the commander in chief would have to sort out these deserters and treat each one as he would judge best in accordance with the man's reasons for leaving Sardinia and returning to France.[33] Dumas thus handled this problem as best he could under the existing conditions.

A similar problem arose when deserters left the French army to go to the enemy. Many of the men in the Army of the Alps were reluctant draftees who had no intention of dying for what they considered to be a "republican" war. On March 15, a small band of thirteen men from a Corsican unit, the 4th Battalion of light infantry, deserted. The group was made up of a captain, a lieutenant, five corporals, and six chasseurs. Dumas deemed the battalion to be untrustworthy for combat duty, or even garrison duty close to the enemy lines, and sent it to the rear to do hospital duty.[34] Individual desertions were known to all of the armies of the French Republic, but this incident was more unusual because the group of deserters was so large. There is no other example in Dumas's command of so many men deserting at one time.

In preparation for the major attacks on the passes, Dumas ordered probing of the enemy positions and sent scouting parties to gain necessary information. A combination of spies sent by Dumas into enemy territory and reconnaissance parties that probed the enemy's forward positions provided him with valuable intelligence. He learned, for example, in the middle of March that the enemy had reinforced its positions at Mount Cenis with a detachment of nine hundred men.[35] He was further informed that there was a reserve detachment of eighteen thousand Neapolitan troops at Alessandria should the French cross the Alps and enter the upper Po River valley.[36] Then early in April, he received a full seven-page report on enemy positions in the passes from an officer who had probed to within musket range of the enemy's redoubts.[37]

Seeing to the feeding, billeting, equipping, and training of the troops consumed much of Dumas's time. His correspondence throughout March and April contains numerous references to the acquisition and distribution of food and wine. Much of the problem was caused by the fact that the terrain on the west slopes of the Alps, where his army was billeted, was a series of river valleys separated by mountains that were impassable in the winter.

Communication and transportation north and south along this front was extremely difficult. Furthermore, there was little surplus food produced in this mountainous region. Nevertheless, it was essential that the troops be fed in order to maintain good discipline, reduce desertion, and enable the army to advance when the time came to attack the passes.[38]

Clothing and equipment were yet other problems. The Army of the Alps received the lowest priority in Paris. The armies on the Rhine and in the north received the major part of what supplies and equipment were available to the government. What was left, and it was little, was distributed between the Armies of Italy, the Pyrenees, the Vendée, and the Alps. In practical terms, this meant that Dumas had to rely on local sources in a region that was not known for its wealth. More than anything else, the troops needed boots and heavy coats, and they had to find them locally. In the first weeks of March, Dumas was able to supply his troops with wooden shoes to facilitate walking on snow.[39] He also provided climbing boots and had specially made climbing irons for ice and snow.[40] For the military equipment needed, he had to plead with Paris. Dumas was fortunate to have Representative Gaston working closely with him and backing up his requests to the local authorities and Paris.[41] Receiving some aid from the government in Paris and a great deal of aid from the local economy, thanks in no small way to Representatives Gaston and Dumas, General Dumas was able to prepare his forces for the expedition against the enemy.

Supplying the army was not the only problem that faced General Dumas in the winter and spring of 1794. His army, like all of the armies of France during the Revolution, had a large number of women who had virtually become a part of his command. These camp followers, or perhaps camp wives is a better term, provided services to the troops and lived off of army rations. The services rendered were not only sexual; the women also prepared meals for their men, did their washing and sewing, and in general "kept house" during the long months of inactivity. While this may have been a very nice arrangement for troops, it was a problem for their commander. He was already having a difficult time feeding and maintaining the men. The extra burden of keeping the women weighed heavily on the resources available in the district. Furthermore, the presence of a large number of women was a negative factor when it came to good discipline and order in the army. Dumas, therefore, took stern measures to remove all of the women from the army. He sent them west into France in large convoys, and those who found their way back to the army were put in prison. Needless to say, this was not popular with the troops, but it most likely improved the overall condition of the army.[42]

Discipline improved in the months following Dumas's assumption of command. Yet there were some problems from time to time with which he concerned himself, even though they were relatively minor affairs. At the end of March, seven or eight soldiers from the Vienne battalion on his extreme left wing had crossed into Swiss territory and caused a disturbance (the nature of which is not documented). The Swiss authorities lodged a formal complaint, and Dumas ordered the men arrested and punished, sending the battalion to the rear so that discipline could be improved. He also paid damages to the Swiss government.[43]

But although Dumas was determined to remain on good terms with the Swiss, he made little effort to appease the powerful local French Jacobin society. When he learned in early March that he had been denounced to the Popular (Jacobin) Society of Chambéry, he reacted angrily. The charge against him, which he flatly denied, was that he had ordered a halt to the work on the defenses at Montmélian. Dumas demanded to know the name of the person who had levied the charge against him so that he could confront his accuser. The Society also had sent a deputation to General Jean-François Dours, who commanded the district of the Maurienne, to demand an explanation of why units of the 23rd Regiment had been moved. This brought an angry rebuff from Dumas. On March 8, he wrote sarcastically to the Popular Society of Chambéry that "a learned society cannot be ignorant of the fact that generals cannot reveal their operations without putting in danger the well-being of their army. They alone are in charge, and they answer with their head."[44] If it was the intention of the Society to intimidate Alexandre Dumas, they had very much misjudged the man. He was not one who could be bullied. He accepted full responsibility for the army under his command and therefore intended to exert control over that army.

The general was once again fortunate to have the support of the representatives of the people with the Army of the Alps in this clash with the local Jacobins. Just five days after his curt rebuff to the Popular Society of Chambéry, the representatives printed copies of the minutes from their last meeting that gave their fullest backing to General Dumas. Over the signature of Representative Gaston, this proclamation declared that "no movement of troops, infantry, cavalry, or artillery will take place without the express order of the commander in chief in consultation with the representatives of the National Convention."[45] This document went on in two more articles to make perfectly clear that General Dumas, with the backing of the representatives, commanded the army, and that he was not in any way responsible to the local authorities, nor did they have any voice in the affairs of the Army of the Alps. Gaston and General Dumas were of one mind on the operations of the army. Indeed, Gaston, the dominant representative with the army, respected Dumas's judgment on military affairs and not only gave the general a free hand but also defended him to the Committee of Public Safety and to the minister of war.

The problems of March were multiplied by yet another unpleasant affair for General Dumas. On the 12th of that month, the minister of war wrote a rather curt letter to him stating that General of Brigade Sarret, who commanded at Briançon on Dumas's right (south) flank, had complained to the Committee of Public Safety that he had been sent a battalion of chasseurs of the Alps that was totally useless to him. The men were "without any training, without arms, and composed of deserters" from the Sardinian army, who were not considered to be reliable. "You would do well," concluded the minister, "to replace those chasseurs with another battalion made up of better men whose patriotism and bravery has already been tested."[46] The battalion of chasseurs sent to Briançon was one of several battalions that had been formed in the region, made up of men from the newly annexed province of Savoy. Indeed, many of the soldiers had deserted from the Sardinian army, and there was still some question as to just where their loyalty would be placed if asked to fight against their former companions-in-arms.[47]

Shortly after receiving this rebuff from Paris, Dumas made a personal inspection of the conditions on his right flank.[48] He rectified the problem of the battalion of chasseurs by sending it to the rear for training.[49] At the same time, Dumas also wished to survey the new line that divided his Army of the Alps from General Jean-Mathieu-P. Sérurier, who commanded the left flank of the Army of Italy. The line dividing the two armies had been vague and uncertain since Dumas had arrived in January. He had been concerned that a gap could develop between the two armies that would be exploited by the enemy and ruin his plans for an offensive in the center of his position. On March 15, the minister of war had written to him, defining in clear terms the southern limit of his command. The Department of Basse Alpes, which Dumas had thought to be a part of his responsibility, would no longer be under his command but under that of Sérurier.[50] At about the same time as the Basse Alpes was shifted to the Army of Italy, Dumas was instructed to send four battalions to that army, which had been ordered to attack the enemy. He protested the loss of these battalions but complied with the orders from the Committee of Public Safety.[51]

During the night of March 23–24, Dumas personally led a detachment of forty-five men to gain intelligence of the enemy in the pass of the Grand Cenis. By daybreak, he had come within a few hundred meters of the Sardinian positions. At that point, the presence of his small force was discovered, and the enemy opened fire. The French suffered two casualties before they were able to withdraw to a safe distance and then make their way back down into the valley to their own secure positions.[52]

It was not the custom for army commanders to do their own reconnaissance. Advancing in the dark to within musket range of enemy positions was both physically challenging and extremely dangerous. Generals would rely on secondary information brought to them by junior officers, who were expected to do the hazardous and unpleasant tasks. This episode provides insight into Alexandre Dumas the man. His bravery would become as legendary in the Revolutionary army as his strength had been in the royal army.

By the end of March, the combination of a slight improvement in weather conditions and continued pressure from Paris made it impossible for Dumas to postpone an attack on the enemy any longer. His army had been ready for weeks while the patience of the Committee of Public Safety and the minister of war was coming to an end. On April 1, he received a copy of a report by a spy sent out to gain the latest information on the enemy positions in the passes. This report confirmed the intelligence that had been coming in throughout the month of March: the enemy positions had been reinforced and were strongly held.[53]

The long-awaited attack on the enemy's position in the Mount Cenis sector took place on the night of April 5, 1794. The pressure from Paris had been constant. Indeed, if Dumas had not shown some initiative, it is likely that he would have been recalled in disgrace to explain why he had done nothing for so long a period of time. During February and March, when he had been pressed to move, he had most certainly given serious consideration to the fate of those who had commanded the Army of the Alps before him. Recall would surely lead at least to prison, if not the guillotine.

Having personally reconnoitered the terrain and knowing the army was ready—indeed, had been ready for some time—Dumas issued his orders for the operation against the enemy positions of the Grand and Petit Mount Cenis. Immediately prior to the attack, those orders were passed along by General Sarret, who had been given command of the six thousand men who were to take part in the action.[54]

The general plan of the operation was to move against the passes on the north and south sides of Mount Cenis at the same time. The principal effort would be made against the south pass (Petit Mount Cenis), which became the right flank. A smaller force would move against the north pass (Grand Mount Cenis), which became the left flank. General Sarret himself would lead the largest corps, 2,130 men strong, on the right, while General of Brigade Louis-Jean-Baptiste Gouvion, the cousin of the future Marshal Laurent Gouvion St. Cyr, led the corps on the left.

Following the attack, there were two reports of the military operations written to General Dumas and two letters to the Committee of Public Safety, written by Dumas and Representative Gaston. By far, the most complete account is the six page report by General Gouvion. The following quote from Gouvion is the best description of what actually happened:

> I am sending to you, citizen General [Dumas], this report of the attack on Mount Cenis which took place the night of the 16th and 17th [of germinal, that is, April 5–6]. . . . The division of the right under the command of General Sarret was 2100 men strong and left from Bramars at 9:00 P.M. the night of the 5th. It advanced up the gorge opposite St. Pierre d'Estravack. The column commanded by this General went by way of a trail that was very dangerous in the winter and a number of men fell into the gorge. Under such conditions the advance of the column was slow. Furthermore, the column was forced to give up that trail and retrace its steps and follow a lower path that had been assigned to another column which had been designated to support their attack. When Sarret's column reached the redoubt in front of the Petit Mount Cenis [at midmorning], which according to different reports had not been occupied by the enemy, they found that it was manned by a strong force supported by artillery, and it was impossible to evade it. Despite these obstacles,

General Sarret decided to attack. Placing himself at the head of his advance guard he attacked. However, they did not reach the redoubt. One by one they were killed or wounded. The snow made it very difficult to advance, and men fell into the gorge.

General Sarret had only forty men when he reached the summit [of the pass] where he was mortally wounded. Many of his grenadiers were also killed or wounded by the same volley [that hit Sarret] and fell into the valley. This spectacle made a great impression on the division and it was taken by a moment of terror and began to withdraw. General Camin, who commanded the 3rd column [Sarret's support column], arrived with his company of chasseurs and tried to stop the retreat. The Piedmontese [Sardinians] who wanted to profit by the failure of our attack were convinced otherwise when they saw [Camin] rallying our troops. . . .[55]

The men, who had been under arms since the afternoon of the previous day and had climbed throughout the night from the valley to the summit of the pass, were exhausted. With their commander mortally wounded and no one stepping forward to take his place, they began the long and dangerous descent.

The columns on the left, led by General Gouvion, had advanced to a point just out of musket range of the enemy positions at the Grand Mount Cenis pass. There they waited throughout the morning and early afternoon for support from the column on the right. General Sarret was to have captured the Petit Mount Cenis pass first and then give aid to Gouvion's attack on the stronger position. When Sarret's support did not arrive, Gouvion withdrew in good order to the valley. He commanded too small a column to attack the strongly held enemy position without support, and he could not spend the night on the side of the mountain in subfreezing temperatures.[56]

The attack was a complete failure. Dumas immediately took measures to reinforce his defensive position in the vicinity of Mount Cenis so as to prevent the enemy taking advantage of the withdrawal of his troops and any possible confusion that might accompany the failed attack. The result was that the status quo was very quickly restored and both armies occupied the same positions that they had occupied on April 5 before the French columns had advanced.[57] The Sardinian army was in no condition to advance into the valleys on the French side of the Alps and had no intention of doing so.

The principal reason for the failure of the attack on Mount Cenis was probably the fatal wounding of General Sarret, who died of his wounds in the village of Briançon on April 7. However, as the enemy seemed to have known that an attack on the passes, either Mount Cenis or the Petit Saint Bernard, was in preparation and had therefore reinforced its position, the French offensive may very well have failed even if Sarret had not been wounded. What is certain is that the turning point of the whole circumstance occurred when Sarret fell on the battlefield and his troops began to retreat.

One of the real mysteries of this affair is why it was that General Dumas did not personally lead the principal column to attack the redoubts at the Petit Mount Cenis pass. There is no question but that General Sarret was a capable commander in whom Dumas had complete confidence, but it would have been more in keeping with Dumas's personality to have at least been with that column on the right where the primary attack was to take place. If the attack on the Petit Mount Cenis positions had been successful, the Grand Mount Cenis pass would have been attacked from front and rear and could not possibly have held out. Thus, the day would have been victorious for the French. On the other hand, if the attack on the right was a failure, the day would have been lost, because Gouvion's force was too small to succeed on its own. In retrospect, one might argue that if Dumas had been in Sarret's place, it is likely that he would have suffered the fate of the dead general. Or it might be argued that Dumas, even if not wounded, could not have captured the pass because of the conditions of the terrain and the strength of the enemy position.

Dumas undoubtedly felt that his presence was not necessary with the advancing columns and that Sarret on the right and Gouvion on the left were perfectly capable of carrying out the missions assigned to them. Yet this defeat seems to have been burned into his consciousness, for he never again sent a subordinate to do the critical work at hand. Dumas would be with his advance guard when the enemy positions were attacked and captured at the Petit Saint Bernard pass. In Italy in 1797, he personally led his troops into battle, and in Egypt when the great Azhar Mosque was attacked, Dumas led the charge and was the first to enter. The affair with the Sardinians was in fact the only serious defeat suffered by troops under his command.

With the front both stable and quiet, Dumas could turn his attention to damage control. The Committee of Public Safety and the minister of war had to be informed of the failure of the attack, but even more important, they had to have an explanation of the failure that would not cost the commanding general his head. Four days after the defeat, Dumas informed the committee and gave his reason for the lack of success.

> In accordance with your orders of 6 pluviôse [January 25] the attack on Mount Cenis has taken place. The dispositions that I had taken and the courage of the troops who were destined to undertake the expedition gave me every reason to believe that it would be successful. I was deceived. The obstacles of nature did not stop me because it was my duty to obey your orders, but I did not calculate on the traitors who informed the enemy of our plan. I have no doubt but that this is what happened.[58]

Dumas was absolutely certain that treason had caused the defeat. He even singled out the towns where he believed the treacherous activities were taking place. "Everything convinces me," he continued in his correspondence with the Committee of Public Safety, "that it was the inhabitants of Sous le Bourg and Sous le Villard who sent spies daily to the Piedmontese with information of our movements."[59] This was followed on April 16 by another letter to the committee in which he wrote, "Two Piedmont deserters have assured us that the inhabitants of Sous le Villard had informed the Piedmontese of our movements and that this was the reason that Mount Cenis had been reinforced by 2,500 men."[60] Then in a letter to the minister of war on April 19, he made further excuses:

> I will limit myself to telling you that the moment of victory escaped us because of the fatigue of the troops and the death of General Sarret. . . . However, the cowardliness and treachery of some individuals . . . also contributed to the disaster of that day. The reports furnished to me have been confirmed by my going personally to the Maurienne and gaining information on the spot.[61]

Although Dumas did not accept any of the responsibility for the defeat himself, neither did he attempt to put any of the blame on the poor unfortunate General Sarret. In fact, he made a special point of exonerating the general. "General Sarret," he wrote to the Committee of Public Safety, "who was in charge of the enterprise, neglected nothing to make it a success, and you may be assured that he conducted it with intelligence, activity and courage."[62]

Representative Gaston also reported to his colleagues of the Committee of Public Safety. After a brief description of the action that took place on April 5 and 6, he indicated that the plan had been a good one. He undoubtedly had approved of the plan, if he had not actively helped draw it up; indeed, if he had had nothing to do with the plan, then he might have been held accountable for neglect of his responsibilities and duties. He further supported Dumas by clearly stating that the cause of the failure did not lie with the Army of the Alps. "The enemy had not been surprised," he wrote; "they knew where the attack would take place and reinforced those positions, and their artillery was properly positioned."[63] Not only did he subscribe to General Dumas's theory of treason, he also took it one step further. As a member of the National Convention and with its support, at least up until that point, he, unlike Dumas, could attack the office of the ministry of war. "We must argue," he continued in his letter, "that the bureau of war is infected with men who are corrupt . . .[that] they sent special couriers to the court at Turin [Sardinia] to inform it of our project against Mount Cenis and the Petit Saint Bernard."[64] Gaston did not accuse General Bouchotte of treason but rather of being manipulated by the corrupt men around him.

Realizing that both he and General Dumas would be held responsible for the failure of the attack on Mount Cenis, Gaston demanded straight out a vote of confidence on the part of the Committee of Public Safety.

> Do you have confidence in the Representatives of the People [with the Army of the Alps] or do you not. In the first case you must give them your full trust. . . . In the second case you must recall them to the [National]

Convention, because if they do not have your full confidence they can be of no use to the army.[65]

In forcing the issue of confidence, the well-respected Gaston, who described himself as a sincere republican *montagnard*, caused the all-powerful Committee of Public Safety either to recall both himself and Dumas in disgrace or to continue to give them both their full support. The committee chose to continue to give their support, and the political crisis passed. Once again, Dumas was fortunate to have Gaston as a buffer between himself and the Paris Jacobins, for men of greater stature than he had lost their command for less cause. Nevertheless, Dumas was on the defensive.

Dumas's correspondence to Paris over the next weeks reflected an obvious pattern of damage control. He went to great lengths to assure his superiors that there was no possibility of the enemy making inroads into France on his sector of the front. He made frequent tours of the forward positions, leaving nothing to chance or to his subordinates. He closed down tightly the frontier and suppressed anything that might even be construed as resistance, subversion, or treason.[66] By the last week of April, the weather conditions were favorable, and the pressures enormous, for a successful attack on the enemy's position.

On April 24, General Dumas was able to inform the Committee of Public Safety from the hospice on the Petit Saint Bernard pass: "Your wishes are fulfilled. Saint Bernard is ours."[67] He could not conceal his joy, and he did not wait four days, as was the case with the Mount Cenis disaster, to send the news to Paris. Furthermore, this time Dumas had gone with the forward units, accompanied by Adjutant General Espagne and even his secretary Laffont, to be sure that there would be no repeat of the failure of command brought about by the wounding of General Sarret.[68]

Dumas described the action in the following terms:

> It was today, April 24 at 5 A.M. in the morning, that we captured a number of redoubts that were on both sides of the pass. This was only possible because the republicans of France did their duty. Every aspect of military virtue was displayed in this memorable attack: persistence over fatigue, bravery in battle, a contempt for death, and the sacrifice of everything in battle. After ten hours of marching throughout the night in the snow across horrible abysses, the troops arrived before the redoubts of Mount Valaizan [Valezian] where cannon balls and bullets fell about our feet. At that point our troops charged and captured the position by force. Once in control [of the redoubt] they turned its cannons on the redoubt of the Chapelle du Saint Bernard which was quickly evacuated . . . and the Piedmontese fled from all of the posts before the victorious French.[69]

The French actually pursued the fleeing enemy for three leagues down the other side of the pass. They had captured twenty pieces of artillery, two hundred muskets, a large amount of supplies, and two hundred prisoners of war. While Dumas could not estimate the losses inflicted on the enemy, he did say they were "considerable." He put French losses at a rather vague "60 wounded and some killed."[70] This vagueness was most likely due to the fact that he wrote this letter the day of the battle and did not have the details of his own killed and wounded.

As Dumas had praised, not blamed, the late General Sarret for the disaster at Mount Cenis, so now he gave the credit for the victory at the Petit Saint Bernard to General Basdelaune. "The success of this affair," he wrote, "is a tribute to General Basdelaune who commanded the troops. . . . I tell you that he has combined intelligence with knowledge and that he executed the attack with firmness and courage."[71] He further added that Representative Gaston would confirm the important role played by General Basdelaune. Gaston did, in fact, support Dumas's praises of the general—and then went a step further. "I have named General Bagdelone [sic] general of division on the field of battle," he wrote to the Committee of Public Safety. "He merited well that act of recognition, and I hope that the Convention will show its approval."[72] It is particularly interesting to note that Dumas gave Basdelaune praise and credit for his role in the attack on the Petit Saint Bernard, because he would have a major confrontation with General Bonaparte in Italy in the winter of 1797 over a lack of recognition. At that time, General Alexandre Berthier would slight Dumas by playing down his role in the capture of Mantua.

Gaston was so pleased with the victory that he began his letter to the Committee of Public Safety with: "I am delivering to you joy!"[73] Like Dumas, he wrote on the day of the battle from the field of battle. His glowing description of the engagement and his overzealous praise of republican virtues is excessive but indicates the high degree of emotion he was feeling at the time. Needless to say, Gaston believed that the victory at the Petit Saint Bernard vindicated both himself and General Dumas in light of the setback just three weeks earlier.

On May 8, as part of a longer letter to the representatives of the people with the Army of the Alps, the Committee of Public Safety, over the signature of Carnot, expressed satisfaction that the Saint Bernard had been captured but reminded them that Mount Cenis was still in enemy hands. In part, Carnot wrote: "The operations of the Army of the Alps at the Petit Saint Bernard has inspired in us great confidence in the generals who conducted that operation, and we hope that Mount Cenis will soon be in our hands, if it is not already."[74] It was rather faint praise with a pointed reminder that the job was only half finished.

With the Petit Saint Bernard firmly in French hands, General Dumas turned his attention once again to Mount Cenis. He was determined to drive the enemy from the strong position it held and to have revenge for the failure of April 5–6. The day after the capture of the Petit Saint Bernard, April 25, Dumas ordered General Basdelaune, with two thousand elite troops who had taken part in the attack, to the Mount Cenis sector of the line. Basdelaune was placed in command of the new preparations for the attack on the passes.

He was now a general of division and outranked General of Brigade Gouvion, who had been the senior general before Mount Cenis since the death of Sarret. As Dumas wrote to the Committee of Public Safety on May 2, he would use reliable troops, who had already displayed their courage at the Petit Saint Bernard, and his most capable and experienced general to undertake this new attack.[75]

Dumas issued detailed instructions to Basdelaune during the first week of May.[76] He then moved his headquarters from Grenoble to Briançon in a most public manner. He also ordered diversionary attacks on the southern flank to make the enemy believe that the next serious strike would be from Briançon against the Montgenévre pass rather than against Mount Cenis.[77] Then on May 11, Dumas ordered an offensive on the enemy position at Mirabauk. The general accompanied the attacking troops, and after the fortifications were captured he led a column in pursuit of the enemy as far as Oulx. At that point he established his advance post. In this successful diversion, the French inflicted about sixty casualties on the enemy and captured several cannons.[78] This was followed on the night of May 12–13 by the army marching on the Grand Mount Cenis pass.

Dumas himself left Briançon secretly and joined General Basdelaune, who was poised for the night march up to the pass. The plan was not unlike that which was successful against the Petit Saint Bernard. It called for one column to advance directly up the valley for a frontal attack of the enemy's position with columns on the right and on the left. Dumas accompanied the column on the right, which was actually commanded by Captain Gerbin of the grenadiers of the 23rd Infantry Battalion. General Basdelaune personally led the column on the left. The advance went as planned. The column on the right reached the enemy position without being detected. The Sardinians were so surprised that the redoubt fell with little fighting. Dumas quickly turned the redoubt's guns against the other enemy positions, and the battle began in earnest. One French column, as per the original plan, reached the other side of the pass and cut off the enemy's line of retreat. With the element of surprise working to their advantage, the French were able to capture all of the redoubts, posts, and positions in the pass within an hour and a half. The victory was complete, and Dumas pushed his advance posts some three leagues farther in the direction of Suse (Suze).[79]

The attack was a tremendous success. The French took eight hundred to nine hundred prisoners of war, killed a "large number" of the enemy (according to Basdelaune), and captured a substantial amount of military supplies and food. French losses were reported at seven or eight killed and about thirty wounded.[80] Dumas had again been with the forward troops and under enemy fire. He would not run the risk of another failure but personally made sure that all went well, or, if something did go wrong, he would be there to make whatever adjustments were necessary. In this manner he was able to direct the battle while on the field of battle. Such command was possible when the engagement was limited in numbers and in a relatively confined area, as was the pass of the Grand Mount Cenis. Indeed, General Dumas was at his best personally leading his men in reasonably small conflicts. He was brave to a fault and very lucky that he was never killed at the head of his men, unlike the equally brave General Sarret.

One may imagine with what pleasure General Dumas wrote from Mount Cenis to the Committee of the Public Safety to inform its members of his latest victory. He had at last fulfilled the instructions given to him by the committee in January when he had taken command of the Army of the Alps. He had also made reparations for the failure to capture the passes in April. He had every reason to expect the approval of the Paris government, and indeed, Paris was pleased. Carnot, the "Organizer of Victory," himself penned the committee's most flattering reply. Addressed to the "Representatives of the People with the Army of the Alps," he wrote:

> Glory to the conquerors of Mount Cenis and of Mount Saint Bernard. Glory to the invincible Army of the Alps and to the representatives who have guided it on the road to victory! We cannot tell you, my dear colleagues, of the enthusiasm that has been created here as a result of the news you have announced. . . . We are placing the greatest confidence in you and in the energy and talents of the brave general Dumas.
>
> Salutations and fraternity
> Carnot[81]

After this expression of satisfaction on the part of Carnot, everyone with the Army of the Alps could sleep well.

With all of the Alpine passes in Dumas's sector of the line firmly in hand, the Army of the Alps was ordered to take up a defensive posture. This included destroying the enemy's redoubts and embrasures on the west side of the passes and building and manning their own redoubts and earthworks on the east side of the passes. That work was taken up in an energetic way with regular reports on the progress reaching Dumas at Grenoble.[82] The commander in chief made inspection tours of the various passes in the months of May and June both to direct the defensive works and to see that his orders were being carried out.[83] Once this work had been completed, the Army of the Alps settled down to await the course of events.

In point of fact, there was little that the Army of the Alps could do once the passes were in its hands. Because of its size—only forty to forty-five thousand men strong—and the general mediocrity of the quality of most of its troops, there was no possibility of an invasion of northern Italy. A number of battalions were composed of newly drafted recruits, many of them from the Savoy, and were deemed questionable in their loyalty to the French Republic. Leading such troops on an offensive campaign into Italy would have been a reckless and hazardous undertaking.

But all was not perfectly quiet along the Alps in the late spring of 1794. In the last days of May, the enemy attacked and held for a very brief time the outpost of the Madeleine. The French had little difficulty retaking the position, as it apparently was more of a probing action on the part of the Sardinians than a serious attack.[84] They continued to probe the French position in early June, then on the 18th made a more serious attack on the French advance position defending the Petit Saint Bernard Pass.[85] Several posts were overrun before General Basdelaune's forces pushed the Sardinians back to their original positions. He reported to Dumas that the enemy had suffered "heavy" losses, more than one hundred men, including senior officers, while exact French losses had not yet been determined.[86] While none of these engagements were serious, they did serve to keep the French alert, and they certainly confirmed the fact that the enemy was ever present and wanted to regain control of the Alpine passes.

At the end of June, Dumas's position in the Alps was excellent, and there seemed little chance that the enemy would be able to dislodge him from the passes. One then can only imagine the general's surprise when he was recalled to Paris. On June 24, over the signature of Robespierre, Couthon, Bertrand Barère, Jean-Nicolas Billaud-Varenne, and Carnot, the order read:

> The Committee of Public Safety orders that Dumas, General in Chief of the Army of the Alps, will present himself before the Committee of Public Safety with two adjutant generals and two aides-de-camp. . . . He will turn over command of the army to the most senior general of division.[87]

After putting his affairs in order and naming General of Division Pierre Petit Guillaume temporary commander in his absence[88]—for he fully expected to return to the army—Dumas acknowledged the orders from the Committee of Public Safety and left Grenoble for Paris on July 7.[89]

However, Dumas did not return to the Army of the Alps. The five and a half months that he served with that army is the only time that he held supreme command of an army with all of the responsibilities involved with such authority. It is true that he would be named commander of the Army of the West after leaving the Alps, but that command was brief, a matter of weeks, and inactive. The rest of his career was served under the direct control of others, primarily General Bonaparte in Italy and Egypt. Thus, his time spent with the Army of the Alps is the only real opportunity to evaluate General Dumas as army commander.

Overall, he was a good commander in chief in this particular situation. His responsibility with respect to the defense of France and the survival of the nation was not great. There was little possibility that the Sardinians would have launched a serious invasion of France over the Alps in dead winter, even if they did wish to regain the province of Savoy. *La patrie* was not in danger in his sector. Nor was the Army of the Alps too large a force for Dumas to handle, because most of the troops were doing garrison duty and less than half, or about twenty thousand men, were actually combat ready. It was that latter half with which he really had to be concerned. Finally, the mission given to him, to capture the passes at the Petit Saint Bernard and Mount Cenis, was of a specific and limited nature. That having been said, how did he handle his army and its mission?

The mass of correspondence from Dumas to the generals under his command, to the representatives of the people with the Army of the Alps, and to the Committee of Public Safety gives ample evidence that he was involved in every aspect of the condition, well-being, training, and preparation of the army.[90] Having spent seven years in the king's army as a private, Dumas understood the army not merely from the point of view of the officer corps but also from that of the rank and file. He may not have been a seasoned army commander—and there were few of them in 1794—but he had had administrative and command experience in 1792–1793 with the American Legion. Saint Georges had left virtually all of the work of organizing, training, and administrating to Dumas. He understood the needs of his army and worked to provide for those needs. He also understood the limitations of the army and what could and could not be expected of the men.

His relations with the political authorities, both local and in Paris, were on much less of a solid footing. Dumas was a true and sincere republican. He was dedicated to liberty, equality, and fraternity, and these were not mere slogans or catchwords for him. But he was not a radical *montagnard* Jacobin republican. He took orders from the legitimate government in Paris and held himself accountable to that government and its representatives with the Army of the Alps. Although he did not attack the Alpine passes as quickly as Paris had wished, he had an excellent working relationship with Gaston and remained on reasonably good terms with the minister of war and the Committee of Public Safety. On the other hand, he rejected any influence or authority on the part of the local government, and his relationship with it was actually quite poor.

In the final analysis, his tenure with the Army of the Alps must be judged as successful and good. The army was stronger when he left than when he had arrived. Discipline had improved, the material conditions of the rank and file were much better, and he had accomplished the tasks that Paris had laid out for him in January. His military operations had been planned very well.

4

UNDER KELLERMANN WITH THE ARMY OF THE ALPS

Fresh from his victories in the Alps, Dumas arrived in Paris—and to a very uncertain future. Two of his predecessors, Generals Kellermann and Carteaux, were still in prison. The fact that Dumas was absolutely convinced that he had done no wrong—indeed, that he had performed very well with the Army of the Alps—might be of little consolation in the atmosphere of Paris during the last days of the Reign of Terror. Since he had been appointed to command the Army of the Alps, two of the most popular and powerful members of the National Convention—Hébert and Danton—had been executed, as had their supporters. Even Marie-Jean Herault de Sechelles, a member of the Committee of Public Safety, had been executed with the Dantonists in April. Maximilien Robespierre, supported as always by Saint-Just and Couthon and tolerated by Carnot and the other members of the committee, was at the height of his power.

In the middle of July 1794, when Dumas arrived in the capital, the Reign of Terror was both at its high point, in terms of executions, and in its last days. It had come into existence gradually over a period of months as a means of solving real and imaginary problems facing France in the wake of the foreign war, the civil war in the Vendée, and economic and social problems brought about by the Revolution in general. However, by the summer of 1794, many of these problems had been solved, or at least had been dealt with to the extent that they no longer required the drastic measures introduced and carried out during the Terror. For example, the French had defeated the Austrian army, the principal threat to France, at the battle of Fleurus on June 26. The frontier was already secure in the south on the Pyrenees and the Alps, where there was little fighting, and after Fleurus the danger from the north was eliminated. In fact, the French army in the north actually invaded Belgium. The military situation was much brighter in July 1794 than it had been at any time since the beginning of the Terror. The civil war in the Vendée had also been relatively quiet since the defeats of the insurgents in the late fall and early winter of 1793.

The sansculottes of Paris had been given much of what they wanted. The Laws of ventôse, passed in February 1794, promised a certain amount of redistribution of wealth with the "sequestration" of the property of "enemies of the people" and its distribution to "patriots." They also hoped to benefit from price controls and the laws against hoarding. At the same time, they were very much opposed to the freezing of wages. Thus, many of the old complaints of the sansculottes had been addressed while their newer problems, like wage control, were attributed to the government of the Terror.

Throughout France, the excesses of the Reign of Terror, which included the unpopular attempt at de-Christianization as well as massive executions (perhaps twenty thousand in the second year of the Terror alone), and the general attitude of the government that only "patriots"—as defined by the extreme left—had rights had caused support of the Jacobin government to decline. Thus, when the Jacobins began to turn on one another, the end was in sight. The precedent was already well established by the summer of 1794 for the final purging of the National Convention. Following the removal of the Dantonists, the Robespierristes were the dominant faction in the government. But when Robespierre launched an attempt to purge the powerful Committees of General Security and Public Safety, all of the threatened representatives (and those who perceived they were threatened) pulled together to remove him and his supporters. Fearing for their very lives—and with good reason in light of the purges of the past spring—the representatives believed that some group would be going to the guillotine. They were determined that it would be the Robespierristes. On the 9th of thermidor (July 26), Maximilien Robespierre, his brother Augustin (by his own request), Saint-Just, Couthon, and eight others who had supported them were denounced, arrested, and, within twenty-four hours, executed.

The 9th of Thermidor, and the reaction that followed it (which is known as the Thermidorian Reaction), was not merely the rejection of Robespierre and company; rather, it was a repudiation of the Jacobin Reign of Terror. France had had more than enough of the political bloodshed, often of the innocent or for trivial matters. If there were still traitors and criminals, let them be given the right of a fair trial and found guilty or innocent on the basis of documents or testimony of wrongdoing. Thus, the jails were almost emptied as political prisoners were released over the weeks and months following the fall of the Jacobins, and a semblance of justice was restored in France.

It is all but certain that the fall of Robespierre and the end of the Terror in July 1794 saved General Dumas when he was recalled from the Army of the Alps. It is true that there was no "paper trail" upon which to base solid evidence to prove exactly what happened to Dumas that July. All that is known is that he arrived in Paris, most likely about the 10th of the month, that he was in Paris during the last two weeks of the Terror, and that he was not arrested or put in prison. It is speculated on the part of his son, Dumas (*père*), that his victories with the Army of the Alps may have saved his life, or at least prolonged it until after the 9th of Thermidor. In any event, the charges against Dumas, the most serious of which was that he had burned the guillotine in

Saint Maurice in January 1794 and had made possible the escape of the men accused of trying to take the church bell of their village, seem to have been ignored. His son was certainly correct when, in concluding this epic portion of his father's career, he wrote "I have said before that my father was a lucky man."[1]

The charges against Dumas, which were never clear because the government never brought formal accusation against him, were simply thrown out or forgotten. By the same token, it was deemed unwise to send him back to Grenoble where the local authorities disliked him. But as he was not to be charged, some other position would have to be found for him. Therefore, on August 2, Dumas was named by the purged Committee of Public Safety as commander of the Ecole de Mars, a military school that had been established in the camp at Sablons.[2] Wasting no time in assuming his new post, he arrived at the military school on August 4, the same day that he received the notification of his appointment.[3] However, even before the new commandant could unpack his clothing, the Committee of Public Safety had reconsidered his appointment, and Dumas received new orders. This time he was sent to the Army of the Sambre and Meuse to command a division on the northern frontier.

But once again, Dumas had hardly unpacked when the Committee of Public Safety changed its mind a second time. He was ordered to the West to assume command of the Army of the West. He reached his new headquarters on September 7, 1794.[4] It is likely that Dumas was sent because the government needed a man with his qualities and ability to pull together an army that had fallen into bad condition. He had improved discipline when he took over the Army of the Alps; he had found the means to improve the material condition of that army with little assistance from Paris; and he had achieved the military objectives given to him by the Committee of Public Safety. What was needed in the West was the same kind of success, and it was hoped that Dumas would be the man to put down the insurrection. And because Dumas was unquestionably a good republican without being a radical Jacobin, a terrorist, or a radical anti-Christian, he seemed to be just the man the Paris government needed for this particular task.

There were actually three armies in west-central France in the fall of 1794: the Army of the West, the Army of the Coast of Brest, and the Army of Cherbourg. Dumas replaced the grateful General Louis-Antoine Vimeux, who joyfully received new orders by a decree dated August 16, 1794. The strength of the Army of the West on paper was forty-five thousand men, but Vimeux had declared that he had only 25,954 combatants and that he was ten thousand muskets short.[5]

Dumas's new command was in miserable condition when he arrived. Under the Jacobin-controlled government in Paris, the Terror had been projected into the war in the Vendée in a most brutal manner. The killing of women and children, as well as of priests and the elderly, had become common practice. Villages were burned and entire populations were massacred.

There were no limits placed on the horror and cruelty of the repression of this insurrection that was both religious and political. The policies of de-Christianization and the purge of monarchists—a term which included at that time all persons who opposed the Jacobin republic—were the principal causes of the revolt against the government in Paris. However, with the end of Jacobin domination on the 9th of Thermidor, the Terror officially came to an end. The problem that Dumas faced when he arrived in the West was that while the attitude of the government in Paris had changed, the conditions in the Vendée had not. The army, both officers and men, had become accustomed to the brutalities of the war. The killing of civilians, rape, plunder, and unrestricted destruction had all become a way of life. Despite his best efforts to restore order and discipline, he soon came to realize that it was beyond the ability of one man, and he received little assistance from either the local political officials or his own officer corps. Thus it was that on October 8, 1794, in an obvious state of despair, he sent to Paris the following depressing report on the Vendée:

Report on the State of the War in the Vendée
Army of the West,
From Headquarters at Fontenay-le-Peuple,
17 vendémiaire, Year II [*sic*]⁶ of the Republic
The Commanding General to the Committee of Public Safety.

I have only deferred my report on the state of the army and the war in La Vendée in order to make it upon reliable information furnished by my own eyes. Otherwise, I would only be merely echoing the views and opinions of others who may have different agendas. I have just returned today from my tour of inspection; thus I am able to speak to you of those things of which I know personally.

To speak plainly, there is no part, whether military or administrative, of the Army of the West that does not call for the stern hand of reform.

You are able to judge from the quality of the new recruits that are being taken in [to the army], the incompetence of the battalions, which are paralyzed because the majority of the men are inexperienced, and the bad composition of the officer corps, which is unable to train the new men.

But this is not the only source of the problem.

The evil lies especially in the spirit of lawlessness and plunder which reigns in the army, a spirit produced by habit and fostered by impunity. This spirit has reached the point that I dare to tell you it is impossible to suppress without removing the [army] corps that are here and replacing them with troops that are well disciplined.

To convince you of the truth of this, it will be sufficient to inform you that soldiers have threatened to shoot their officers for having tried, by my orders, to prevent pillage. You would at first be astonished at these excesses; but you would quickly cease to be so on reflecting that it is a necessary result of the system carried out until now in this war. . . . *La Vendée has been treated like a town taken by assault. Everything has been sacked[,] pillaged, burnt.* . . . You will not find, even among the general officers, any power to bring back into the rank and file the love of justice and of decent behavior. . . .

Military virtues are most necessary in a civil war. How, without these virtues, can the measures you have prescribed be carried out? . . .

I believe that the war might be promptly ended by adopting the measures which I propose, and which consist in—

(1) A complete change of the army.

(2) A complete change in the general officers.

(3) A careful selection to be made of the officers destined for service in La Vendée. . . .

So long as things remain in the same state, it is impossible for me to answer your expectations, and to guarantee you the end of the war in La Vendée.[7]

This most interesting letter, frank, blunt, and far reaching in its recommendations, was certainly not what the men in Paris wanted to hear. It is also the most logical explanation of why Dumas did not remain very long with the Army of the West. Yet, it was an excellent evaluation of the situation in the Vendée, and his recommendations for improving conditions in the West were sound, if not very practical, in a country already heavily engaged on all of its frontiers. His report was tantamount to a letter of resignation, and Dumas was forthwith relieved of his command. The Army of the West was merged with the Army of Brest, and General Louis-Lazare Hoche reluctantly took command of the combined forces.

On November 10, Dumas was sent back to the Army of the Sambre and Meuse to command a division.[8] But he did not remain long with this new command; in fact, there is no real evidence that he ever reached the Army of the Sambre and Meuse. Just when Dumas requested to be relieved of his command is uncertain, but on December 7, the Committee of Public Safety gave him a convalescent leave to retire to his home at Villers-Cotterêts to recover his health.[9]

That one's health was failing and it was necessary to retire from the army for a number of months was the standard excuse for quitting an undesirable command. It always helped if one could give some reference to a wound, old or recent. More often than not, it was fatigue that was being dealt with, but just plain fatigue was not an adequate reason for temporarily leaving the army. In the case of Dumas in the fall of 1794, it was very likely that the government in Paris was quite relieved, even pleased, to send him home for a while. He had, after all, posed a problem while with the Army of the Alps, and his report on the conditions in the Army of the West indicated that he wanted to be reassigned. With the general at Villers-Cotterêts, the government could forget about him, at least for the time being. The country was not in

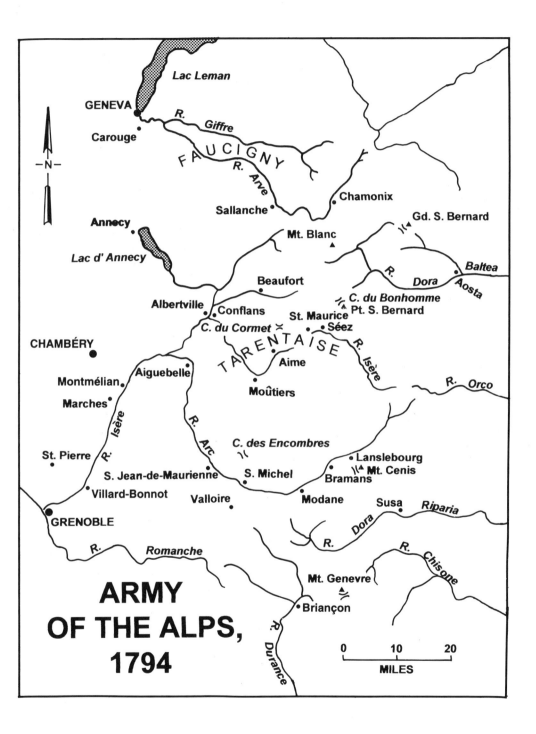

Lac Leman

GENEVA

Carouge

R. Giffre

F A U C I G N Y

R. Arve

Chamonix

Sallanche

Annecy

Lac d' Annecy

Mt. Blanc ▲

Gd. S. Bernard

R. Dora

Baltea

Aosta

Beaufort

C. du Bonhomme
Pt. S. Bernard

Albertville

Conflans

St. Maurice

Séez

CHAMBÉRY

C. du Cormet

T A R E N T A I S E

Aime

R. Isère

Aiguebelle

Montmélian

Moûtiers

R. Orco

Marches

R. Isère

C. des Encombres

St. Pierre

R. Arc

Lanslebourg

Mt. Cenis

S. Jean-de-Maurienne

S. Michel

Bramans

Villard-Bonnot

Valloire

Modane

Susa

Riparia

GRENOBLE

R. Dora

R. Romanche

R.

Mt. Genevre

R. Chisone

Briançon

ARMY
OF THE ALPS,
1794

R. Durance

0   10   20

MILES

serious danger, and Dumas was quickly and easily replaced. Both parties were satisfied with the solution, and Dumas spent the next ten months at home.

Villers-Cotterêts was still a quiet little town in the provinces that had not been seriously troubled by the war or the period of the Terror. While he lived with his in-laws, with whom he was on very good terms, the winter, spring, and summer passed quickly. His great love of hunting was satisfied in the excellent forests that extended east from the edge of the town. One aspect of Dumas's life that had changed was that his wife, Marie-Louise, had given birth to a daughter, Marie-Alexandrine-Aimée.

The months of quiet repose that Dumas spent at Villers-Cotterêts were neither calm nor peaceful in Paris. The Thermidorian Convention struggled to walk a fine line between the royalists to the political right and the Jacobins terrorists on the left. By the summer of 1795, what the French people wanted more than anything else from their government was stability. Six years of revolution with its continuous changes of government, foreign and civil war, de-Christianization, and terror left the nation longing for a stable regime in Paris that would abolish the excesses and extremes of the Revolution while it protected its basic gains. At the same time, there were movements afoot to change once again the political status quo of the Thermidorian year. The Jacobins were still smarting from their downfall and felt that the Thermidorians had betrayed the Revolution. On the other hand, the royalists were having a revival under the less radical regime of the Thermidorians.

The first serious rising took place in May and is known by its revolutionary calendar name of Prairial. The spring had been particularly difficult in Paris because of the severe food shortage; thus, it took little effort on the part of the old-line Jacobins to bring people, primarily of working-class districts of eastern Paris, into the streets. The rising was put down, but rather than strengthening the Thermidorian government, it encouraged the royalist right, which no longer had to worry about the Jacobin left. With the left crushed, the right then decided that it had a reasonable chance to overthrow the government.

The Thermidorians had written a new republican constitution, and by the end of the summer of 1795 they were ready to present it to the people for a vote. It provided the framework for the regime to be known as the Directory. It called for a bicameral legislature with males over twenty-one years of age voting and a five-member directory as its executive. At the same time, the government also proposed the Two-Thirds Law. This law mandated that two-thirds of the new legislators must come from the ranks of the existing National Convention. In this manner, two new legislative bodies, the Council of Five Hundred and the Council of Elders (*Anciens*), would be controlled by the Thermidorians and would guarantee that there would be no purge of the men who had governed France during the Reign of Terror. Both the new Constitution of the Year III and the Two-Thirds Law were passed in September.

Early in October, before the new constitution would come into effect (on October 27), the royalists attempted to do what the Jacobins had been unable to do in May. With the support of the various disgruntled factions of Paris, as many as twenty-five thousand insurgents marched on the Convention, which could count only six thousand troops for its protection. Seventeen sections of Paris declared a state of insurrection on October 4. The following morning—13 vendémiaire—they attacked the government.

The government was truly in danger and needed all of the support it could obtain. It also was in desperate need of a reliable general, a sincere republican who was at the same time not a left-wing Jacobin, to command the troops loyal to the government in Paris. One name that came up was that of General Alexandre Dumas. He had been denounced by the Jacobins of the southeast; he had been a successful army commander with the Army of the Alps; and he was disgusted by the excesses of the Army of the West. Furthermore, he was available just fifty miles north of Paris without a command. Thus it was that on October 6, he received the following letter:

> Paris, 13 vendémiaire, year 4
> [October 5, 1795] of the
> French Republic one and
> Indivisible.
>
> The representatives of the people in charge of the Army of Paris and the Army of the Interior order General Dumas to come immediately to receive orders from the government.
>
> [signed] J. J. B. Delmas
> Laporte[10]

It would seem that the government, or some members of the government, planned to give Dumas command of the troops in Paris to put down the insurrection. However, events in Paris moved quickly. Although Dumas left for the capital immediately, he did not arrive until the 7th, by which time the insurrection had been put down. As conditions worsened on October 6, deputy Paul-François Barras, who because of his military background had been given overall authority to crush the insurrection, named General Napoleon Bonaparte to command the troops in Paris. Bonaparte, using the artillery at his disposal (the rebels had none), put down the rising, with the loss of several hundred dead, and restored order to the capital. Thus, when Dumas arrived in Paris, the fighting had been ended, and General Bonaparte was the hero of the hour. In point of fact, 13 vendémiaire is frequently cited as the principal reason that Bonaparte was given command of the Army of Italy early in 1796. It is said that the government of the Directory felt indebted to him for having saved it from the insurgents.

Dumas remained in Paris after the failed coup d'état of Vendémiaire. He was ready to return to active duty and requested the minister of war to find him a command. To enhance his position with the new government, a number of fellow officers wrote the following testimony with respect to his actions at the time of the insurrection.

Paris, 14 brumaire, in the 4th
Year of the French Republic
[November 7, 1795].

We, general officers and others, certify and attest to the fact that citizen Alexandre Dumas, general of the army, arrived in Paris on October 7, and that he rallied with his brothers in arms in support of the National Convention to defend it against the rebels who had taken up arms against it those days.

Signed J. J. B. Delmas
Laporte
Gaston
[et al.][11]

Beneath the signatures is written: "Certified as being true. Commanding General of the Army of the Interior. [signed] Buonaparte."[12]

With the threat of the political left and right temporarily reduced and the government of the Directory in place (after October 27, 1795), life in Paris struggled to regain something that might be interpreted as normal. The war continued with Austria, England, and Sardinia, even though Prussia and Spain had signed separate peace treaties with France. On November 14, 1795, General Dumas was once again employed. This action was carried out in spite of the fact that a recommendation within the ministry of war stated that he should not be reinstated on active service. The minister of war, Jean-Baptiste-A. Aubert Dubayet, wrote in the margin of that recommendation: "General Dumas has been returned to active duty in Belgium."[13] In fact, Dumas had been ordered to Belgium two days before the minister of war had received the negative report. In support of Dumas, eighteen deputies had signed a document testifying to the fact that he was a true and sincere republican.[14] Thus, he had been sent to Belgium to put down resistance to the union of the old Austrian Netherlands to the French Republic. His orders were to take with him a sufficient force "to impose respect for the law" and then to remain in Belgium until he received further orders.[15]

The "insurrection" was not of a major or even serious magnitude, and Dumas was able to restore order without the loss of life. His mere presence at the head of a troop of French veterans was enough to cause all resistance to melt away. The population had little affection or attachment to the Hapsburg dynasty in far-away Vienna. On the other hand, there was concern with respect to the French Republic in light of the excesses of the most recent Reign of Terror. Dumas remained in Belgium several weeks and was then ordered once again to the Army of the Sambre and Meuse.

He arrived at his new headquarters at Sedan on the Meuse on November 22, 1795, and reported to the minister of war three days later that all was calm and quiet.[16] But if the military situation was uneventful at Sedan, all was not well with Dumas. On December 4, he asked to be relieved of his command for reasons of health.

As long as I thought that I could be of use to my country, I desired to be on active service. But today I no longer have any doubt of the impossibility of rendering that service because of the excrescence of flesh over my left eye that occupies my thoughts to the point that it confuses my clearness and accuracy. Therefore, I am giving to you, citizen, my resignation of my rank of general of division which I ask you to present to the Executive Directory for its acceptance.[17]

This abnormal outgrowth over the eye, which at times made it impossible for Dumas to wear his hat, is attributed to an old saber wound he received in a duel shortly after he had joined the Queen's Dragoons.[18] It would continue to be a problem for him the rest of his life.

When, after three weeks, no action was taken by the war ministry, Dumas again wrote to the minister. He declared that he had done everything he could to serve the armies of the Republic, but there was nothing more that he could do and he could no longer be of any use. The tumor made it impossible for him to concentrate on his duties, and he again requested that he be allowed to return to his home to convalesce. Finally, he asked that his replacement should be named so that he could turn over his command and withdraw.[19] But the minister of war was reluctant to allow Dumas to leave the army. Instead of permitting him to retire, Dubayet gave him command of the Upper Rhine,[20] and reluctantly Dumas took up his new duties. However, his health did not improve.

On January 19, 1796, Dumas again wrote to the minister of war imploring that he be allowed to retire from the army because of the poor state of his health.[21] Once again, instead of being allowed to leave the army, he was ordered to Landau in the first week of February.[22] However, he never left his headquarters at Blotzhein, for by February 11 he had received permission to leave the army and to go to Paris. On that day he wrote to the minister of war: "I cannot thank you enough for the order you have sent to me to go to Paris."[23] After waiting for his replacement, General François-Xavier Mengaud, Dumas left on February 22 for the capital.

In Paris, Dumas had surgery to remove the tumor over his left eye. The operation was apparently successful, at least temporarily, and after a brief period of convalescence in Paris, he returned to Villers-Cotterêts. Reunited with his family, he was able to relax and receive the excellent care he needed to completely regain his health. By the end of April, he informed the Directors that he was recovering quite well from his operation,[24] and on May 30 he informed Paris that his health was much better.[25] Finally, toward the end of June, Dumas asked the minister of war to send him back to the Army of the Rhine and Moselle. However, a report to the minister suggested that Dumas be assigned to either the Army of the Alps or the Army of Italy, and the minister wrote at the bottom of that report, "Alps."[26] Thus, Dumas returned to the army he had once led, but not as the commander in chief—Kellermann once again held that post. Instead, Dumas held the rank of division commander.

Virtually everything had changed between the time General Dumas had left the Army of the Alps in July 1794 and when he returned in August 1796. The Reign of Terror had ended; the political clubs, the Jacobins, had lost their power and influence; the representatives of the people were no longer a force with which to be reckoned; Sardinia had been forced out of the war, thus leaving General Kellermann to preside over an empty command; and General Bonaparte had led the Army of Italy on a victorious campaign into the Po valley. It was indeed a different war. In fact, for the Army of the Alps, it was not a war at all.

With the end of the Terror, General Kellermann had been brought to trial on November 8, 1794, and acquitted of any wrongdoing. He was restored to his rank of general of division in January 1795, and in March of that same year he was given command of the Army of the Alps. In March 1796, General Bonaparte took command of the Army of Italy. While Kellermann sat in Grenoble with his advance posts in the Alpine passes looking down into Piedmont, Bonaparte marched his beleaguered army into northern Italy. He defeated the Sardinians and drove the Austrians to the east. In just one month and two days, Bonaparte had forced the Austrians east of the Adda River and occupied Milan. While the most difficult fighting was yet to come, northwestern Italy was under French control or influence.

When Dumas joined the Army of the Alps at the end of August, Bonaparte and the Army of Italy were heavily engaged in a bitter struggle for northern Italy. This campaign, which had gone well for the French through the summer of 1796, was by no means settled, as the Austrians were determined to drive Bonaparte back into France and to reoccupy all of the Po valley. Nevertheless, Bonaparte's initial success in forcing Sardinia out of the war meant that the Army of the Alps had little to do and hardly any reason to exist. There was no longer an "enemy" on the east slopes of the Alps, nor was there any thought of the Army of the Alps advancing into Piedmont. In fact, the army was slowly being stripped of its manpower to strengthen Bonaparte in Italy where the fighting was taking place. Kellermann was simply to occupy the Alpine passes and watch and be sure that Sardinia remained peaceful.

On August 22, 1796, Kellermann ordered Dumas to establish his headquarters at Saint Jean de Maurienne and to replace General Jean-François Carteaux in command of the 2nd Division.[27] In the absence of any military threat, Dumas's only real concern was the traffic across the Franco-Sardinian border—a truly minor matter in light of the military demands under which he had labored in 1794 when he had headed the Army of the Alps. He was obviously disappointed with this assignment on several levels. First of all, he had once commanded this army, and now he had to serve under Kellermann as the commander of a division that was hardly a brigade in strength. Although Kellermann was perhaps better than average and quite experienced, Dumas did not hold him in much esteem as an army commander. He clearly believed that if he was to serve in the Army of the Alps, he should command. After all, he had captured the passes at Mount Cenis and the Petit Saint Bernard, not Kellermann, and thus he deserved the command and Kellermann should have been serving under him.

Perhaps a more telling reason for Dumas's unhappiness was that the war was no longer being fought in the Alps. General Bonaparte had taken it into the Po valley, and there was nothing of any serious nature to be done on the west side of the mountains. Dumas felt that the government should have sent him to the Army of Italy to command a division where the fate of the campaign was still in question in the fall of 1796. To serve under Kellermann in a noncombat area was, if not an outright insult, a major disappointment. It led to Dumas expressing his internal frustration in insubordination, pettiness, constant complaining to Paris, and quarreling with his commander in chief.

Almost immediately upon taking up this new command, Dumas became obsessed with the only real problem with which he had to deal: the large number of persons returning to France from Sardinia. The province of Savoy had already been annexed to France. Now, with an end to the war between France and Sardinia, many who had fled Savoy into Piedmont between 1793 and 1796 wished to return to their homes, even if that meant living under French republicanism. After all, the Terror had ended more than a year earlier, and life as an émigré in Piedmont was not the most desirable. However, France still had laws on the books with respect to those who had left the country since the beginning of the Revolution. The problem was to what extent did those laws apply to the inhabitants of the former Duchy of Savoy, which had not been a part of France until 1793. Furthermore, there was the problem of the young men of Savoy who had been in the Sardinian army at the time the duchy was annexed and had remained in that army until the end of the war and now wished to return to their homes in France. There were, in other words, many gray areas with respect to the law and the returning émigrés and soldiers.

Dumas stepped fearlessly into this gray area and created waves. He became paranoid on the issue of returning émigrés and refractory priests (Catholic priests who had refused to support the revolutionary changes in the church). This may be partially explained by his experience as commander of the Army of the Alps in the spring of 1794. At that time, he had been absolutely convinced that some of the inhabitants of Savoy had been passing information of a military nature to the enemy and that the failure of the first attack on the passes at Mount Cenis—and the death of General Sarret—was the result of the enemy having been informed of French plans. In Dumas's mind, the refractory priests and the émigrés were responsible for this treachery that had led to failure—failure that ended up on his doorstep and for which he had been held accountable. Now these same priests and émigrés were returning to France. He believed that if they were allowed to enter the country, they would once again be enemies of the Republic.

By September 1, just five days after he had arrived at Saint Jean, Dumas was complaining to the local authorities that they were not arresting émigrés returning to France and that the whole problem of émigrés was not being properly handled.[28] A few days later, he wrote to Kellermann to assure him of his zeal in finding and apprehending those who would disturb the public tranquillity and peace, meaning the returning priests and émigrés.[29] And on September 6, he wrote to the Executive Directory at Paris:

> I believe, citizen Directors, that it is the duty of those who love their country to provide you with an exact account of all political observations. The Mount Blanc [department] border is completely open to refractory priests and foreigners. They will soon be flooding all over France.[30]

This was followed on September 9 by a second letter to Paris in which Dumas expanded on the theme of the refractory priests and émigrés returning to France, the open frontier, and the potential danger to the region and to France as a whole. At this time he asked for instruction from the Directors on how he should handle the situation.[31]

In writing directly to the government in Paris, Dumas had gone over the head of his commanding officer. Proper channels would have had him go through General Kellermann with such a letter. More than that, he should have addressed his letters to Kellermann in the first place, not to the Directors. Perhaps it was that Dumas was accustomed to communicating directly to Paris; or perhaps he knowingly and intentionally went over Kellermann's head. The latter seems the more likely. Dumas had been an army commander and knew perfectly well the chain of command and proper protocol. He would not have tolerated such conduct from his subordinates. In any event, the ensuing clash between Dumas and Kellermann was, after those two letters, inevitable.

Kellermann was informed in the last week of September that his division commander was complaining directly to Paris. On the 27th of the month, he wrote to the Directors expressing his displeasure and frustration. He denounced Dumas and justified his handling of the problems on the frontier. "My answer to these charges made behind my back [that the frontier was wide open] is that they are false."[32] By an order that he had issued on July 22, 1794, all of the passes over the Alps had been closed, he continued, except to official couriers with proper passports. If there were undesirable people crossing the border in General Dumas's section of the frontier, it was the general's fault for not carrying out his orders. In fact, he added, Dumas seldom carried out his orders. But then, perhaps feeling that he was reacting too harshly, Kellermann added: "However, I can excuse him because he has been so short a time in the Maurienne."[33]

Having justified himself to the government in Paris, Kellermann next turned his pen to General Dumas. On the last day of September, he wrote to his division commander:

> I was very astonished, General, to receive a letter from the Directory by which I was informed of the observations that you had made to it that

the the Department of Mount Blanc is entirely open to refractory priests and émigrés. . . . and that there exists no defense to stop these individuals without passports. . . .

Did you not read the orders that had been given to you directly on 13 fructidor [August 30]? If you read those orders you will see that all individuals who could be considered as émigrés, even those who had served in the war in the army of the king of Sardinia, are not to be received on the territory of the Republic without carrying some sort of acceptable passport. A number of orders have been given on this subject, mainly on 4 and 9 thermidor [July 22 and 27]. If you had read them you would have retracted and rethought that which you have written to the Directors. The action [you took] was not in keeping with the lines of command nor with its principles. Before writing to the Directory you should have made those observations to me and to have spoken to me.[34]

Kellermann then added, in a rather sarcastic manner, that if Dumas did not understand the daily orders he received, he would direct special instruction to the general.

Of noble birth, Kellermann had served thirty-five years in the king's army before the Revolution. He had risen to the rank of general (*maréchal de champ*) by 1788. Although he embraced the Revolution, he was neither a revolutionary nor one who owed his career to the Revolution, as did Alexandre Dumas. Refined, moderate, and pragmatic, Kellermann had no desire for a confrontation between himself and one of his subordinate generals. Dumas, on the other hand, had become a fiery republican and patriot with a deep devotion to the ideas of the Revolution and the nation-state. He did not shy away from confrontation, and when he believed his cause just—and he always did—his righteousness knew no limits.

Rather than accepting the rebuke from his commanding officer, Dumas justified his actions and assumed the role of the grieved party. Immediately upon receiving Kellermann's letter, he answered it in a most abrupt manner. Wrapping himself in the flag, so to speak, he wrote the following on October 1, 1796:

I know perfectly well, General, that the Executive Directors provided you with a copy of the letter I had written to them. That letter was dictated by love of my country. But what I did not know was that it would serve for you as a pretext to regard me as an informer and a traitor. My loyalty and frankness make it my duty never to denounce a person except in good conscience. I have never discarded this principle, and I will not begin now in the Army of the Alps to violate it. Thus I ask you general not to feel injured by my action and to resume with me normal correspondence.[35]

Dumas then addressed the problem of refractory priests and émigrés. He said that they were entering the country with false passports and that he had informed both him (Kellermann) and the Directory in Paris of this condition. Finally, in a conciliatory gesture, he wrote: "I have received, General, with great pleasure the new instructions that you have sent me. I will observe them and execute them with the greatest effectiveness."[36]

But on October 4, Dumas wrote another antagonistic letter to Kellermann. After complaining that the tranquillity of the region was being threatened by émigrés, he said that he had heard there was a contingent of 150 men at Saint Pierre about whom he had no knowledge. He went on to state that he had sent an aide-de-camp to that unit and was informed that although they were on the territory under his authority, they were not under his command but rather reported to General Charles Morard La Bayette de Galles.

> I was not directly informed of these troop movements [in my district] as I should have been. I view all of this with great astonishment and I demand, general, a clear explanation from you. Am I in the army that you command? Am I a general of division? . . . Since I no longer need to give orders in my division, . . . I will send the *procè verbaux* addressed to St. Pierre to the Directory along with copies of my correspondence with you. It will see that for love of the Republic, that I should not be treated in this manner.[37]

He went on to offer his resignation, declaring that he would make every sacrifice for the good of the Republic.

Dumas had crossed the line. There was no longer any possibility of his remaining under Kellermann in the Army of the Alps. No army commander could accept that insubordination from an officer under his command, even if he held the equal rank of general of division. Dumas's correspondence in those days showed clearly his total lack of respect for Kellermann, and this despite the fact that the army commander was his senior in age and in time in grade. Kellermann had been a general of division when Dumas was a corporal, and he had saved France from invasion when he turned back the Prussian army in September 1792. Dumas had no good grounds for holding Kellermann in such low esteem. The problem was that Dumas thought that he should have been in command of the Army of the Alps, as he had been in 1794. He simply could not bring himself to serve under another commander, even if he was a competent and able soldier.

An angry and frustrated Kellermann first answered Dumas and then turned to Paris to rid himself of this insubordinate general. "I received your letter today, general," he wrote Dumas on October 4, "the style of which astonished me. It is not what one expects within his own command."[38] He then went on to explain that the 150 men at Saint Pierre were not under his command because they were destined to join the Army of Italy along with the 1st Battalion of the 29th Demi-brigade. He then listed all of the units that were directly under Dumas's command.

Having set the record straight with his division commander, Kellermann poured out his frustration to the minister of war in a four-page letter, dated October 5:

> By many orders, of which I am sending you copies, I have maintained the closest surveillance of the border, and no émigré or refractory priest has entered the territory of the Republic.
>
> General of Division Dumas has, without doubt, forgotten all of the orders given on that subject as he has written to the Directory that the department of Mount Blanc was totally open to refractory priests and émigrés. The Directory has informed me of his letter of September. . . . All of the letters that I receive from the General are filled with complaints and contain the most insulting language. . . . Copies of these letters are attached to this dispatch.[39]

Dumas, he continued, had a most vivid and troublesome imagination that would be a problem for the government. He concluded:

> I am an enemy of intrigue who has served his country loyally and with zeal. My frankness will not permit me to detour. Thus for the good of the service it appears to me that I must demand that General of Division Dumas no longer be employed in the Army of the Alps.[40]

Kellermann followed the only real course of action open to him at that point. Dumas could not remain under his orders after what had taken place. The two men were incompatible, and Kellermann was quite correct in saying that for the good of the service, Dumas should be transferred to another command. "Tragedies do not arise from encounters in which right clashes with wrong. Rather, they occur when right clashes with right."[41] Both Kellermann and Dumas believed that they were right, that they knew what was in the best interest of France, and that they were acting in that best interest.

The fundamental problem between these two men was their perception of the good of the nation. Dumas spoke in terms of the Republic and of republicanism. Kellermann, a man of the Old Regime who accepted the Revolution, spoke of the nation and of *la patrie*. Dumas had developed a deep hatred of the refractory clergy of the Revolution and the émigrés, most of whom were aristocrats. In part, this may have been the result of the two brief periods he had spent in the West in direct contact with the insurrection of the Vendée where the principal supporters of the revolt were non-juring clergy and aristocrats. Kellermann on the other hand, an aristocrat himself by birth, was much more moderate in his attitude toward the clergy and the émigrés. Thus, what Dumas considered to be a threat to the Republic, in light of the experience in the Vendée, Kellermann, who had never served in the West, viewed as a local nuisance that could be handled with a minimum of effort.

Nevertheless, irrevocable damage had been done. The Directors and the minister of war had to choose between Kellermann and Dumas. The commanding general was supported, and troublesome Dumas was removed and replaced. On October 13, 1796, the minister of war wrote to General Dumas:

> The Executive Directory has judged it appropriate, citizen, that you should be employed at your grade [general of division] with the Army of Italy. I am enclosing a copy of your service record that you will present to the commanding officer of that army [General Napoleon Bonaparte]. . . . The good of the service dictates that you leave for your new assignment as soon as possible. You should acknowledge having received this letter and of your arrival at your new destination.[42]

The minister of war and the Directory were getting Dumas out from under Kellermann as quickly and assuredly as possible. There was no way that the letter could be misunderstood, nor was there reason or desire on the part of Dumas to misunderstand. He was extremely unhappy at Saint Jean and equally happy to be going into the Po valley, where there was an active campaign with sieges and battles, excitement, and a reputation to be made. Dumas needed no further encouragement. He received his orders from the minister on October 15 (or very soon thereafter),[43] packed his belongings, informed Kellermann that he had received instructions to leave immediately for Italy, and then did so.[44]

To pay his expenses and those of Captain Paul-Ferdinand-S. Dermoncourt, his aide-de-camp whom he took with him, Dumas requested from Kellermann six hundred livres. He explained that the money was absolutely necessary to make the journey into Italy.[45] There is no record of Kellermann giving Dumas the money he asked for, but the commander in chief may well have thought that a small price to rid himself of one who had become a thorn in his side.

On the same day that the letter was written to Dumas informing him of his transfer, the minister of war also wrote to Kellermann: "I am informing you, General, that I am ordering General Dumas, whom you have asked me to remove from your command, to the Army of Italy."[46] To replace Dumas, the minister of war sent General Hyacinthe-François-J. Despinoy, who held the same rank as Dumas (general of division) and who wanted to leave the Army of Italy.[47] In this way, Dumas and Despinoy, neither of whom were happy in their positions, were simply exchanged, and the government in Paris solved two problems to the satisfaction of everyone involved.

5

WITH BONAPARTE IN ITALY

General Dumas arrived in Milan in mid-November 1796, thankful that he had left behind him the bickering with Kellermann and the seemingly unsolvable and annoying problems of the Army of the Alps. At last he believed that he would command a division in combat where the war was being fought. However, he remained in Milan for several weeks until General Bonaparte was ready to find him a suitable place in the Army of Italy. Indeed, Bonaparte had not asked for an additional general of division, and in particular, he had not asked for Dumas, whom he knew primarily by reputation—a brave soldier with limited combat experience and a temperament that left much to be desired. In fact, Bonaparte already had more generals of division than he had divisions. André Masséna, Jean-Mathieu-P. Sérurier, Pierre-François-C. Augereau, and Barthélemy-Catherine Joubert (named December 7, 1796) were all generals of division who had been with the Army of Italy since the beginning of the campaign of 1796. Furthermore, General of Division Alexandre Berthier was Bonaparte's chief of staff. In July, General of Division Gabreil-Venance Rey had been sent by the Directory to Italy, and in August General of Brigade Claude Dallemagne had been promoted to general of division. Then in October of the same year, General of Division Guillaume-Marie-A. Brune had also been placed under his command. Dumas arrived in November, and in December General of Division Henri-Jacques-G. Clarke, albeit on a political mission, also arrived.

From the very beginning of their relationship, General Dumas did not hold Bonaparte in high esteem. Dumas was seven years older and two years senior in the rank as general of division than his new commanding officer. Clearly, Dumas believed that he had a better right to command the Army of Italy than did Bonaparte. With this attitude on the part of Dumas even before he arrived, one might anticipate a stormy, or at least a difficult, relationship between these two men.

Napoleon Bonaparte (Napoléone Buonaparte before he changed the spelling) was a twenty-seven-year-old native of Corsica. Of lesser Corsican (and after 1768, French) nobility, he was educated at the military school at Brienne and the Ecole Militaire in Paris. Trained in the Army of Louis XVI as an artillery officer, young Bonaparte had been a captain in the summer of

1793 when Dumas was promoted to general of division. When Dumas commanded an army in 1794, Bonaparte, with the temporary rank of colonel, took part in the siege of Toulon, for which he was given the rank of general of brigade. In 1795, he commanded the troops in Paris that put down the insurrection of 13 Vendémiaire. When, in January of the following year, General Barthélemy-Louis-J. Scherer, commander of the Army of Italy, asked to be relieved of his command, Bonaparte became the recipient of the gratitude of the Directory. Scherer had become frustrated over what he considered to be unreasonable and unattainable demands by the government in Paris. Bonaparte was promoted to general of division and given command of the Army of Italy. In March, when he took command of the army, he was twenty-six years of age; Dumas, at thirty-three, was regaining his health at Villers-Cotterêts.

When Bonaparte arrived at his new headquarters at Nice on March 25, 1796, he found an army in miserable condition and his high-ranking subordinates in a most disgruntled mood. As he had just been promoted to general of division before leaving Paris, all of the generals of division with the Army of Italy were his senior in time of grade. In particular, Generals Masséna and Augereau, two of the senior generals of division, believed that one of them should have been given command of the army. They, with the entire officer corps, which had undergone several years of campaigning and privation with the army, resented the fact that a "boudoir général" with virtually no combat experience would be given command of the army.[1] The new general would have to prove himself under enemy fire to win their respect.

The Army of Italy had been, since the beginning of the war in 1792, the same sort of stepchild as the Army of the Alps. The principal theater of operation was in the north and on the Rhine. The soldiers' pay was always in arrears. Supplies of every kind were always lacking: shoes, uniforms, munitions, artillery. Morale was low and discipline poor. The enemy was superior in numbers, well supplied, and operating in a mountainous area that provided good defensive positions. There seemed little hope that the new, young, and inexperienced Bonaparte would be able to accomplish what his more experienced and older predecessors had been unable to achieve.

But against all predictions, great odds, and numerous obstacles, Bonaparte pulled his army together and marched it over the maritime Alps and into the valley of the Po River. He drove between the Sardinian and Austrian armies and forced King Victor Amadeus of Sardinia to sign an armistice that led to his withdrawal from the war. In a series of marches and battles, Bonaparte then drove the Austrian army east of the Adige River by the middle of June and laid siege to the fortified city of Mantua. During the summer and fall of 1796, Bonaparte fought off three attempts on the part of the Austrians to drive him out of northern Italy.

When Dumas arrived in Italy in the middle of November,[2] General Bonaparte was scrambling, quite literally, for his very life. An Austrian army under General Joseph Alvintzy was threatening to relieve the besieged city of

Mantua and drive the French from the middle Po. On November 15 at Arcola, Bonaparte had come under direct enemy fire trying to cross the Alpone River. The Austrians were defeated and driven off, and northern Italy was temporarily secured. But Alvintzy immediately began to plan his next march against the French.

Dumas languished in Milan without a command for a month. It is most likely that during that month he became acquainted with both General Bonaparte and his wife, Josephine. The commanding general was in and out of Milan during the latter part of November and the first half of December. Josephine also spent part of her time in Milan.[3] She had been born and raised on the island of Martinique and was considered to be a Creole, a term sometimes used to refer to mulattoes. Thus Josephine and Dumas, with their common background, understood one another and became friends.

Bonaparte had no need of an additional general of division, and certainly not for one who had been removed from his previous post because of insubordination and general trouble-making. By November 1796, Bonaparte had proven his ability as an army commander and had won the respect and the support of the officers and men of the Army of Italy. His generals, including Masséna and Augereau, were no longer resentful and were working well with him. The army was functioning like a well-oiled machine, and Bonaparte had no intention of replacing any of his senior officers with the newly arrived General Dumas, of whom he had not heard particularly good accounts. Nevertheless, in mid-December Bonaparte gave Dumas a command at the siege of Mantua. General Charles Kilmaine was temporarily in command of the siege while General Sérurier recovered his health at Leghorn. Dumas was given one of the two understrength divisions that made up Kilmaine's command; General Claude Dallemagne commanded the other division. Within the city were about twenty-four thousand Austrian troops under the command of General Dagobert Sigismond Würmser.[4]

By December 1796, the Army of Italy had been campaigning in northern Italy for eight months with only brief lulls in the marching and fighting. It had suffered heavy casualties in major battles and perpetual skirmishes. Fatigue and sickness, which knew no rank, had also depleted its numbers. Its strength had been maintained by a steady flow of reinforcements from France, primarily from the Army of the Alps.

Bonaparte controlled the Po valley as far east as the Adige River at Legnago. However, the Austrians had repeatedly sent new armies and new generais into Italy in futile attempts to drive him back into France. The Austrian general Alvintzy had withdrawn to the north where he regrouped his forces and waited for reinforcements. His general strategy was to advance south against the French and raise the siege of Mantua. The French army in Italy was numerically inferior to the combined enemy forces of Alvintzy and the besieged garrison of Mantua. It also lacked many of the necessities needed to wage war, the most visible being uniforms. At Mantua, the most urgent need was siege artillery. The fertile Po valley provided adequate food, but war matériel, most of which had to come from France, was in short supply.[5]

Mantua was the strongest fortified city in northern Italy, and perhaps in all of Europe. It was situated on the south bank of the Mincio River, which widened out at that point to form three lakes that surrounded the city on the west, north, and east. The city's south approach was dominated by impassable marshes. Two causeway-bridges crossed the river; one of these led due north to the fortified villages of San Antonio and La Favorita, the other to the east toward San Giorgio. The French had no siege guns or equipment, although it is doubtful that such guns or matériel would have made any difference, for Würmser was well supplied militarily. In addition to the large number of troops, he had three hundred guns to defend the approaches to the city. Indeed, at no time during the seven-month siege did Bonaparte give serious thought to an attempted attack on Mantua to take it by force. He realized that the garrison would have to be starved into submission.

Dumas arrived at Mantua on December 18 and took command of his division, which was assigned the north bank of the Mincio River. He established his headquarters at Roverbella on the high road to Verona. General Dallemagne's 2nd Division blockaded the city on the south bank of the river. The day after Dumas reached Mantua, and before he could even unpack, General Kilmaine, who had fallen sick (the marshes about the city made it one of the most unhealthy climates in northern Italy), was allowed to retire and take to his bed to recuperate. Dumas, as senior general of division, was given temporary command, but this would last only until December 29, at which time General Sérurier, his health greatly improved, returned and took charge of the siege that he had been conducting through the summer and early fall.

The siege of a major fortress was a command that Dumas deemed worthy of his rank, and he directed all of his energy to familiarize himself with the terrain upon which he might have to fight, the troops who would do the fighting, and the enemy he would face. He personally visited all of the units of the besieging force and inspected all of the defensive positions designed to prevent the Austrians from breaking out of Mantua. He began almost immediately to issue orders to strengthen his position. Unaware of the fact that he would command for only a brief period, he did not act as a caretaker waiting for a new commander but rather as if he would be responsible for the siege until its conclusion. His voluminous correspondence from the last days of December gives testimony to the seriousness with which he took his duties. On Christmas Day alone, Dumas wrote fourteen letter or orders, some of them several pages in length. He wrote every day to his two division commanders, giving them detailed instructions.[6]

The most important and most interesting episode that took place while Dumas commanded the siege of Mantua was the apprehension of a spy and the acquisition of his correspondence. In a long letter to General Bonaparte, Dumas related the circumstances surrounding the affair. Upon assuming command of the army before Mantua, General Dumas had doubled the guard at

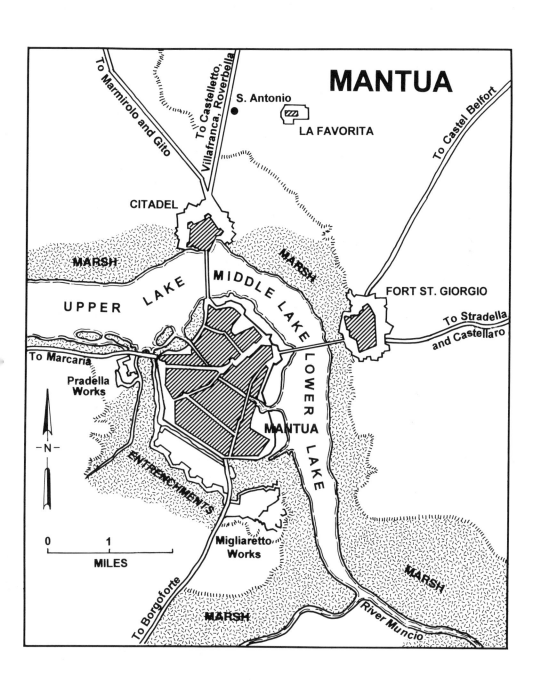

MANTUA

To Marmirolo and Gito

To Castelletto, Villafranca, Roverbella

S. Antonio

LA FAVORITA

To Castel Belfort

CITADEL

MARSH

MARSH

UPPER LAKE

MIDDLE LAKE

FORT ST. GIORGIO

To Stradella and Castellaro

To Marcaria

LOWER LAKE

Pradella Works

MANTUA

-N-

ENTRENCHMENTS

Migliaretto Works

0   1
MILES

To Borgoforte

MARSH

MARSH

River Muncio

all approaches to the city. On the night of December 24, three men were taken into custody after trying to get through the French lines to enter the besieged city. When Dumas was informed, they were all brought to his head-quarters, and he personally interrogated the men. "I paid the most attention to one of them," Dumas wrote, "because I believed him to be charged with the most important mission."[7] The reason for his assumption was most likely because that young man had the characteristics of an aristocrat. He was, in fact, an officer in the Straroldo Regiment, a royal regiment of the Austrian army.[8] This man was searched and researched, but nothing of an incriminat-ing nature was found. Nevertheless, Dumas was sure that he was a spy and carrying a dispatch for General Würmser. He accused the young man of hav-ing swallowed the dispatch, but the accusation was denied. To frighten him into admitting that the dispatch was in his stomach, Dumas ordered him to be taken out and shot. But when Dumas's aide-de-camp, Captain Dermon-court, and several soldiers began to take him from the room and presumably carry out the order, he confessed that he had indeed swallowed the dispatches.

Dumas then instructed Dermoncourt to find a pharmacist and to ob-tain from him a potion that would cause the young spy to regurgitate every-thing that was in his stomach. The potion was acquired and consumed by the spy. After several hours of vomiting, the desired result was achieved, and the spy produced a small ball the size of a hazelnut that was coated with wax.[9] Within the little ball were two letters to General Würmser, one from the Holy Roman (Austrian) Emperor Francis II and the second from General Alvintzy, who commanded the relief army that was coming to lift the siege of Mantua. Dumas immediately made copies of the two letters, which were in French, and sent the originals to General Bonaparte with a cover letter.[10]

The information contained in the two letters was extremely important to Bonaparte and aided him greatly in planning his own actions over the next weeks, which led to the battle of Rivoli and the eventual capitulation of Mantua. In his letter, Francis had instructed General Würmser to hold out in Mantua as long as he possibly could, as a relief army commanded by General Alvintzy was on its way to raise the siege. If, however, he consumed all of the necessi-ties to continue his resistance, which was primarily food for the more than twenty-four thousand troops in the city, then he was to destroy everything that could be of use to the enemy and break out of the siege to the south. He was to march to Ferrara or Bologna, or, if necessary, even as far south as Rome. The emperor assured him that he would be well received and that his troops would be welcomed and generously supplied. These orders were strictly a matter of survival for Würmser and his army, and it is interesting to note that he was not ordered to march north to try and join Alvintzy or east to attempt to reach the safety of Austrian-held territory.[11] This information was of par-ticular interest to Bonaparte, as it was generally believed that an attempt on the part of the Austrians to break out of Mantua would be to the north of the Mincio River, not to the south. The French had, since the beginning of the siege, concentrated the bulk of the besieging forces on the north bank of the

Mincio. The south bank of the river was also occupied by the French in some strength, but the object was more to prevent the Austrians from making sorties to get food or other needed supplies to continue their resistance.

The letter written by General Alvintzy to Würmser was of even greater significance. Alvintzy was at Trent, some seventy miles to the north, with twenty-eight thousand men. His first attempt, in the fall of 1796, to raise the siege of Mantua having failed, he was regrouping and planning a second advance against the French. However, he wrote Würmser, he could not be ready to move south with confidence of success for three to four weeks, and he repeated the emperor's plea to hold out as long as possible. In any event, he urgently requested that Würmser send him news of his situation and to keep him informed of his actions. Alvintzy did not explicitly say it, but what he had to know was if and when Würmser evacuated Mantua and marched south. This was essential information because Alvintzy had counted upon Würmser to break out of Mantua to the north as he approached the city from the north, and thus they would catch the French between their two Austrian armies. But if Würmser marched south away from Mantua, having abandoned the city, while Alvintzy marched south to relieve the city, the situation of the Austrians in Italy would be lost even before a battle had been fought.

In a postscript to his letter, Alvintzy wrote:

> In all probability my movement [south] will not begin until January 13 or 14. I will advance with thirty thousand men by way of the plains of Rivoli while General Provera with ten thousand men will advance on the Adige at Legnago with a large convoy of supplies. When your hear the cannons, you will make a sortie in order to support his advance.[12]

This information was of the greatest value to General Bonaparte. It is true that he already knew that Alvintzy and Provera were preparing to march to the relief of Mantua, but this dispatch confirmed the enemy's plans and indicated from which direction they would come. But most important, it gave him a timetable. Alvintzy would not be ready to move until January 13 or 14. Thus, Bonaparte was able to rest his weary army and to form a tentative plan of his own while he waited for the enemy to advance. The letter from the Emperor Francis also confirmed what the French generally believed, namely that the central Italian princes, including the pope in Rome, were not only sympathetic toward the Austrian cause but also could be counted upon to give active support and comfort to an Austrian army should it reach their territories. This information would be used after the defeat of Alvintzy and the capitulation of Mantua to justify Bonaparte's march into central Italy in order to force the principalities to support France.

Bonaparte could not have been more pleased. He treated Dermoncourt, who brought Dumas's dispatches to him, most courteously and sent the aide-de-camp back to Mantua with a flattering letter for his general. "I have received the letters you sent to me by your aide-de-camp. It is impossible to have received more important information. . . .I congratulate you on your good success and your intuition."[13] Bonaparte also noted Dumas's fine achievement at some length in a letter to the Directory. He gave several details of the episode and sent copies of the two letters.[14] Needless to say, Dumas was also very pleased with himself.

On December 29, General Sérurier, his health having improved, returned to resume command of the siege of Mantua.[15] Dumas again took command of the division blockading the city on the north (left) bank of the Mincio. Under Sérurier, the besieging army continued to work on improving its position. Although the French were reasonably sure that the coming battles would take place on the north bank of the Mincio, they also believed that Würmser had most likely received (by a second or third courier) orders to break out to the south if he had to evacuate the city before help could arrive. Thus, it was necessary for Sérurier to maintain a large part of his ten-thousand-man army on the south bank and to strengthen his position there in the event that it became the principal point of battle.

Dumas established his new headquarters at St. Antonio, which was located about two-thirds of a mile north of the Citadel—a well-fortified bridgehead on the north bank of the Mincio held by the Austrians—on the high road to Verona. The bulk of the French army was between his position and Rivoli. The major part of his command blockaded the Citadel. To the east of St. Antonio, but still on the north bank of the river, was the Austrian-held fort San Giorgio. General of Brigade Sextius-Alexandre-F. Miollis, under Dumas's command, with about seven hundred men, stood guard before San Giorgio to prevent an enemy exit at that point.

Dumas briefed General Sérurier with respect to all that had taken place since he had arrived at Mantua and continued to correspond with him on a daily basis.[16] In the first days of January 1797, Dumas evacuated all of the civilians from the villages and farms on the north bank of the Mincio as per instructions from General Bonaparte.[17] He also reported to Bonaparte that the Austrians in Mantua had been using artillery to send signals out from the besieged city. He was unable to interpret these messages or to determine for whom they were meant, but they had continued for several days.[18] It is most likely that General Würmser, who was approaching the limits of his ability to hold out in Mantua, was desperately trying to make contact with General Alvintzy or General Provera, whom he hoped might arrive before the middle of January.

Having commanded the besieging army for a brief period, Dumas realized that there was little that General Sérurier could do to improve the conditions of his troops, who were suffering from shortages of every kind. He therefore bypassed his immediate superior and wrote directly to General Bonaparte. Indeed, Dumas had developed the habit of going over the head of his immediate superior while serving under General Kellermann in the Army of the Alps. In a letter to Bonaparte, dated January 3, 1797, Dumas complained of shortages and again brought to the attention of the commander in chief the poor general condition of the troops on the eve of what was anticipated to be a major battle. His army continued to live off of the land at the expense of the civilian population, which was becoming increasingly restless. He placed the real blame on the commissioners who were being paid by the French to supply the needs of the army. These civilians, Dumas charged, were making themselves rich while his troops were suffering. He begged the general to look into this matter and correct the problem.[19]

Dumas had developed a dislike for the commissioners, whom the government would hire to supply the armies, when he had commanded the Army of the Alps. His experience with their inefficiency and outright dishonesty, both of which caused suffering among the troops, annoyed him and caused him numerous problems. The combination of the lack of adequate supplies, particularly food, and the fact that the troops' pay was perpetually in arrears forced the men to live off of the land. This meant leaving the army to search for food and whatever else they needed. The result was stealing, plundering, and looting, all of which weakened discipline and authority and led to a general reduction in the efficiency of the army. Thus, while Dumas was striving to improve the effectiveness of his command, he was faced with a corrupt and inefficient system of supply that worked against all of his efforts.

While Dumas was preparing to give battle on two fronts, against a sortie by Würmser and the advancing forces of Provera, Bonaparte and the bulk of the Army of Italy were making preparations to meet Alvintzy's army coming down the Adige. After his defeat at Arcola in mid-November, the Austrian commander had retired to the east and taken up a position on the Brenta River from Padua north to the mountains. Late in December, he had marched north and then west to Trent on the Adige and pushed his advance units south. Alvintzy had left behind General Provera at Padua with nine thousand men and General Bajalich with six thousand men farther up the Brento. His strategy was to advance all three armies against the French to converge on Mantua. With twenty-eight thousand troops, he would himself march down the Adige past Rivoli to Verona. Bajalich would advance westward from the Brento and meet him at Verona. After capturing that key city, they would move south together to Mantua. At the same time, Provera would march west from Padua across the Adige at Legnago and on to Mantua. The combined Austrian forces moving on the besieged city would be forty-three thousand men, and when added to the twenty-four thousand inside of Mantua, who were expected to break out of the city as the relief columns approached, Alvintzy and Würmser could put sixty-seven thousand troops in the field and overwhelm the combined French force of about forty-three thousand men. These figures are, of course, somewhat unrealistic. In the first place, between eight thousand and ten thousand of Würmser's men in Mantua were either in the hospital or too sick to bear arms. Furthermore, the Austrians would have to leave troops along their lines of march to garrison towns and protect their flanks. But by the same token, the French had their own sick and flanks to protect. The total ratio of men clearly favored the Austrians.

General Bonaparte was fully aware that he had fewer troops than did his adversary. However, he also knew the enemy's plan, thanks to the information he had received from Dumas. In the first week of January 1797, he posted General Joubert with his division of 10,300 men thirty-five miles north of Verona at Rivoli on the west bank of the Adige. Augereau, with a division of 10,500 men, was strung out along the lower Adige from Verona to a point east of Legnago. Masséna, with 9,400 men, was at Verona with General Charles-François-J. Dugua's cavalry (six hundred strong) behind him. General Gabreil-Venance Rey, with 4,100 men, was south and west of Lake Garda in the event the Austrians were to advance down the west side of the lake. Bonaparte's strategy was one of wait and react.

In the second week of January, Alvintzy began his movement down the Adige, pushing his advance guard south until it came in contact with Joubert. When Bonaparte was sure that Alvintzy had committed himself to an advance on Verona, he ordered Masséna and part of Rey's division to the plains of Rivoli. On January 14, the two armies met just north of the small village of Rivoli in a battle that finally decided the fate of Italy. Napoleon defeated the Austrian army and drove it back north to Trent. It was the last attempt to try to drive the French from the Po valley.

At the same time Alvintzy marched on Rivoli, Bajalich and Provera advanced on the lower Adige. On January 11, Bajalich's march on Verona was checked, and he began to withdraw. Provera crossed the Adige upriver from Legnago on the night of January 13–14 and made straight for Mantua. Augereau's division was spread too thin to prevent a major force from crossing the river. On the 15th, Provera's advance units engaged General Miollis's small force before San Giorgio. Dumas had been informed of Provera's advance on a daily basis, and even two or three times a day once the Austrians had crossed the Adige. Miollis was as prepared as possible with half of Dumas's division (fifteen hundred men) at his disposal. Fortunately for Miollis, Würmser, who thought the gunfire at San Giorgio was a diversion to lure him from the safety of his fortress, did not attempt a sortie on the 15th to support Provera's advance.

Provera expected active cooperation at least from Bajalich, who he thought would be approaching Mantua from the north with six thousand men while Alvintzy occupied the bulk of the French army about Verona. However, on January 15, when Provera reached the besieged city, he found himself with Augereau's division on his flanks, Sérurier's 2nd Division (Dumas) in front of him, and no help from Bajalich, who was too far to the northeast of Mantua to be of any assistance. After an unsuccessful attack upon   Miollis's strong position at San Giorgio, Provera moved off to his right toward La Favorita—the palace of the duke of Mantua about two miles north of the Mincio River and a mile east of St. Antonio—and St. Antonio. At the same time, he got word to Würmser that he had arrived and that the garrison should make a sortie so that together they could destroy Sérurier's considerably outnumbered force.[20]

Sérurier had become pessimistic and greatly concerned for the safety of his army. He had written to Dumas on January 14 that he was ordering the commander of the 64th Regiment, which was at Formigosa (a town just southeast of Mantua on the Mincio), to unite with Miollis at such time as he was no longer able to hold his position. In the event that that should take place, Sérurier continued, he would retire on Goito, about fifteen miles north and west of the Mincio. Two hours later, he again wrote to Dumas:

> I had dared to presume, general, that there would not be a sortie against General Dallemagne [to the south]. To the contrary, I [now] believe that the enemy will present itself in strength at Governolo and Formigosa to secure for himself these points and the Po to re-supply Mantua.[21]

Dumas reacted in a rather predictable manner. He held General Sérurier in low esteem and believed that he should have been in command of the siege of Mantua because he was senior in time to Sérurier with the rank of general of division and had already commanded an army. Dumas thus replied to Sérurier that he could do whatever he pleased—that is, retire on Goito—but that he, Dumas, would not move one inch from his positions blockading Mantua.[22]

Poor Sérurier was already having the same problems with Dumas as Kellermann had. Dumas would obey only those orders and instructions that he chose to obey. Ever since he had commanded the Army of the Alps in 1794, he resented having to serve under any general who was not his senior in time in rank—and combat and the guillotine had greatly thinned the ranks of his seniors. It is reported that when Bonaparte heard of this exchange of letters, he said that if Dumas had written to him in that tone, he would have had him shot.[23] But then, Bonaparte was always threatening to have his generals shot. Such blustering was designed primarily to intimidate his subordinates, and he never carried out such orders.

By January 15, Sérurier's position certainly did look grim. Augereau had been slow in reacting to the Austrian crossing of the Adige, and he was not close enough to Mantua to give immediate support. Indeed, it would be Masséna's exhausted regiments that would save Sérurier and seal the fate of both Provera and Würmser. During the battle of Rivoli on January 14, Bonaparte had received news that Provera had crossed the Adige the previous night. With the battle won, Bonaparte had ordered Joubert to escort the Austrians back up the river toward Trent, and after he had given Masséna's men a one-hour rest and food he ordered them to the relief of the French blockading force at Mantua. Masséna had left Verona on the 13th, marched to Rivoli, where he fought on the 14th, and then marched thirty-five miles back south on the 15th, where he fought again on the 16th. The real heroes of this phase of the campaign were his 57th and 18th Regiments (demi-brigades).[24]

At 5:00 A.M. on January 16, two strong columns of more than a thousand men each broke out of the Citadel and attacked Dumas at St. Antonio. With only six hundred men under his direct command, Dumas was driven out of the town. But General Claude Victor (Perrin), who was the lead unit of Masséna's division, arrived with the 57th Regiment from Roverbella, where it had been given only two hours of rest after its march from Rivoli. Thus reinforced, Dumas and General Victor recaptured St. Antonio and drove the Austrians back into the protection of the Citadel.

Dumas was in the forefront of the fighting and was exposed throughout the morning to enemy fire. He was at his best on horseback leading his dragoons against superior numbers. That morning, though he had two horses killed under him, his division captured six enemy flags. This action was critical to the success of the French victory that day because it prevented a linkage between Provera and Würmser.

In the official account of the fighting that took place that day, it was Victor who received all of the praise. To be sure, it was the determined fighting of the 57th that brought victory at St. Antonio and before the Citadel, for which the regiment became known as "the Terrible." However, it was Dumas, the senior officer on the field, who commanded the operation and who was slighted when the laurels were handed out.[25]

While Dumas and Victor were heavily engaged at St. Antonio on the morning of the 16th, Provera, just a mile or so to the east, attacked Sérurier, who had taken up a defensive position with only fifteen hundred men at La Favorita. Masséna's 18th Regiment arrived early in the morning to support him, as did Dugua's cavalry. Later in the morning, Masséna himself arrived with the rest of his division and attacked the Austrian right while Miollis marched out from San Giorgio on to the enemy's left rear. Provera's encirclement was completed when Augereau's lead battalion under General Jean Lannes arrived from the east. By noon, the Austrian commander realized that he was surrounded and outnumbered. With no relief in sight and no hope of breaking out of the encirclement, he concluded an honorable surrender. Würmser, informed of Alvintzy's defeat at Rivoli and Provera's surrender, had no choice but to give up the mighty fortified city of Mantua. His supplies were exhausted, and his troops were suffering great hardship and being reduced daily by sickness and death. There was no longer any possibility of relief. Thus, on February 2, he surrendered Mantua and the French gained control of that strategic city.[26]

In the official account of the fighting that had taken place on January 16 and the immediate events that led up to the battles,[27] General Dumas's role was ignored. Sérurier, who by that time was quite angry with Dumas for the latter's insubordination and crass correspondence that showed no respect for a commanding officer, did not mention him in his report of the day's action. It is true that Sérurier, who had spent the day at La Favorita fighting Provera, had little knowledge of Dumas's engagement at St. Antonio, but there was probably a bit of spite involved as well. He could have gained information of Dumas's actions if he had wished to do so. In any event, when Bonaparte's chief of staff, General Berthier, who was not on the field of battle, wrote the official account of the fighting, he only mentioned Dumas in passing: "General Dumas was in observation at St. Antoine before the Citadel."[28] There is no indication that Berthier meant to intentionally slight Dumas. The two men had had little contact with one another, and nothing that might be construed as unpleasant had occurred between them. Berthier was simply writing on the basis of the information that he had available at headquarters. When the document was written, he was most likely with Bonaparte at Verona.

Dumas was furious when he learned that his role in the fighting of January 16 had been reduced to one of "observation." In a state of anger, he sat down at once and wrote to Bonaparte:

> I have learned that *jean-f...* [Berthier] who was charged with preparing for you a report of the battle of the 27th [January 16][29] has reported me as resting in observation during that battle.
>
> I would not like to wish him the same observation as I had [that day], considering that he would have made *caca* in his pants.
>
>

Salut et fraternité
Alex Dumas[30]

Bonaparte was quite naturally angered by this crude and vulgar letter. He was not accustomed to having his subordinates express themselves in such barracks-room language, or to be so critical of his chief of staff. Nevertheless, he recognized the injustice, however innocent the mistake might have been, and he told Berthier to acknowledge Dumas's role in the fighting. The chief of staff, himself now angry by the uncalled-for insult of questioning his courage in battle, took pen in hand and added a sentence in the margin of the original document. Thus, when the final account of this phase of the campaign appeared, it read:

> General Dumas was in observation at S. Antoine, before the Citadel, where he successfully fought the enemy with a company of *guides à pied* of the army and captured a redoubt which the enemy had taken on the right side of S. Antoine.[31]

While the addition to the bulletin may well have satisfied Dumas and eased his anger, the letter he had written to Bonaparte made a permanent enemy of Berthier. This soldier was ten years older than Dumas and had worked his way up through the ranks of the royal army. He had been a lieutenant in the army fifteen years before Dumas enlisted and had been a general when Dumas was still a private. He was an outstanding staff officer upon whom Bonaparte would rely on every campaign until 1815. He deserved more respect than was shown by Dumas; indeed, he had earned that respect. To make an enemy of Berthier was certainly a grave mistake on the part of Dumas, as Berthier would be not only chief of staff for the future Egyptian campaign but also minister of war under the Consulate when Dumas was in great need of influential friends. Thus, within a few short years, Dumas would have reason to regret his rashness.

Dumas was not the only one overlooked in the original account of the fighting of January 16; the role of the troops he commanded was also neglected. In support of their general and thus of themselves, the officers of the 20th Regiment of dragoons, who had fought with him, wrote the following to General Bonaparte:

ARMY OF ITALY

DIVISION OF BLOCKADE OF MANTUA,
20th REGIMENT OF DRAGOONS

We, the officers of the 20th regiment of dragoons, the undersigned, certify that the general of division Dumas lost a horse killed under him in the battle of the 27th [January 16] of this month before Mantua, and another killed by a bullet.

Written at the bivouac of Marmirolo, the 29th of nivôse of the year V of the Republic of France [January 18, 1797].

Signed: Bontems, adjutant; Baudin, adjutant; Dubois, second Lieutenant; L. Bonefroy, second Lieutenant; A.-J. Bonnart, *chef de brigade*; Le Comte, Lieutenant; Lebrun, lieutenant; Dejean, captain; Bouzat, lieutenant.[32]

On the day following the combat at St. Antonio and La Favorita, Bonaparte reorganized the entire Army of Italy. On January 17 alone, Berthier informed twenty generals of their new assignments.[33] Even before Würmser surrendered Mantua, Sérurier's command was being dispersed. On that day, Dumas received orders to give up his command of the 2nd Division and to report to General Masséna, where he would assume command of a brigade. His dissatisfaction was great because this was an appointment for an officer with the rank of general of brigade, not general of division. He immediately wrote to Bonaparte: "I have received your order, General, from the chief of staff [Berthier] for me to go and serve under the orders of General Masséna. I do not have to tell you how astonished I was."[34] He went on to say that it was strange to get such orders the day after a victorious battle. "I had hoped for better consideration after having commanded armies, having never been beaten in battle, and finding myself the most senior general of this army." He continued by pointing out that on the previous day, with only six hundred men, he had held back an enemy army of almost twice that number. "I might add that I had a horse killed under me in combat and a second horse killed by a bullet under me, and that was only the highlight of the battle. General, you have made an error on my account." He then went on to declare that he had served Sérurier well and concluded: "I will obey, I will go [to Masséna] and await your response for my new disposition. But as I cherish my honor, no one has the right to rob me of it. If you will give me a suitable command . . . I will serve you well."

This rambling letter provides a window into the soul of a proud, brave, frustrated soldier. He believed that he was not receiving the respect he deserved, that his ability and his past performance were unappreciated and unrewarded. It was of no concern to him that the Army of Italy had more generals of division than positions requiring that rank. Bonaparte was continuing to employ those generals who had been with him since the campaign had begun. Independent commands and command of divisions remained in the hands of Masséna, Augereau, Sérurier, and Joubert. These were men who had proven themselves under Bonaparte's direct command and upon whom he had come to depend. Dumas, on the other hand, had held command under Bonaparte for only a month. Clearly, Dumas felt that he was being downgraded. It was not that he held Masséna in low esteem, it was that he believed that he could command a division as well as any man in the Army of Italy and that he outranked them with respect to time in grade. Therefore, he had a "right" to the command of a division. It should finally be noted that there is no indication that Bonaparte's use of Dumas was in any way affected by the fact that he was a mulatto. Bonaparte used or did not use men on the basis of their ability and loyalty to him and to the degree that they might further his ambitions. Color or race were of little concern to the future emperor.

In the official report that Bonaparte sent to the Directory on the battles of mid-January, he had praise for General Miollis's defense of San Giorgio on the 15th and his supporting role at La Favorita. General Victor was given all of the credit and the highest praise for his actions on the 16th. In fact, Bonaparte promoted Victor, pending confirmation from Paris, to the rank of general of division on January 18 as reward for his services. But in this long report (six pages in the official correspondences), there is not one word of the role of General Dumas either by name or by implication that his troops even took part in the combat. The reference to Würmser's sortie reads:

> On the 27th [January 16] at one hour before daybreak, the enemy attacked La Favorita, while at the same time Würmser made a sortie and attacked the lines of the blockade at St. Antonio. General Victor, at the head of the 57th Regiment, fell upon all those he found before him. Würmser was forced to re-enter Mantua from which he had just left.[35]

Indeed, Dumas had just reason to feel that he had been slighted.

No sooner had the cannons been silenced at La Favorita than Bonaparte put his army once again on the march. He formed three columns. On the right, Augereau advanced just north of Venice, while Masséna, forming the central column, advanced just south of the foothills of the Alps. The neutrality of Venice was ignored and the French crossed the Brenta River and moved on to the Piave River. At the same time, Joubert, who made up the French

NORTHERN ITALY, 1796–97

Brenner Pass

AUSTRIA

Lienz

Drave River

Rienza River

To Vienna

Brixen

Villach

Merano
Klausen

Botzen

Isarco R.

Noce R.

TYROL

Avisio R.

Trento

Brenta River

Feltre

Campoformio

LAKE GARDA

Adige River

Bassano

Piave

Treviso

TREVISAN

River

Rivoli

Vicenza

Verona

Padua

VENICE

VENETIAN REP.

GULF OF VENICE

Gito
St. Antonio St. Giorgio
La Favorita
Castello
Mantua

Legnago

Adige River

POLESINE

Rovigo

Po River

ADRIATIC

SEA

Ferrara

N

Bologna

0   10   20   30   40   50
MILES

left, fought his way up the Adige toward Trent. With Austrian influence expelled from northern Italy, Bonaparte also took advantage of his favorable situation to march south personally with a strong force to bring the lesser Italian states and the pope into line with France and to punish those who had been leaning toward Austria.

In accordance with his new orders, Dumas turned over command of his division to General of Division Louis-François Chabot and reported to Masséna at Marmirolo. He was immediately given command of the advance guard. Masséna did not know Dumas personally, but he was familiar with his reputation for courageously leading his troops, and that was just what he wanted at the head of his division. He was also aware of his sharp tongue and his inability to get along with the commanders under whom he had served. The solution was to keep him busy pressing on the heels of the enemy. Dumas pursued the enemy through Vicenza and Bassano, and when the Austrian rear guard made a stand before Feltre, he overran their position and occupied the city. During the few weeks that he served under Masséna's orders, Dumas distinguished himself by his personal leadership and bravery. Although a general of division, he would lead reconnaissance parties out in front of his own lines and engage in hand-to-hand fighting with enemy patrols. On several of these occasions, his life was seriously—and one might add unnecessarily—in danger.[36] The legend of the strength, bravery, and daring deeds of the great mulatto was taking shape and spreading through the army.

Dumas's advance to the east had been so rapid that it was necessary for Masséna to order him to halt so that the rest of the division could catch up with him and so that Augereau, who was moving at a much slower pace on Masséna's right flank, could move up and secure that flank. Bonaparte then secured his front from the mountains to the sea and ordered Joubert, Masséna, and Augereau to hold their positions.

Before Bonaparte launched his final drive out of Italy and into southern Austria, he received long-overdue reinforcements. General of Division Jean-Baptiste Bernadotte came with an entire division from the Army of the Sambre and Meuse, and General Antoine-Guillaume Delmas brought several regiments from the Army of the Rhine and Moselle. Together these units numbered more than twelve thousand troops and raised Bonaparte's field army to about forty thousand men, with a total strength of perhaps sixty thousand.[37] Bonaparte was certainly pleased to receive the reinforcements; however, he was not glad to have yet another general of division sent by the Directory. He had actually requested that the minister of war not send him any additional generals of division, as he could not find suitable employment for all of them already with his army. Bernadotte was a very experienced and senior general whom he would have difficulty placing under any of his present generals of division. However, since Bernadotte had arrived with his own division from the Sambre and Meuse, it made good sense to Bonaparte to keep him at the head of that division and to have him report directly to himself rather than to put him under either Masséna or Augereau. Why then did he see fit to put

Dumas under the orders of Masséna when he was also senior in rank? The explanation would seem to be that Bernadotte arrived in Italy with his own division, whereas Dumas arrived with hat in hand and no division. Bonaparte had never served under or with Bernadotte and knew him no better than he had known Dumas when Dumas had arrived, but Bernadotte did have more combat experience than Dumas and a good military reputation. If Dumas had come to the Army of Italy at the head of a division that he had commanded in combat, it is very likely that Bonaparte would have allowed him to continue at its head. Needless to say, Dumas was not so understanding, and he took Bonaparte's decision to be favorable treatment of Bernadotte and unjust treatment of himself.

The month of February was spent in resting the Army of Italy after the strenuous marching and fighting of November, December, and January, incorporating the newly arrived units into the army, and imposing French control upon central Italy. In the case of the latter, Bonaparte not only forced very "French" treaties upon the pope and the lesser princes but also extracted large sums of money from those rather well-to-do former Austrian friends and allies. Some of the money was sent to Paris where it bought for General Bonaparte a great deal of goodwill. The rest was used to take care of the needs of the Army of Italy and to enhance the popularity of the commander in chief.

During the course of this first Italian campaign, Bonaparte began the custom, which he would continue after he became First Consul and would accelerate as emperor, of personally rewarding officers and men under his command. Although he had no authority to do so, he gave swords of honor, which were appropriately engraved, to those who had distinguished themselves in battle. Such honors, bestowed on the parade ground in front of their comrades, were greatly appreciated by the men who received them and bound them even closer to their commander in chief. In early March 1797, Bonaparte granted large sums of money, at the expense of the province of Mantouan, to most of his generals and a number of colonels and lesser officers. In all, thirty-eight officers received either five thousand or ten thousand livres each, with General Joubert being the only one to receive twenty thousand livres. In this generous act, General Dumas was not forgotten. He received ten thousand livres, which was the highest amount given to any officer except Joubert.[38] Whatever his faults—and they were numerous—Bonaparte was generous toward those who served him. There is no record of Dumas's reaction to this handsome gift, but he must have been pleased that he had not been left out of the recognition as he had been in January.

Dumas remained with the advance posts of Masséna's division during the month of February while General Bonaparte managed the affairs of France with the pope and the lesser princes of central Italy. Then sometime about the middle of March, he was ordered to leave Masséna and join General Joubert at Trent for the advance up the Adige into the Tyrol. He was given command of the advance guard, replacing General Louis Baraguey d'Hilliers, who had been promoted to general of division on March 10 and sent to Lavis. The exact date of Dumas's appointment is not clear. The first mention of him in the correspondence of General Joubert is in an order dated March 19. Thus, Dumas was most likely ordered to Trent sometime after Baraguey d'Hilliers was promoted (March 10) and transferred and the time Dumas reached his new command by March 19.[39]

Dumas was fortunate to have been sent to serve under Joubert. Although Masséna did not treat him poorly, he was skeptical about having Dumas under his command. On the other hand, Joubert liked Dumas and respected and admired him for what he was. Joubert was a fine soldier and a good division commander when serving under a capable commander like Bonaparte. But he lacked the self-confidence that would have made him a great commander. Dumas, for his part, had more than enough self-confidence for both men. While Joubert would give Dumas rather exacting instructions from time to time, he generally left him a free hand to conduct the advance guard.

Joubert had served very briefly in the king's army before the Revolution and in a national guard unit before joining the 3rd Battalion of Volunteers of the Ain. Early in 1792, he had received a commission, and when the war broke out, he was with the Army of Italy. This sincere republican had been a general of brigade when Bonaparte took command of the Army of Italy, and Bonaparte promoted him to general of division on December 7, 1796, after eight months of outstanding service. Joubert would spend his entire military career with the Army of Italy and would find death on the field of battle in 1799 as its commander in chief.

Bonaparte gave Joubert command of three divisions following the battle of Rivoli. This strength was necessary if he was to drive Alvintzy back up into the Tyrol. Bonaparte had become very fond of Joubert during the Italian campaign, and this important assignment reflected Bonaparte's recognition of both his ability and the significant role he had played in defeating the Austrians at Rivoli.

Dumas had reason to be resentful of being placed under the orders of a man who was not only younger in age and junior in time in rank but also who had so recently been promoted. However, Dumas had come to realize and accept the fact that he was not a favored companion, that he was not yet one of "the men of Italy." He was still the newcomer whom Bonaparte had not asked for and owed nothing. In fact, Bonaparte was still angry with him for the insulting letter he had written in January, by which he had made an enemy of Berthier. It was up to Dumas to take whatever command was given to him and establish a reputation within the Army of Italy. He had performed well at Mantua, although his relationship with Sérurier had been poor, and he had distinguished himself at the head of Masséna's advance guard. It would be to his advantage to continue to serve well in order to convince the commander in chief that he should be given a division that would be in keeping with his rank.

Joubert not only liked Dumas but also knew that this fine soldier could be an asset if handled properly. Dumas was given command of the advance guard, the same position in which he had served with success in Masséna's division. As Joubert commanded the equivalent of an army corps on the Adige, he was able to give Dumas several regiments. Thus, the advance guard could, with some stretch of the imagination, be considered a division, and indeed, Joubert in his correspondence referred to it as such, a fact that gave Dumas great personal satisfaction.[40]

When Dumas joined Joubert's command, there had been a lull in the fighting for a number of weeks, during which time General Bonaparte had prepared for the drive into Austria. Joubert commanded about twenty thousand men in the immediate vicinity of Trent. He had one strong division and two understrength divisions, commanded by Generals Antoine-Guillaume Delmas, Claude Dallemagne, and Louis Baraguey d'Hilliers. The remains of Alvintzy's army, twenty-four thousand men now under the command of General P. Davidovich, had taken up a defensive position on both sides of the Adige River just north of Trent where two smaller rivers joined the Adige. The Avisio River, which flowed from east to west, joined the Adige about five miles north of the city, and the Noce, flowing west to east, entered the Adige some ten miles north of Trent. The Austrians were divided into two parts with General Kerpen occupying the right bank of the Avisio (thus the left bank of the Adige) and General Laudon on the left bank of the Noce (the right bank of the Adige.)

On March 17, Bonaparte ordered Joubert to attack the enemy and to occupy the towns of Botzen and Brixen, which lay on the road to the Brenner pass and the interior of the Tyrol.[41] On March 20, Dumas, supported by Baraguey d'Hilliers's division, was ordered up the left bank of the Avisio to Segonzano and Castello in order to outflank the Austrians and force their withdrawal from the Avisio.[42] Always at the head of his advance guard, Dumas fought in hand-to-hand combat with the enemy on numerous occasions. So frequently and so furiously did he engage the Austrians that they began to refer to him as the *Schwartz Teufel* (Black Devil).[43] After taking his men across the Avisio at Segonzano, he led them in close fighting with enemy troops, who opposed their advance. Again at Castello, he was found at the head of his troops with saber in hand, striking down enemy cavalrymen. Dumas's strength was such that he would unhorse a man with one blow. As the campaign progressed, so also did the legend of this powerful mulatto general.

On March 22, Joubert began to write to General Bonaparte of Dumas's deeds on the field of battle. "Dumas has charged with the greatest success a corps of enemy cavalry with a much smaller force. He has scattered the Austrian dragoons and captured many horses."[44]

The enemy withdrew to the north on both sides of the Adige as the French applied pressure. Dumas led the advance, fighting a serious engagement at Tramin, and forced the Austrians to evacuate Botzen. Joubert left General Delmas with a modest force at Botzen to hold that important junction of the river Isarco (Eisack), which flowed south from the Brenner pass, with the Adige, which flowed southeast to Botzen. By doing this, Joubert separated the two Austrian generals, leaving Laudon on the upper Adige while pushing Kerpen up the Isarco. Twenty-five miles up the Isarco from Botzen, there was again heavy fighting at the picturesque village of Klausen. The French advance guard, with Dumas at it head, stormed across the bridge to dislodge the enemy from a strong defensive position, where it had hoped to stop the French offensive.

On this occasion, Dumas, with a troop of about thirty dragoons and some light infantry, was routed by a squadron of Austrian cavalry. Panic took hold of his small force, and all but a dozen of his dragoons fled back across the bridge over the Isarco. With this handful of men and his aide-de-camp, Captain Dermoncourt, Dumas was unable to stop the Austrian counterattack. When the French were driven back to the bridge that led over the river to Klausen, panic again took hold of the remaining dragoons, and they fled headlong over the bridge to the perceived safety of the town. Only Dumas and Dermoncourt remained to block the enemy's advance.[45]

In the fighting that took place on the bridge at Klausen, Dermoncourt was seriously wounded after slaying several Austrians. Dumas was then left alone on the bridge, holding an entire squadron of Austrian cavalry at bay. The bridge was narrow so that no more than two or three Austrians could face Dumas at any one time. Furthermore, the carcass of his dead horse, killed under him, helped to block the enemy's advance. Before his second aide-de-camp, Lambert, arrived with a troop of dragoons to relieve the exhausted general, he had killed eight or nine enemy soldiers and wounded twice that number. By the time his dragoons returned to the fight, seven balls had pierced Dumas's coat, and he was bleeding from three saber wounds. Yet Dumas's luck continued to hold, for none of the balls had drawn blood. Furthermore, none of the three saber wounds—to the arm, thigh, and head—was of a life-threatening nature.[46]

Following the fighting at Klausen, Joubert wrote to Bonaparte of the progress he was making into the Tyrol. In this report, he singled out Dumas and praised his courage:

> Dumas with the officers of his staff and about thirty dragoons were harassed by enemy fire from a redoubt. They crossed the Isarco under that heavy fire. I must mention the conduct of General Dumas, who charged at the head of his cavalry and killed many enemy cavalrymen with his own hand. His courage contributed greatly to the success of the day. He received two [*sic*] light saber wounds in the engagement when he resisted alone the Austrian cavalry on the bridge [at Klausen].[47]

Just two days after the fighting at Klausen, Joubert reported to Bonaparte that once again in heavy fighting Dumas had had his horse killed under him.[48] Joubert then gave Dumas, who had lost in battle all of the horses that he had brought to the Tyrol, one of his own fine animals.

Within the space of one week, Joubert commended Dumas in three of his four reports to the commander in chief. Bonaparte could hardly overlook such praise from a man whom he respected enough to give an important independent command. And indeed, Bonaparte was duly impressed. However, Dumas's courage and bravery had never been brought into question; it was his acid tongue and pen that made his enemies. But his courage and feats on the field of battle helped rebuild friendships. On April 1, when Bonaparte wrote to the Directory of the conduct of the campaign against the Austrians, he took the opportunity to praise Dumas:

> General Joubert has arrived at Brixen, always pressing the enemy. General Dumas at the head of the cavalry has killed with his own hand many enemy cavalrymen. He has been twice [*sic*] wounded by enemy sabers, and his aide-de-camp Dermoncourt has been seriously wounded. The General had, for many minutes, held a bridge all alone against the enemy cavalry who were trying to cross the river. By doing so, he was able to delay the enemy advance until reinforcements arrived.[49]

Perhaps the future emperor was making amends for having slighted Dumas's role in the fighting about Mantua in January, but it is more likely that Bonaparte was putting behind him his displeasure with Dumas and recognizing his bravery and his service, two qualities much admired by the commander in chief. Furthermore, it was indeed most unusual, even in the French army, for a general of division to stand alone on a bridge and engage enemy cavalry in hand-to-hand fighting. It certainly eclipsed General Bonaparte's show of bravery at the bridge of Arcola, which has been portrayed on canvas and in bronze.

Such recognition on the part of Bonaparte must certainly have pleased Dumas. He had indeed come into his own as a member of the Army of Italy and henceforth would be one of the "men of Italy." His reputation spread throughout the army, and while General Berthier never forgave him for the insults of January 1797, nor Kellermann for his insubordination while serving under him in the Army of the Alps, Dumas was becoming a legend in the French army.

Dumas's capture and defense of the town of Klausen and its bridge over the Isarco opened the way to Brixen, which commanded the critical junction of two rivers. The Isarco valley extended to the northwest up to the Brenner Pass, while the Rienza flowed from east to west. Joubert now had to make a critical decision. His options were to continue the pursuit of Kerpen, who was retiring up the Isarco toward the Brenner pass; or to hold his positions at Brixen and Botzen; or to march off to the east to join Bonaparte and the main French army, which was advancing on Vienna. His decision to join the main army was based upon several factors. Perhaps most important was the general uprising of the Tyrolean population against the French invasion. More than six thousand Tyrolese had already joined the Austrians on the Adige above Botzen, and Kerpen's force was growing larger with each passing day. This also meant that Joubert was operating in unfriendly territory with his line of communication back to Trent under constant guerrilla attack. He was running short of the necessities to continue the campaign, and food was becoming increasingly difficult to obtain as the population became hostile. With only three hundred thousand cartridges for his men, Joubert informed Bonaparte that he would avoid all battle and only engage in such combat as was necessary. His news of the main army's advance to the northeast toward Vienna was spotty, and he was not receiving orders from the commander in chief.[50]

While Joubert was still at Brixen, he received an urgent plea for reinforcements from General Delmas at Botzen. When General Laudon learned that Delmas had only a weak division with him, he decided to attack and cut Joubert's communication. However, Joubert sent Dumas with his cavalry division on a forced march back to Botzen to support Delmas. Dumas and Delmas decided to take advantage of the fact that the Austrians were not aware of the French reinforcements. They attacked Laudon at dawn, routed his Tyrol militia, and forced him to retreat up the Adige towards Merano. Dumas rested his men the night of the battle and returned to Brixen the next day. In all, he had been gone only three days.[51]

Joubert, having decided to march east to link up with the main army at Villach, realized that he could not leave Delmas and his small force at Botzen. On April 5, with Delmas's division approaching Brixen, Joubert started for Lienz, which lay in the upper valley of the Drave. Dumas led the advance guard on this treacherous march. "'For twenty-four hours' he [Joubert] told his father, 'I was myself under the murderous steel of the Tyrolese, risen *en masse*; and I kept them off during a march of twenty leagues through the most terrible country.'"[52]

In late March, Bonaparte had planned to leave Dumas, with a division and that of Delmas, on the upper Adige in the vicinity of Botzen to prevent the Austrians from once again marching down that river into northern Italy and threatening his rear. If attacked by superior forces, Dumas was to withdraw to a suitable defensive position and stand his ground.[53] However, on April 3, Bonaparte tried to make contact with Joubert by way of the Drave, Lienz, and down the Rienza to Brixen. But the courier could go no further than Lienz. At the same time, a second courier was sent by way of Trent and up the Adige. This second messenger seems to have reached Joubert, but after the general had already begun his march to the east. The April 3 letter suggested that Joubert do just that—move to the east—to make contact with the main army in the Drave valley.[54]

In the same letter, the following instructions were included:

> General Baraguey d'Hilliers having been promoted to general of division, the general in chief has named him to command the division vacated by the illness of General Sérurier. He [Bonaparte] has named General Dumas to replace Baraguey d'Hilliers, and wishing to give that general [Dumas] a mark of satisfaction, he is leaving him at the same time in command of the cavalry division in the Tyrol.[55]

This letter, which Berthier could hardly have been pleased to write, is another indication that Bonaparte was ready to forgive Dumas for his indiscreet actions of the previous January. An expression of "satisfaction" from the commander in chief was not given lightly.

On April 7, the day before Joubert reached Villach, the Austrians asked for and received a five-day truce, which was later extended and, in fact, ended the campaign. Bonaparte's army was at Leoben, just one hundred miles from Vienna, and the archduke Charles was not at all sure that the army he commanded could prevent the French march on the Austrian capital. Actually, Bonaparte's position at Leoben was not as strong as the Austrians believed it to be. General Jean-Victor Moreau, who commanded the French forces on the Rhine and who was to cooperate with Bonaparte by attacking into southern Germany, was still not ready to move; thus, there was no pressure against the Austrians on the Rhine. In addition, the Tyrol had risen en masse against the French; General Laudon was threatening to advance down the Adige onto Bonaparte's overextended lines of communication; and Charles was assembling a respectable force to defend Vienna. Nevertheless, the Austrians were weary of the war and fearful of Bonaparte's unchecked advance toward the Danube. Both parties were ready to talk peace, and on April 18, negotiations began at Leoben, which led to the Treaty of Campoformio (October 27, 1797).

At just about the same time that Dumas joined Joubert's command in March 1797, he received most disturbing news from Villers-Cotterêts. His younger daughter, Louise-Alexandrine, who had been born in February 1796, had died on February 13, 1797. He had left Villers-Cotterêts for Paris shortly after her birth and had seen little of the child before he rejoined the army. He had learned from a letter he received from his wife in the first week of March that Louise-Alexandrine was very ill, and he wrote a tender letter back to her expressing his deep concern and insisting that he be told how serious the illness was.[56]

Shortly thereafter, he received the news that his daughter had died. From Brixen on April 1, he expressed his grief in a letter to his "closest friends" in Villers-Cotterêts.

> These victories [referring to the successes of the campaign up the Adige] were necessary to help ease the bitter pain caused by the irreparable loss of my dear and adorable unfortunate Louise, whose memory is always present before my eyes and occupies my mind day and night. I am also constantly worried about the condition of my wife as the result of this experience.[57]

In his biography of General Dumas, d'Hauterive suggests that the death of Dumas's daughter may have caused his reckless behavior and led him to vent his sorrow on the unfortunate Austrians who crossed his path.[58]

With an armistice in place but the outcome of the campaign still in doubt, Dumas was back in the good graces of Bonaparte. In fact, on April 8 the commander in chief, without knowing the situation in the Tyrol, wrote to

Joubert: "Generals Delmas and Dumas will remain with their divisions at Botzen, where Dumas will be in command of the Tyrol."[59] Joubert was in the process of leaving the Tyrol, and thus the order was never carried out; nevertheless, it was a further indication that Bonaparte was ready to give Dumas an independent command of his own.

After Joubert had moved down the Drau valley and linked up with the main army, he gave Dumas temporary command of his divisions while he went to army headquarters to confer with Bonaparte. Upon his return, Dumas was informed that the commander in chief wished him to come to headquarters. Dumas was not sure of the reception he would receive. He had not spoken with Bonaparte since the siege of Mantua. To his great satisfaction and surprise, Bonaparte met him with, "Greetings to the Horatius Cocles of the Tyrol!"[60] This most flattering comparison of Dumas's stand on the bridge at Klausen and the legendary heroic stand by Horatius Cocles[61] vanquished all apprehensions on Dumas's part, and the two men embraced one another as if there had never been a problem between them.

With the armistice extended for an indefinite period of time and peace talks under way, Bonaparte reorganized the Army of Italy and turned his attention to the governing of northern Italy.[62] He incorporated Joubert's divisions into the main army and decided to strengthen his weak cavalry. Throughout the Italian campaign of 1796–1797, his cavalry had been inadequate for collecting intelligence, protecting flanks and lines of communication, and meeting the Austrians in pitch battles. General Dumas, who was by far the most experienced cavalry officer under Bonaparte's command, was given the task of reorganizing the cavalry and increasing its numbers to a full-strength division. At the same time, Dumas was named military governor of the province of Trevisan.[63]

The principal reason for Dumas and the cavalry to be at Treviso, which lay about twenty-five miles north of Venice, in May was to bring pressure on the government of the Venetian Republic. The French army already occupied most of the Republic, but the city of Venice, lying on the islands just off the coast, was out of the easy reach of the French army. The armistice with Austria gave Bonaparte the time and the troops to bring pressure on Venice. On May 2, he declared war on the Venetian Republic. Thus, in addition to organizing the cavalry, Dumas was ordered to impose a land blockade against the city of Venice and to close off its freshwater supply.[64] Then the divisions of generals Baraguey d'Hilliers and Victor were ordered to Venice. With no hope of the Austrian army coming to its rescue, the city submitted to the wishes of General Bonaparte. The territory of the Venetian Republic was divided between France, Austria, and the Cisalpine Republic in October by the Treaty of Campoformio.

In the third week of May, Dumas took up residence in the city of Treviso.[65] The province of Trevisan had been one of the richest in Italy. It lay along the right (west) bank of the Piave River, and its land and climate were excellent for agriculture. The city of Treviso had also been one of the wealthier in northern Italy. Over the centuries, many of the richest Venetian senators and merchants had built fine homes in the city and lavish country estates throughout the province. But with the decline of Venice, Treviso also began to fall on hard times, and this was only exacerbated by the recent war. Nevertheless, the district was perfect for both official and unofficial pillage and looting. Very much to the credit of the new governor, neither was allowed to take place during the two months he was in command. Shortly after his arrival, Dumas reported to Bonaparte that the city of Treviso was not cooperating with him;[66] but by the time he left for another assignment, he had become very popular because of his fair and just administration of the province.[67]

Even before his arrival at Treviso, Dumas had begun the task of assembling the cavalry regiments of the Army of Italy. On May 19, he reported to Bonaparte that four regiments had already arrived at Treviso: the 1st and 7th Hussar Regiments and the 3rd and 8th Regiments of dragoons. He was still waiting for the 14th Dragoon Regiment and confessed that he had no idea of where it was.[68] On the same day, he wrote to General Berthier asking him, as chief of staff for the army, to find the 14th Dragoon and order it to Treviso.[69] Then on May 24, after he had had an opportunity to inspect the regiments at Treviso, Dumas wrote to Bonaparte that

> the regiments of cavalry you have placed under my orders are lacking everything that is necessary—both clothing and equipment. This country and its environment offers only the bare necessities. I implore you to give me the authority to requisition that which is lacking both in armament and equipment.[70]

On June 16, Bonaparte ordered Dumas with his cavalry division to the city of Rovigo, where he became the governor of the province of Polesine.[71] This move was made because the cavalry division was no longer needed to blockade Venice and Polesine provided more forage for the large number of horses. Lying between the lower Adige and the Po, its fertile soil provided ample fodder for the cavalry regiments. Dumas remained throughout the summer and early fall at Rovigo. His principal tasks were to maintain good discipline amongst his troops to keep them from preying on the helpless Italian population and to prevent the military commissars and government officials from "officially" looting the province. By protecting the population from the unjust pillaging of the French, he was better able to gain its cooperation to provide the just needs of his division. However, when Bonaparte became frustrated with the slow progress of the peace negotiations with Austria, as well as the heavy demands of his own government in Paris, he ordered the army to reassemble in the vicinity of Campoformio. Dumas was called to the army, and for several weeks with his brother officers, he wined, dined, and danced in an almost continual festive atmosphere. In the end, the Austrians made concessions, and Bonaparte, ignoring the more extreme demands of the Directory, signed the Treaty of Campoformio, which brought peace to the continent of Europe after five years of war. Only England remained at war with France. Dumas returned to Rovigo in the last week of October, where he remained until he was given permission to retire to Villers-Cotterêts to spend time with his family.

Bonaparte preceded Dumas back to France and was received as the hero who could make both war and peace. He was the toast of Paris, and every door was opened before him. When Dumas went to Paris on his way to Villers-Cotterêts, Bonaparte introduced him to the Executive Directory as the "Horatius Cocles of the Tyrol," and he too was treated as a conquering hero.[72] Without any question, Dumas's return from Italy marked the high point of his career. His reputation as a soldier was well established and his finances were in good condition; only the loss of his younger daughter marred this happiest period of his life.

6

THE EGYPTIAN CAMPAIGN

Alexandre Dumas was enjoying the life of a country gentleman at Villers-Cotterêts when he received orders from the minister of war in April 1798 to report to Toulon. He had been living in the home of his father-in-law with his wife and daughter, Marie-Alexandrine, since his return from Italy in December. Too active a man to sit by the fireside and rock, the general spent most of his time hunting with friends of the family. He enjoyed the out-of-doors life made possible by the great forests that surrounded the small town of Villers-Cotterêts. However, family life, gratifying as it was, and hunting, which pleased him very much, were not enough to prevent this energetic man in the prime of his life (he was thirty-six years of age) from becoming bored. Life at Villers-Cotterêts was simply dull and uninteresting. This was particularly true for a man who had been active in Parisian society and was accustomed to the exciting life of a military commander at war. Dumas was ready to undertake another campaign. Little did he know just how profound an effect it would have upon his life.

The destination of the army being assembled in southern Europe was a closely guarded secret. It is not clear whether or not General Dumas knew that he was going to Egypt at the time he agreed to take part in the campaign. The decision to send a French expedition to Egypt was made by the Executive Directory, but the idea seems to have come from General Bonaparte with the support of Charles-Maurice de Talleyrand-Perigord, who in 1798 was the minister of foreign affairs.

France had been at war for five years, and a succession of governments, while they had prevented defeat, had been unable to achieve victory. It was Bonaparte who had given the nation both victory and peace on the continent. It was true that England remained at war with France, but the island nation did not have a formidable army; and while the naval war continued, the land war had ended. The young Bonaparte was popular in Paris and was named a member of the National Institute. He tried to maintain a low profile, but many in the government saw him as a potential threat to an already weak regime.

To keep General Bonaparte occupied and, it was hoped, away from Paris, he was named commander of the Army of England. Encamped along the

English Channel with its headquarters at Boulogne, this army was designated as the one to be used for an invasion of the British Isles. However, the general, after reviewing his troops on the Channel and seeing and hearing of the strength of the English home fleet, decided that an invasion of Britain was not possible because the French navy could not secure the English Channel for a sufficient length of time to transport an army across that body of water. Therefore, he resigned his command and began to look eastward for a possible expedition.

In 1795, he had unsuccessfully applied for a position as military attaché in the French embassy at Constantinople. Then in August 1797, the conqueror of Italy proposed that Egypt be taken to harm English commerce and to protect that of France. Bonaparte had long been intrigued and fascinated with the eastern Mediterranean. He believed Alexander the Great to be one of the greatest military commanders. He was also very much aware of the fact that the Roman Empire had included most of the Middle East. "The time has not yet passed," he wrote to the Directory on August 16, "when we will feel that to destroy England it will be necessary to seize Egypt. The day by day decline of the Ottoman Empire forces us to consider ways to preserve our commercial interest in the Levant."[1] Then in 1798, with the support of the minister of foreign affairs, he proposed that he lead a military expedition to Egypt. Such an expedition would accomplish several objectives and open other possibilities. It could capture the island of Malta in the central Mediterranean and turn it into a strategic naval base that would considerably strengthen the French position in that sea. It could establish a French colony in Egypt that would greatly benefit France by enhancing its trade with the eastern Mediterranean and providing a base for a French military presence in the region. Finally, it was thought that Egypt might be used as a base from which the French might strike at India, which had become England's most important overseas holding since the loss of the American colonies.

France had lost most of its overseas holdings in the eighteenth century and was in the process of losing Haiti as well as her other Caribbean islands. The prospects of gaining what was thought would be a lucrative colony in north Africa was appealing to the government. Furthermore, the Directory was willing to send General Bonaparte any place he wanted to go, so long as it was far from Paris. Thus, the proposed expedition was approved and planning began immediately.

Serious preparations for the expedition were under way by March 1798. General Bonaparte was involved in every aspect of the complicated planning. That Bonaparte and the Directory viewed this expedition as something more than purely a military campaign may be seen in the large number (about five hundred) of nonmilitary personnel who were to accompany the army. Among those who sailed with the expedition were more than 160 learned men from every academic field. The former Army of Italy provided the troops and most of the officers for the new army. This could help explain, in part, why General

Dumas was given a command. However, there were generals who had served primarily with the French armies on the Rhine and in the north to whom Bonaparte gave important commands; among the most notable were Generals Louis-Charles Desaix, Louis-N. Davout, and Jean-Baptiste Kléber. The regiments of the former Army of Italy had been scattered throughout southern France, Switzerland, and the northern Italian states after the Treaty of Campoformio. For this reason, and because no one French seaport could handle the number of men and ships required to transport the army, five ports of departure were used. The men and matériel were assembled at Toulon and Marseille in southern France, at Genoa and Civita Vecchia on the Italian coast, and at Ajaccio on Corsica.[2]

Dumas received his orders on April 24 and immediately left Villers-Cotterêts to report to Toulon. There were rumors of a Mediterranean expedition, but few outside of the government in Paris knew where it would land. Sardinia and Sicily were the two islands most often mentioned, but these were only uneducated guesses. Dumas believed that he was rejoining his division, which would take part in the expedition, wherever it might go. After four months of rest and recreation, he seemed to have been in good health and in good spirits, ready to take on a new adventure under his old commander in chief. Upon his arrival at Toulon at the end of April, Dumas, as the senior general of division, assumed command of the army that was preparing to embark. However, this command was of little consequence, because the commander in chief was on his way from Paris.

Bonaparte left Paris on May 5 and arrived at Toulon on the morning of the 9th. The city was the scene of great activity and confusion as last-minute preparations were carried out under the watchful eyes of the commanding general. There is no indication that Dumas was involved in any of the preparations. Furthermore, it is not certain just when General Dumas was actually named to command all of the cavalry on the expedition. General Berthier, whom Bonaparte had chosen to serve as his chief of staff, still remembered quite vividly the insults of Mantua and still disliked Dumas. But Bonaparte remembered accomplishments of the cavalry commander of the Tyrol, with whom he had become much better acquainted in the summer and fall of 1797. Yet, Dumas's name does not even appear on the table of officers and military units assigned to the expedition, dated April 14.[3] The first official mention of Dumas appears in a general order put out by Bonaparte at sea on June 23, just one week before the expedition landed in Egypt. "The general in chief has determined the following commands," the order reads; ". . . General of Division Dumas command of the cavalry of the army."[4]

The fleet sailed from Toulon on May 19. Bonaparte and his staff sailed on *The Orient*, Admiral François-Paul Brueys's flagship. The one-hundred-gun ship of the line was the pride of the Mediterranean fleet. Dumas sailed on the *William Tell*, which was also a ship of the line. An English squadron under Admiral Horatio Nelson had been sent from Gibraltar to Toulon because of persistent rumors of the preparations for a French expedition. However,

Nelson arrived off of Toulon a few days after the French had sailed. Bonaparte reached his first destination, Malta, on June 9 without a major incident. The French had sailed south by way of Ajaccio and then along the east side of the island of Sardinia while Nelson, believing that the destination of the expedition was the eastern Mediterranean, sailed down the west cost of Sardinia. A violent storm did substantial damage to the English fleet, resulting in Nelson's frigates returning to Gibraltar and his ships of the line taking refuge at the island of San Pietro, off of the coast of Sardinia, for repair. The French fleet was sheltered from the fury of the storm by the island of Sardinia and reached Malta with no more than the usual wear and tear of the twenty-day voyage. It was at Malta that the French squadron from Civita Vecchia, under the command of General Louis-Charles Desaix, rendezvoused with the main fleet. Bonaparte had picked up the Genoa and Ajaccio squadrons along the way.

The island of Malta was key to the control of the central Mediterranean Sea. It belonged to the Order of the Knights Hospitaler of Saint John of Jerusalem, or the Knights of Malta, as the order came to be known. The knights had their origins in the Holy Land during the crusades of the twelfth century, but when the Christians had been driven out, the order had made its headquarters on the island of Rhodes. Then in 1522, the Turks, under Suleiman the Magnificent, captured Rhodes and allowed the order to leave. To perpetuate the order, the Holy Roman Emperor Charles V gave it the island of Malta in 1530. Since that date, the Knights of Malta had continued to wage their perpetual war against all Moslems in the Mediterranean. But the once-mighty order had been in a state of decline for several centuries by the time the French arrived. Although it was still relatively wealthy, its military power was only a shadow of what it had once been, and the knights, most of whom were French by the end of the eighteenth century, served no purpose other than their own comfortable existence. In addition to the French, the English, Austrians, and even the Russians (the tsar Paul I was the honorary grand master of the knights) wished to control Malta.

It required only a small portion of the French army to occupy the island and its formidable fortress because there was no real fight left in the knights. Bonaparte put an end to the order, which led to a number of the younger knights actually joining the French army. He also set about reorganizing the government and social structure of the island in light of the French Revolution. By June 19, the French fleet had taken on water and supplies and, leaving a small garrison behind, weighed anchor and sailed to the east. [5]

The day before the fleet departed from Malta, Dumas had the opportunity to write a letter to his wife and entrusted it to Monsieur Bouchard, who was returning to France. After one month at sea, Dumas's discontent was already beginning to show:

> I am giving this letter to citizen Bouchard, who has seen perhaps more clearly than the rest of us by having me obtain for him permission to leave [the expedition]. I believe that all prudent men should do the same because

a project of this gigantic magnitude requires very serious consideration. Nevertheless, so that I will not be blamed by you again [for leaving on this expedition] I must say that I will follow, as will all of my comrades, my career blindly even though it is more a question here [Malta] of deportation than of expedition. I am risking everything because I have nothing to regret. [6]

With the campaign just one month under way—albeit that month was aboard a crowded ship—Dumas's skepticism was apparent. "Deportation" is a strong word, not that Dumas ever shied away from strong terms. He had always been quick to express his feelings bluntly. It would also appear from this letter that his wife had not been pleased with his decision to undertake the campaign. After all, France was at peace with the continent and in no immediate danger from England. She undoubtedly felt that he should have stayed home and that this was more of an adventure than a necessity. The fighting in 1792–1797 had been to save France and to suppress rebellion in the West, but this expedition was more difficult to explain. Dumas justified it in terms of following his career, an explanation that his wife apparently thought unsatisfactory.

The French armada made its way to the east at a snail's pace because of the numerous slow troop and cargo ships. Nelson did not reach Malta until after the French had departed. While Bonaparte was capturing the island and reorganizing its government, the English had been repairing the damage caused when Nelson's flagship, the *Vanguard*, had been dismasted. Seaworthy once again, but with unreliable information that the French were at Malta, Nelson resumed the chase. On his way to Malta, he had learned, incorrectly, that the French had sailed east from the island on June 16. In fact, Bonaparte did not leave Malta until the 19th. Believing that the French destination was Alexandria, Nelson passed through the straits of Messina and made way, under full sail, for Egypt. In his vigorous pursuit of the enemy, he actually passed the French fleet on June 22 and 23 and reached Alexandria before his quarry. Finding the harbor empty, Nelson thought that he had been mistaken and that the French must be going to Anatolia, or perhaps Syria, or Rhodes or Cypress. In fact, he had no idea of where the French fleet was or where it was headed. All that he could do was search the entire eastern Mediterranean. Thus, there was a good bit of luck involved in the French armada reaching the Egyptian coast safely.

The French sighted land on the morning of June 29, and Bonaparte, who knew that there was an English squadron looking for him, decided that he would have to act quickly. It was imperative that he land his army before Nelson found him. He ordered parts of several divisions to be put ashore in small boats at Marabout, about eight miles west of Alexandria. This amphibious operation, for which neither the army nor the navy had any practice, went surprisingly well. Despite rather rough seas, which took the lives of a handful of men, more than four thousand troops were landed on the sandy beaches

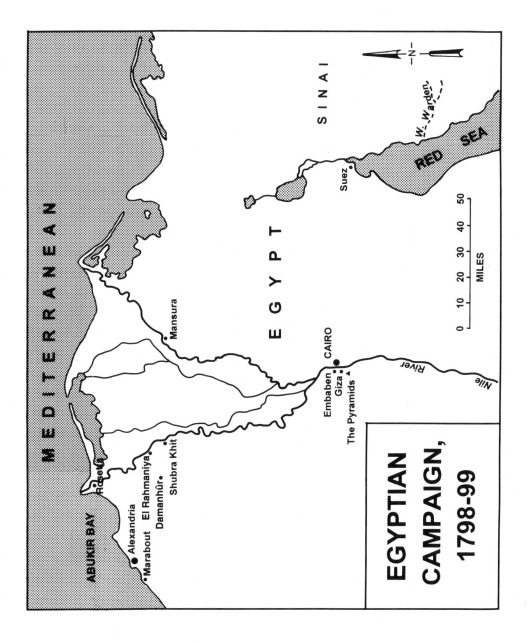

EGYPTIAN
CAMPAIGN,
1798-99

the night of July 1–2. Bonaparte went ashore at 2:00 A.M., and the army was soon on the march. Dumas came ashore that night, but all of his cavalry remained aboard ship. Armed with his hunting rifle, Dumas marched to Alexandria at the head of the army beside Bonaparte, General of Brigade Maximilien Caffarelli,[7] who despite his wooden leg commanded the engineers, and General Elzear-Auguste-C. Dommartin, the commander of the artillery, who had left his men and guns aboard ship.[8] Without cavalry, artillery, siege equipment, or even water (no canteens had been issued to the men), the French arrived before the ancient city about 8:00 on the morning of July 2.

The French soldiers had had no water since leaving their ships. As what water was available was in Alexandria, they needed little encouragement when Bonaparte ordered them forward to attack the dilapidated fortification of the city. There had been no preparations on the part of the Egyptians for the defense of the city, as the appearance of the French expedition was a total surprise. With light casualties, one of whom was General Kléber, who was wounded at the wall in the very early phase of the attack, the city was in French hands within a few hours.[9]

General Dumas, without a command, managed to take part in the capture of Alexandria, albeit in a minor role. When Bonaparte was told that some of the city's fathers had been favorably impressed by the appearance of Dumas, tall and dark-complexioned like the Arabs themselves, he sent for him. "General . . . he said to him, take twenty of my guides [the forerunners of the imperial guard] and go to the Arab tribe that has returned to me some prisoners. I want you to be the first [French] general whom they will see; the first leader with whom they deal."[10] His mission was to bring them back to Alexandria to be rewarded. Dumas carried it out without any incident, and Bonaparte, who was trying to win over Arab support, was generous with his gifts. Bonaparte was obviously taking advantage of the fact that Dumas was a tall, muscular mulatto. His impressive appearance had the desired favorable effect upon the Mameluke, the ruling class of Egypt, and, indeed, upon the Arab population in general.

The once great city of Alexandria had ceased to be of any real significance centuries before the French arrived. It was the first of many disappointments the Europeans would experience in what had been heralded as a land flowing with milk and honey. One of General Bonaparte's staff officers, Adjutant General Pierre-François-J. Boyer, described the city to his parents:

> That town [Alexandria] has nothing of antiquity about it except its name. Imagine ruins inhabited by a people impassive, and taking everything as it comes—a people who, pipe in mouth, have no other occupation than to lounge on a bench in front of their door, and who pass their day like this, troubling themselves very little about their families or children! Imagine mothers wandering about, their faces covered with black rags, and offering passers-by to sell them their children! Men half-naked . . . foraging in the muddy streams, and like pigs, munching and devouring everything they find! Houses twenty feet high at the most, the roof of

which is a platform, and the interiors as stables, with four blank walls. Remember, too, that amid this mass of squalor and wretchedness are the foundations of the most celebrated city of antiquity and the most precious monuments of art.[11]

With Alexandria in French hands, Bonaparte began at once to land the rest of his army. He still had no exact knowledge of Nelson and the English fleet. If they should arrive while his troops, artillery, and supplies were aboard ship, the expedition could still suffer a catastrophe.

While the army was coming ashore, Bonaparte was already issuing orders to General Desaix to begin the march to Cairo and the Nile.[12] Dumas's cavalry came ashore with only a few hundred horses; indeed the French had brought from Europe only about twelve hundred horses.[13] This number included horses for the artillery, supply wagons, officers' personal use, and the like, as well as those for the cavalry. The animals, scarce as they were, were in poor condition from having been six weeks aboard ship. With few of his men mounted, Dumas's command was of limited use to the army. It is true that some horses were purchased in the immediate vicinity of Alexandria, but they were needed for the artillery and supply wagons. Few of them found their way to the cavalry. It was not until after the army had settled down in Cairo that the cavalry was mounted.

Several days before the army landed in Egypt, the commander in chief put out an order of the day in which he made final changes in the command and structure of the cavalry. Dumas was named commanding general of the cavalry of the army. His command was to be comprised of General of Brigade Charles-Victor Leclerc commanding the 7th Hussards and the 3rd Dragoons; General of Brigade François Mireur commanding the 22nd Chasseurs and the 20th Dragoons; General of Brigade Joachim Murat commanding the 14th and 15th Dragoons; and General of Brigade Louis-N. Davout commanding the 18th Dragoons.[14] On paper, this was a superb command. No other unit in General Bonaparte's army could boast of three outstanding generals. Murat would be one of the finest cavalry commanders of the Napoleonic army. He would marry Napoleon's sister Caroline and become a marshal of the empire and later king of Naples. Davout was to distinguish himself as one of the most capable Napoleonic generals. He went on to establish his reputation by defeating the Prussians at Auerstädt (1806) and was named a marshal of the empire and prince of Eckmühl. He also married General Leclerc's sister, Louise-Aimée. Leclerc, who married another of Napoleon's sisters, Pauline, was given command of the expedition to Saint Domingue (Haiti) in 1801. The unfortunate General died of yellow fever the following year. The even more unfortunate General Mireur's life came to an end less than two weeks after he had set foot on Egyptian soil. Davout was later put under the orders of General Desaix and fought numerous engagements with the Mameluke in middle and upper Egypt, while Murat distinguished himself at the head of his dragoons in Syria, but Dumas made neither campaign. It is perhaps ironic that General Dumas never commanded this cavalry, led by such good generals, in a serious battle.

Bonaparte remained in Alexandria for six days, issuing orders and proclamations. Nominally, Egypt was a part of the Ottoman (Turkish) Empire. However, in fact, it was dominated by the Mameluke, many of whom were neither Turkish nor Egyptian by birth. Young boys of ten or eleven years of age were purchased as slaves by the ruling class of Egypt. Most of them came from the region between the Caucasus Mountains and Syria, although they might have been from any part of the Near East or Ottoman Empire. Although they were slaves in the households of the ruling class, they were raised to be warrior-rulers, and upon reaching their maturity (about eighteen years of age or so), they became Mamelukes in their own right. It was this Mameluke caste, which numbered about ten thousand men, that ruled Egypt and made up the backbone of the Egyptian army.

On the night of July 2, General Desaix's division camped just outside of the Rosetta Gate of Alexandria. It had come ashore that same day, and the following night it began the march to Cairo, the occupation of which was Bonaparte's immediate military and political objective. The first leg of this journey was across a strip of desert from Alexandria to Rahmaniya, on the Nile River, by way of Damanhûr. The distance was not great by European standards, about forty-five miles from Alexandria to Damanhûr and another fifteen miles to Rahmaniya. The problem was not the distances, it was the weather and the terrain. In early July, the temperature could rise well over 100 degrees in the day. The French soldiers, in their woolen European uniforms and carrying more than forty pounds of equipment, were miserable in the heat. When possible, the army marched at night; but even this posed a problem. The road to Damanhûr was little more than a camel trail along the abandoned Nile-Alexandria canal, and marching at night on the uneven ground was slow and unpleasant.

A greater hardship was the lack of water. The maps that the French were using showed towns along the dry canal, and it was assumed that, as in Europe, there would be food and water. But the "towns" were little more than a few dirt shacks clustered about a cistern. The inhabitants had fled before the French march, and the Bedouin, the desert people, had filled in the cisterns with rocks, dirt, and whatever was at hand. The army had not been issued canteens. It has been speculated that this had been intentional in Europe so as not to indicate the destination of the expedition. Desaix's division had had no time to make adequate preparations to carry water for a three-day march into the desert. A few soldiers found jugs or containers, but the vast majority carried no water with them. The march was thus a miserable experience for the four divisions that took that direct route. The heat, lack of water, and Bedouin raiders, who killed or captured any stragglers, worsened the already low morale of both the officers and men.[15]

Adjutant General Boyer described the march:

When you leave the town [Alexandria] to go to the Nile, you find a perfectly bare desert, wherein, at intervals of fifteen miles, you meet with one bad well of brackish water. Imagine an army obliged to cross these arid plains, which offer not the slightest shelter to the soldier from the unbearable heat that prevails. The soldier, carrying provisions for five days, loaded with his knapsack, and clothed in wool, is, after an hour's marching, overwhelmed by the heat and by the weight on his back; he disburdens himself, and flings away his food, thinking only of the present, and giving no heed to tomorrow. Then comes thirst, and he has no water. Thus it is that, amid the horrors of this picture, soldiers may be seen dying of thirst, exhaustion, or heat; others, at the sight of their comrades' sufferings, blowing out their own brains. . . . And this is the Egypt so famed by historians and travelers![16]

Bonaparte sent four of his divisions (Desaix's, Louis-André Bon's, Jean-Louis-E. Reynier's, and Honoré Vial's [Menou's division before he was wounded in the attack on Alexandria]) to Rahmaniya by way of Damanhûr. His fifth division, commanded by General Charles-François-J. Dugua, who replaced Kléber after he was wounded during the assault on Alexandria, was sent to Rahmaniya by way of Rosetta, that is, east along the coast to the west leg of the Nile and then south along the left bank of the river. Murat and his dragoons, most of them on foot, accompanied Dugua. Their march, while longer in miles, was easier on the men. There was no real shortage of water on the march, and Rosetta was a city that provided supplies.

The greater part of Dumas's command remained with him at Alexandria in the days immediately following the landing. The drastic shortage of horses actually made the cavalry more of a handicap than an asset. Unable even to buy horses except in very small numbers, Bonaparte had to come to terms with a cavalry on foot. On July 4, he wrote the following to Berthier:

> All of the cavalrymen who are not mounted and who wish to carry their saddles will be mounted first. All of the others will leave their saddles at the regimental depot at Alexandria and will follow the regiments. They must serve with the infantry of the division to which they are attached.[17]

At the same time, he wrote to Desaix, who was already a day's march into the desert, "General Leclerc is leaving at this instant with the men of the 7th Hussards on foot, the 3rd Dragoons, and your artillery."[18] On July 6, Bonaparte wrote a long letter to the Executive Directory in Paris in which he gave an account of his actions since leaving Malta. On this date he placed Desaix at Damanhûr and Dugua at Rosetta and was himself making last-minute preparations to leave Alexandria.[19]

On the morning of July 7, Dumas was ordered to be at General Bonaparte's residence at 5:00 in the afternoon with those men of his command who were mounted. They were ordered to be prepared to march immediately to Damanhûr.[20] Bonaparte's entire headquarters staff, as well as everyone left in Alexandria who was going with the army to Cairo (that is, the nonmilitary personnel), assembled at the appointed hour and set out at once in pursuit of the army. Those cavalrymen who were not mounted (and no numbers are available) were ordered to join the foot guide, Bonaparte's personal bodyguard, to make the march across the desert. Dumas, with Bonaparte and a small part of his command, reached Damanhûr in about twenty-four hours after a long, hot march, but with less discomfort than the main army, which had spent three days in the dry, burning desert. What they found at that dilapidated town on the edge of the desert was a dejected, disgruntled, and demoralized army that was more than ready to leave Egypt immediately and to return to France, even if that meant six more weeks of seasickness.

The grumbling and discontent was found at every level of the army, from the lowest drummer boy to the generals of division. Years later, Napoleon would write that "the generals murmured louder than the soldiers."[21] The army felt that it had been sent out into the desert without the proper preparations and that the extreme suffering had been the result of poor and incompetent planning. Egypt, which they had been led to believe was a land of milk and honey, had turned out to be a miserable wasteland.

The extent of the dissatisfaction and frustration on the part of the generals may be seen in an anecdote related by General Auguste-Daniel Belliard in his history of the Egyptian campaign:

> One could see in a moment the despair of Dumas, Jean Lannes and Murat who threw their hats on the ground and stamped on them in anger. They all declared that they had been sacrificed and that the General in Chief himself had been duped by the Directory, and that he had been sent off like an innocent child.[22]

On the night of either July 9 or 10, an incident took place in General Dumas's tent that began the true decline of the relationship between himself and Napoleon Bonaparte. Dumas had been given three watermelons, and he invited several of his friends to his tent to share in the feast of these melons after the heat of the day. Among those present were Generals Murat, Lannes, and Desaix. The conversation quickly turned to the miseries of the campaign. Everyone expressed their frustrations freely and complained bitterly about every aspect of the campaign. If one is to believe Dumas's son—and his opinion is in keeping with his father's personality, character, and reputation—General Dumas was the most outspoken critic of the expedition and of its commander in chief.[23] However, despite the implicit confidentiality of the conversation, everything that was said in Dumas's tent that night was reported to General Bonaparte. Although the person who betrayed the confidence of his comrades was never discovered, it was generally believed that it had been one of those present in the tent.[24]

The morale of the army was already quite low at Damanhûr, and

Bonaparte was anxious to push forward toward Cairo and to engage the Mameluke in a major battle. He did not want a confrontation with his generals at that critical point of the campaign. Therefore, he chose to ignore what had taken place in Dumas's tent for the time being—but he certainly did not forget. Not surprisingly, Dumas, presented to Bonaparte as the "ringleader" (it was, after all, in his tent where the meeting had taken place, and he was the most outspoken), would bear the brunt of Bonaparte's wrath when the time arrived for him to bring up the affair.

The army rested several days at Damanhûr and then resumed its march. It reached the west leg of the Nile on July 12 where Dugua's division and Murat's cavalry joined the main body. So happy were the French to see the great river that they waded in and drank to excess. Unfortunately, the water of the Nile was poorly suited to the constitution of the Europeans, and within days dysentery had become rampant throughout the army, resulting in a number of deaths. Nevertheless, having an ample water supply was preferable to the desert conditions of the march from Alexandria to Damanhûr. On the 13th, the French saw for the first time a major Mameluke army at Shubra Khit. There was not a serious engagement, only skirmishing, for the Mameluke retired south up the Nile when Bonaparte offered battle. The French continued their advance on Cairo. After another rest, this time at Wardan (July 18–20), Bonaparte came within sight of Cairo and the Pyramids of Giza, which were some fifteen miles farther south and west.

The Egyptians had divided their army between their two principal leaders. A substantial portion of the army, under the command of Murad Bey, was waiting for the French on the west bank of the Nile. Murad Bey commanded about six thousand Mamelukes and eighteen thousand fellahins. The Mamelukes could be best described as a neo-medieval cavalry. Superbly mounted and elegantly dressed, they tended to wage war without the support of infantry or artillery. Ibrahim Bey, with a large number of fellahin, a mixture of foot soldiers and militia, took up a position on the right (east) bank of the Nile, on which side was Cairo.[25] The fellahins were poorly armed with little training and even less discipline. They were generally inferior troops, even by Egyptian standards. They were certainly inferior to the well-trained and well-armed soldiers of the French army.

As the French approached Cairo, they found the Egyptian infantry in a weak fortified position in the town of Embaben, across the river from the capital. The Mamelukes were just south of the town. Bonaparte formed his five divisions into hollow squares with Desaix, supported by Reynier, on the desert (right) flank and the other three divisions—Dugua, Vial, and Bon—on the Nile flank. The regimental artillery was placed at the corners of the squares, and the baggage was protected inside the hollows. What little cavalry the French did have was greatly inferior in numbers and in the quality of horses. General Dumas had been able to buy very few horses since the army's arrival in Egypt, and the horses brought from Europe were not in the best condition after the sea voyage and the march to Cairo. Bonaparte had no intention of using what little cavalry he did have against the greatly superior numbers of the Mameluke; thus, the cavalry was divided into two parts and placed inside the squares of Desaix and Dugua. It is most likely that Murat and his mounted men were with Dugua's division, as they had marched with that unit from Alexandria. Thus, it may be assumed that Dumas was with Desaix.[26]

The battle opened with the French squares advancing. While Bon's division attacked the position at Embaben, the Mamelukes charged the squares of Desaix and Reynier. The discipline of the French soldiers held the squares firm, and despite great valor on the part of the Mamelukes, they were unable to break the squares on any side. When it became apparent that Bon would overrun the defenders at Embaben and that the squares could not be penetrated, Murad Bey led his Mamelukes south past Giza and up the Nile valley. The infantry was left to the mercy of the French. On the right bank of the river, the tens of thousands of Ibrahim Bey's army stood and watched the disaster across the Nile, and then withdrew to the east. So complete was the French victory that the city of Cairo immediately opened negotiations with General Bonaparte. On July 25, Bonaparte entered the city and could claim at least nominal control of the delta region.

Six days after the battle, Dumas wrote a brief account of the affair:

> We have fought a battle here the same day that we arrived on the Nile at Cairo. The Mamelukes, who have a great deal of spirit, crossed over from the right bank to the left bank of the Nile. It goes without saying that they were vicious and that we drove them into the river.[27] This battle will be called, I believe, that of the Pyramids. Without any exaggeration, the enemy lost seven to eight hundred men, a great part of them drowned trying to swim across the Nile.[28]

With the occupation of Cairo, the French began to settle down while they kept what was left of the Egyptian army at bay. General Desaix led his division up the Nile in pursuit of Murad Bey and his Mamelukes. Ibrahim Bey and his masses fled to the east. Bonaparte began to reorganize the government while General Dumas looked to the care and mounting of his cavalrymen.

Cairo had been portrayed to the French as the capital of a wonderful country in the heart of the rich Nile valley. But just as Alexandria had proven to be little more than a shantytown on the Mediterranean, so Cairo turned out to be an even greater disappointment. Just a few days after the French had occupied the city, Dumas wrote a rather discouraging letter to his good friend General Kléber, who was still back in Alexandria recovering from his wounds.

At Boulak, near Cairo, July 27, 1798

> We have at last arrived, my friend, in the land so much desired. But my God! it is far from the most pessimistic picture of our imagination. The horrible *villasse* of Cairo is inhabited by a lazy rabble squatting in front of

their miserable huts, smoking and drinking coffee, or eating watermelons and drinking water.

One can easily lose himself for an entire day in the dirty narrow streets of this famous capital. The only habitable quarter is that of the Mamelukes .... I have written to *Chef de Brigade* Dupuis [Dominique-Martin Dupuy], he is actually general and commander of Cairo, to reserve for you a house ... I have not yet received a reply.

The division [Dumas's] is at a kind of village named Boulak, near the Nile, a few miles from Cairo. We are lodged in very nasty abandoned buildings. ...

You cannot imagine the fatiguing marches we have made in order to reach Cairo. We always arrived [where we would camp] at three or four in the afternoon after having suffered the heat of the day, usually without food. We were forced to garner what was left by the divisions that preceded us in the miserable villages that, in most cases, had been pillaged. We were harassed all along our march by the hordes of thieves called Bedouins, who have killed men and officers at twenty-five paces from the column .... I swear to you, it is a worse war than that of the Vendé.

... I do what I can to keep peace between the various parties here, but it is not going well. The troops are neither paid nor fed, and you can imagine how that causes the complaints. It is perhaps even worse among the officers than the men. One can only hope that in about eight days the administration will be well enough organized to make the necessary distribution—but that will be some time yet.

All of the best to you,
Dumas[29]

Dumas was not alone in his disappointment with what he found at Cairo. Part of the disillusionment, undoubtedly, was due to the glowing seventeenth- and eighteenth-century accounts the French had heard of Egypt that had raised their expectations. The letters written home by the French officers, and captured by the English, testify to the general dissatisfaction that seems to have been universal. General Dupuy was not sure whether being governor of Cairo was an honor or a duty.[30] In a letter to his wife, he described the city as "'abominable; the streets here breathe of the [bubonic] plague as the result of the garbage; the people are dreadful and dazed.'"[31]

With lower Egypt, including Cairo, under his control and the enemy in flight, Bonaparte could settle a few old scores. Coming up to a group of generals who were standing about talking, Bonaparte dressed them down. Referring to the affair that had taken place in Dumas's tent at Damanhûr, he said vehemently to Dumas, "You have proposed treason, ... take care that I do not do my duty; your five foot ten inches will not prevent you from being shot within two hours."[32] There is a second account of this same incident that quotes Bonaparte as having said, "I was firm, I went up to that negro general, Dumas, and I threatened to have him shot."[33]

Shortly after this, Dumas had a second serious encounter with General Bonaparte regarding what had taken place in Dumas's tent at Dananhûr. Noticing that his commanding officer had been treating him coolly since the army had left Damanhûr, Dumas went to see Bonaparte to ask for an explanation. His son relates the following meeting between the two men.

The explanation was not difficult to get. Seeing him [Dumas] Bonaparte frowned, and, pressing his hat closely to his head, exclaimed,—

"Ha! it is you; so much the better. Step into this room."

And with these words he opened a door.

My father went in first: Bonaparte followed, shutting and bolting the door behind him.

"General," he then said, "you are behaving badly toward me; you are trying to demoralize the army; I know all that went on at Damanhour [*sic*]."

My father stepped forward, and, placing his hand on the arm which Bonaparte kept on his sabre-guard, he said,—

"Before answering you, General, I will ask you what was your meaning in shutting that door, and with what object you are kind enough to grant me the honor of this interview?"

"With the object of telling you that in my eyes the highest and the lowest of my army are equal before discipline, and that, should occasion require, I will shoot a general as soon as a drummer-boy."

"Possibly, General; but I still think that there are some men whom you would not shoot without thinking twice over it."

"What! not if they stood in the way of my plans?"

"Take care General; a moment ago you spoke of discipline, now you are speaking only of yourself. Well, I would like to give to you an explanation. Yes, the meeting at Damanhour [*sic*] took place; yes, the generals, discouraged after their first march, did ask one another what was the object of this expedition; yes, they did think that they saw in it a motive that was not in the public interest, but of a personal ambition; yes, I did say that for the glory and honor of my country I would go around the world, but that if it was a question only of your fancy I would stop with the first step. Now what I said that evening I am repeating to you, and if the miserable person who reported my words to you has said anything different to what I am now telling you, he is not only a spy, but worse than that, he is a liar."

Bonaparte looked at my father for an instant, and then said to him with a certain affection:

"Thus, Dumas, you make a distinction in your mind. You put France on one side and me on the other. You believe that I separate my interests from those of France, my fortune from hers."

"I believe that the interests of France must be put before that of any man, no matter how great that man might be. I believe that the fortune of a nation must not be subordinated to that of any individual."

"Then you are ready to separate yourself from me?"

"Yes, from the first moment that I think that you separate yourself from France."

"You are wrong Dumas," Bonaparte said coldly.

"That is possible," replied my father; "but I do not approve of dictators, no less that of Sylla [Lucius Cornelius Sylla or Sulla] than that of Caesar."

"And what is it that you want?"

"To return to France on the first occasion that presents itself."

"Very well, I promise you that I will not put any obstacle in the way of your departure."

"Thank you General, it is the only favor that I will ask of you."

And bowing, my father walked to the door, opened the bolt, and departed.[34]

Alexandre Dumas (*père*), after reporting the above conversation between Bonaparte and his father, felt the need to add the following statement to reassure readers of its accuracy:

A quarter of an hour after [the conversation with Bonaparte], my father repeated to Dermoncourt that which had taken place between himself and Bonaparte, and twenty times since then Dermoncourt has in turn told the story to me without ever changing a single word of that conversation that had such a great influence on the future of my father and on myself.[35]

The affair in the tent at Damanhûr followed by the confrontation between Dumas and Bonaparte marked the turning point in the relationship between these two soldiers. Up until this time, their relationship had been quite normal. It is true that there had been words in Italy the previous year, but it was General Berthier with whom Dumas had been angry. Even though Bonaparte believed that on that occasion Dumas had stepped over the boundaries of good taste and proper behavior, the offending general had been quickly rehabilitated, put to good use, and given high command in the expedition to Egypt. Bonaparte had forgiven, though it is questionable if he ever forgot. However, this time was different: it was Bonaparte himself whom Dumas was criticizing, and at a very bad time. It took all of the ability of the commander in chief to hold the army in line and to move it into position to give battle. He needed the support of his officers, in particular his generals, if the campaign was to be successful. There certainly is no question that Bonaparte's strong dislike—hatred may even be appropriate here—of Dumas dates from the general's departure from Egypt. One might question the accuracy of the wording of the conversation recorded by Dumas's son, but the general thrust was that Dumas wanted to leave Egypt and Bonaparte wanted him to stay. However, there were complications that would delay Dumas's departure.

News of the battle of Aboukir Bay, which took place on August 1, 1798, reached Cairo quickly. Admiral Nelson, after searching the northeastern Mediterranean in vain for the French armada, had returned to Alexandria and found the French fleet anchored in Aboukir Bay. Bonaparte had instructed Admiral Brueys to find a safe, defensible anchorage for his thirteen ships of the line (which would not fit in the shallow harbor of Alexandria), either along the Egyptian coast or at Corfu, which was under French control. Admiral Brueys decided upon Aboukir Bay, some fifteen miles east of Alexandria. When Nelson came upon the French fleet, he immediately attacked and destroyed or captured all but two of Brueys's ships. With the destruction of the French Mediterranean fleet, Nelson had isolated General Bonaparte and his Army of Egypt. There was no longer any possibility of receiving reinforcements or supplies from France. Even instructions, letters from home, and newspapers would seldom reach Egypt from Europe. Thus, although Bonaparte had said he would not put any obstacle in the path of Dumas's departure for France, the English fleet provided the obstacle. It would be months before Dumas was actually able to leave Egypt.

With the French in control of lower Egypt and General Desaix pursuing Murad Bey up the Nile, Dumas settled down to the care of his cavalry. Unhappy as he was in Egypt, he had no intention of leaving the army immediately, even if that had been possible. Horses were purchased, and gradually his command was mounted. Bonaparte used his cavalry to do escort duty, to go on scouting patrols to gain information, to make quick strikes against bandits, and to put down disturbances or would-be insurrections in the delta region. For example, on November 23, Bonaparte ordered three hundred cavalrymen under the command of General Davout to cross the Nile by night and attack a band of Arabs. He was to drive them out of the delta region and take control of their fifteen to eighteen hundred camels.[36] This was typical of the operations carried out by the cavalry in the fall of 1798. Then, after months of pleading by General Desaix, Bonaparte sent him a thousand cavalrymen in the first week of December. This unit was commanded by Davout and provided Desaix with his first real cavalry support.[37]

Dumas himself saw little action at the head of his cavalry while serving in Egypt. As general in command of all of the cavalry, he served more in the capacity of a staff officer. He remained most of the time in Cairo while Murat or Davout or a lesser ranking officer led detachments of his command whenever needed. On one occasion, he did lead his cavalry in action.

On October 16, Bonaparte wrote to General Berthier:

> You will give orders to General Dumas to leave immediately with the 15th and 20th regiments of dragoons on patrol from here [Cairo] to El-Khânqah, and to take possession of the horses as well as the rest of the convoy of an Arab tribe that has appeared, within the hour, near El-Mataryeh.
>
> . . . He will spend the night with his cavalry at El-Mataryeh or at El-

Merg; he will attack the Arabs and then remain there the rest of the day. He will report to me everything that he sees and I will send him further orders.[38]

Nevertheless, Dumas found his work dull, boring, and a waste of his time and energy. It is not at all surprising that when the great insurrection broke out in Cairo, Dumas was one of the first into the street with sword in hand.

The rebellion, which began on Monday morning, October 21, was the result of a combination of reasons and frustrations that had built up since the French had landed. Nicolas the Turk (Mou' Allem Nicolas El Turki),[39] who was sent to Egypt to report on the French occupation by Emir Bechir, the prince of Druzes, proved to be a keen observer. The Egyptians, he wrote, never accepted the French occupation. They even conjured up the recollection of the French crusading king Louis IX, who was driven out of Egypt in the thirteenth century. The men "were exasperated by seeing their women and daughters going about unveiled with the French and cohabiting with them. Death was preferable in their eyes."[40] Despite the fact that the French administration was much more favorable for the masses of the people, he continued, the occupation was despised. The foreign unbelievers, with their corrupt and offensive life-style, provided the rallying point around which the upper classes, who had been hurt the most, were able to muster the masses for the insurrection. Finally, Nicolas believed that "the inhabitants of Cairo, seeing that the revolt of Mansura . . . was not severely punished, believed that they could themselves revolt."[41]

Abdurrahman Gabarti , an educated native of Cairo, believed that the principal cause of the revolt was a property tax that was imposed upon the people.[42] This tax was heaviest upon the middle and upper classes, but it also fell upon the shop-keepers and small landowners to the extent that it was universally unpopular and thus an immediate cause of the revolt.[43]

The rebellion took the French totally by surprise despite the fact that it was widely known throughout the Arab population. On the day preceding the revolt, "Rebiul Akhir went throughout the city [of Cairo] declaring that 'all true Moslems were to assemble the next day at Azhar [Mosque] and to merit the glory of martyrdom in fighting the infidels.'"[44] That the French remained ignorant of what was about to take place attests to the great gulf that existed between themselves and the Moslem population.

On the morning of October 21, great numbers of men converged upon the Azhar Mosque. They came by the thousands not only from the city of Cairo but also from the suburbs and neighboring villages. The insurrection began with the killing of Christians, isolated and small groups of soldiers, and small guard units or patrols. General Dupuy was at once informed. With no knowledge of the extent of the disorder, he went into the streets with only a handful of men. He was mortally wounded within an hour and carried off by the few soldiers who survived that early encounter.[45]

General Bonaparte had left Cairo early on the morning of the 21st before any news had reached headquarters of the insurrection. He had crossed the Nile and gone to Giza to inspect an arms depot, a routine inspection that came to an abrupt end when he was informed that the city of Cairo was in full revolt. By 9:00 A.M., the commander in chief was back at headquarters and issuing orders in a frantic attempt to regain control of the situation. However, as the insurgents controlled the streets, it was difficult to communicate with the various barracks in the different parts of the city. Many of the isolated French units fought throughout the day either with no orders or with instructions that were hours out of date.[46]

Dumas had been in bed with a fever the day before the revolt and had still not fully recovered his strength when his aide-de-camp, Captain Dermoncourt, came to him and said that there was turmoil in the streets. As with Dupuy, he knew nothing of the magnitude of the disturbance. Rushing into the street only half dressed but with his sword in hand, he quickly gathered together the soldiers in the immediate vicinity who had been acting without leadership or direction. At the head of this small makeshift force, he scattered the insurgents and sent them running for cover wherever he went. The fighting continued throughout the day. After securing the treasury building, Dumas, at the head of a troop of his dragoons, made his way across the city and rescued those members of the Egyptian Institute who had been under attack most of the day. The fighting stopped when the sun set but resumed the following morning.[47]

By the morning of the 22nd, the French had the situation well in hand. Bonaparte sent four attack columns throughout the city, and by noon most of Cairo was firmly in their hands. The principal resistance was centered in the great Mosque of El Azhar. This enormous mosque and the complex about it had been the command center of the rebellion. On the 21st, the insurgents had gathered some one hundred dignitaries who had formed themselves into a "divan of defense." The last task was to take the great mosque.

Dumas, with his dragoons, was ordered to El Azhar the morning of the second day of the insurrection with orders to put an end to all resistance. Bonaparte had massed artillery on the high ground near the mosque, and shortly after sunrise it was ready to go into action. When the resistance continued, the artillery opened fire on the mosque and the surrounding quarters held by the rebels. By noon, the French were in position for the final assault, and it was General Dumas who had the dubious honor of leading the attack. The great doors of the mosque were destroyed by French artillery, and Dumas led his men into the structure. His son gives the following colorful description:

> The doors were broken down by cannon fire, and my father, launching his horse forward, was the first to enter the mosque.
> As fate would have it, there was a large stone,[48] about three feet in height, inside the mosque directly in the path of my father's horse. On seeing this object the horse stopped quickly, raised up on his hind legs

and came down with his front legs on the stone, remained for a moment immobile with fiery eyes and smoke coming out of his nostrils.

It is the angel! the angel! the Arabs cried out.

Their resistance was only that of desperation among a small number; the great majority were resigned to their fate.[49]

The French quickly gained control of El Azhar and took eighty members of the divan of defense prisoner. Under cover of darkness that night, between two thousand and twenty-five hundred Arabs escaped from the city and made their way to safety at Suez. Although Bonaparte had all eighty members of the rebellious divan executed, he granted a general pardon to the people of Cairo and made an effort to restore normal, if not amiable, relations with the local Arab population.

The energetic role of General Dumas in putting down the insurrection, and in particular his fearless attack on the great mosque, favorably impressed Bonaparte. The next time the two men met, Bonaparte greeted him with: "Good morning Hercules . . . so it was you who brought down the Hydra . . . . I am going to have a painting made of the taking of the great Mosque. Dumas, you have already posed for the principal figure."[50] And indeed, for a few weeks there were better relations between the two generals. Unfortunately, it was not to last. Dumas remained determined to leave Egypt, an action Bonaparte would never accept graciously. Thus, when Anne-Louis Girodet painted his now-famous portrait of Dumas entering the great mosque, the figure was not the dark-complexioned mulatto with black curly hair in the uniform of a general of division, but rather a blond, fair-skinned dragoon with no distinguishable rank. Between the taking of the mosque and the painting of the picture, General Dumas had fallen far from grace.

But there was one other incident that occurred in the fall of 1798 that also improved the relations between Dumas and Bonaparte. As a general of division, Dumas had been given the home of a very wealthy Mameluke. Before the owner had fled from Cairo as the French occupied the city, he had hidden a treasure in gold, silver, and precious stones in his house. Dumas found this treasure, valued at about two million livres. He sent the treasure to General Bonaparte with the following letter:

Citizen General,

The leopard does not change its stripes, the honest man does not change his conscience.

I am sending to you a treasure that I have just found, and which is estimated at close to two million [livres].

If I am killed, or if I die here of sadness, you will remember that I am a poor man, and that I leave behind me in France a wife and a child.

Greetings and brotherhood

Alexandre Dumas[51]

Bonaparte must have been very pleased, because the financial burden of the army of occupation was weighing heavily on the commander in chief. He had been trying to come up with innovative ways of raising money when this windfall fell into his lap. But the basic cause of the conflict between Dumas and Bonaparte remained; and although their relationship may have improved from time to time, it was destined to reach a breaking point because Dumas would refuse to remain in Egypt.

Sometime after the uprising in Cairo, one final interview occurred between Dumas and Bonaparte. Dumas had been suffering from depression in the weeks preceding the insurrection, and although the few days of fighting and the immediate aftermath of that excitement had lifted his spirits for a while, he had fallen back into a severe depression that actually affected his health. Thus he went to Bonaparte to request a leave of absence so that he could return to France to recover his health. Bonaparte tried one more time to convince him to remain with the Army of Egypt. He even went so far as to tell him that he himself would return to France as soon as affairs in Egypt were settled and promised that he would take Dumas with him. But nothing that Bonaparte could say would change Dumas's mind. He was determined to depart, and he insisted upon a leave of absence. In the end, Bonaparte realized that such an unhappy officer would be of little use either to himself or the army. Dumas was given official permission to leave Egypt, and it became only a question of time until his departure.

In preparation for his return to France, Dumas sold all of the furniture and articles he had acquired. He then took all the money he had and purchased four thousand pounds of *moka* coffee and eleven Arabian horses (two stallions and nine mares), keeping only enough to hire a ship for the return voyage. These arrangements were made during the months of December and January. By February 25, 1799, all was ready, and together with several other officers who were also returning to France, he awaited the proper moment when the winds would be favorable and the British blockade lax.[52]

7

THE PRISONER OF WAR

For some months before Dumas put to sea aboard *La Belle Maltaise*, events in Europe had been moving at a rapid pace, and not in the best interests of France. The Second Coalition (made up of states at war with France) was being formed in the fall of 1798. With General Bonaparte and a French army of thirty-five thousand men isolated in Egypt as the result of the destruction of the French fleet at Aboukir Bay, England was able to bring Austria back into the war in order that Austria might regain control of Italy, influence in Germany, and her dignity, all of which she had lost in the Treaty of Campoformio. Angered by Bonaparte's seizure of the island of Malta, Russia also joined the coalition. The emperor Paul I, who had taken Malta under his personal protection and who aspired to regain his position as grand master of the Order of the Knights Hospitaler of Saint John of Jerusalem, was slighted enough to go to war. The Ottoman Empire was also angered by the French occupation of Egypt and joined the coalition. Finally, the Kingdom of the Two Sicilies joined the alliance against France.[1]

The Kingdom of the Two Sicilies was actually the Kingdom of Naples, which included the island of Sicily. On the throne of Naples sat King Ferdinand, and next to him, Queen Caroline. The king was of the house of Bourbon and thus a distant relative of the executed Louis XVI. The queen was the daughter of Maria Theresa of Austria and the younger sister of Marie Antoinette, also executed by the French. Both Ferdinand and Caroline hated the French Republic and Frenchmen. The court at Naples rejoiced when the news of the destruction of the French fleet at Aboukir reached Italy.[2] It required little encouragement on the part of the English, who desperately desired the use of Italian ports to supply and refit their Mediterranean fleet, to persuade the Francophobe rulers of Naples to join the Second Coalition.

In November 1798, General Jean-Etienne Championnet was sent to Rome to command a French army of some twenty-two thousand men in central Italy. His instructions were to invade the Kingdom of Naples and force it to abide by the treaty it had with France to close its ports to the English navy. However, the French army was not ready for such a military operation when Championnet arrived, and before he could even assemble his scattered forces, a Neapolitan army under the command of the Austrian general

Karl Mack von Leiberich marched north to capture Rome. Ferdinand did not declare war on France but rather announced that his intention was to restore the pope and drive out the foreigners—the French. The premature commencement of hostilities by the king of Naples did catch the French by surprise as fighting in northern Italy had not yet begun. Championnet withdrew to a position north of Rome and allowed Mack to occupy the city on November 27 without a fight. But when the Neapolitan army advanced to the north and attacked the assembled French army, Championnet easily defeated it and sent it retreating to the south. The French reoccupied Rome on December 15 and moved in pursuit of the enemy into Neapolitan territory.[3]

The French invasion of the Kingdom of Naples met little resistance from the Neapolitan army. When reformers had wished to change the color of the soldiers' uniforms, King Ferdinand is reported to have replied: "Dress them in blue, red, or yellow, they will run all the same."[4] However, there was fierce resistance on the part of the Neapolitan population. Nevertheless, Championnet entered the city of Naples on January 23, 1799, and then attempted, unsuccessfully, to pacify the southern provinces of the kingdom. Ferdinand and Caroline had not waited for the arrival of the French. They had fled their capital on December 23 under the protection of Admiral Nelson and the English fleet. They established their court at Palermo and awaited the course of events. Back in Naples, Championnet announced the end of their reign and proclaimed the Republic of "Parthénopéenne."

It was political rather than military affairs that brought about the downfall of General Championnet. Despite his successes, the government of the Directory relieved him of his command, and General Etienne-Jacques-J.-A. Macdonald was named to command the French force, recently renamed the Army of Naples. Then in the early spring of 1799, an Austrian army, supported by a Russian corps, took the offensive in northern Italy. Macdonald was recalled from Naples as the fighting in the north went in favor of the Second Coalition. This enabled Ferdinand and Caroline to return to Naples and take vengeance on all who had been sympathetic to the French. While it was true that there was a faction in southern Italy that would have liked to have seen an end to the Bourbons and the monarchy, by the spring of 1799 anti-French feeling in the Kingdom of Naples was at a feverish high pitch. It was General Dumas's great misfortune to arrive at the port of Taranto on the south coast of Italy under these hostile conditions.

In April or May 1801, immediately following his release from prison, General Dumas wrote a long account of his captivity and mistreatment at the hands of the Neapolitans entitled "Report Made to the French Government by General Alexandre Dumas, Relative to His Imprisonment at Taranto and Brindisi, Ports of the Kingdom of Naples."[5] The report, which at times is in great detail, is the only source of information on Dumas during the two-year period from his departure from Alexandria on March 7, 1799, until his arrival in French-held territory in central Italy in April 1801.

Dumas chartered *La Belle Maltaise* early in 1799 along with other officers and civilians who had, like Dumas, obtained leave from General Bonaparte to return to France. The two most prominent of his companions were General Jean-Baptiste-F. Manscourt du Rozoy and citizen Dieudonné (Déodat) Dolomieu. Manscourt was a fifty-year-old aristocrat who had risen in the ranks of the king's army before the Revolution. He had become acquainted with Dumas while serving as General Sérurier's chief artillery officer at the siege of Mantua in 1796-1797. Like Dumas, he was returning to France because of his poor health. Dolomieu was a mineralogist and one of the civilian *savants* Bonaparte had taken to Egypt. He had been an influential member of the recently established Egyptian Institute in Cairo.

Upon chartering *La Belle Maltaise*, Dumas was informed that before putting to sea, the ship would require some repairs. The general gave the ship's captain, Felix, the sum of one hundred louis to make the vessel seaworthy for the journey to France. Unfortunately, the French were to learn too late that the captain had kept the money and the ship had not been repaired. Nevertheless, on March 7, when the winds were from the east and the English blockade was lax, *La Belle Maltaise* set sail for France.

Shortly after the ship had sailed from Alexandria, a storm engulfed the southeast Mediterranean. By morning of the second day at sea, *La Belle Maltaise* was taking on water. A conference was held of the principal passengers and crew, and it was decided that since they were some forty leagues west of Alexandria and there was a strong wind blowing from east to west, it would be very difficult to return to port. The prevailing wisdom was to continue to the west with the favorable winds and hope that the ship would make the distance to France. However, on the third day of the voyage, the vessel was taking on more water than the crew could bail out. It became clear that to prevent it from sinking, the ship would have to be lightened. The ten cannons, which constituted the ship's only defense, were the first to go overboard. The next day, nine of Dumas's eleven Arabian horses were cast into the sea along with all of his bales of coffee, as was everything else, except the personal effects of the passengers, that was not necessary for the voyage. Despite this lightening of the ship, it continued to ride lower in the water with each passing day. Finally, a second conference was held, and it was decided that the captain should make for the closest port because the ship was in danger of going down within days. After taking a reading of their position, it was determined that southern Italy was the closest land and the seaport of Taranto their destination.

Upon approaching Taranto, the ship was anchored some distance from land, and Captain Felix was sent ashore. The passengers realized that because they were coming from Egypt, they would have to spend thirty days in quarantine. Europe in general and southern Italy in particular lived in constant fear of the bubonic plague. This apprehension was based on solid ground as the plague was common in the eastern Mediterranean. In fact, the French army would lose a considerable number of men to the plague in the spring and summer of 1799 when Bonaparte led ten thousand men into southern

Syria on an ill-fated campaign. It was then necessary to inform the local officials that the ship was coming from Egypt and to ask permission to land.

The captain returned to the ship and informed the passengers that they would be permitted to land under the condition that they submit to thirty days of quarantine. They readily agreed, for as Dumas wrote in his report, "On the tenth day we reached land, and it was none too soon. Another twenty-four hours at sea and the ship would have sunk."[6] The passengers were allowed to come ashore one at a time, and as each did so he was searched by four Neapolitan captains who had sailed with the French from Alexandria. Dumas, out of the goodness of his heart, had allowed the four captains to sail with the French because their ships had been destroyed off of the Egyptian coast and they wished to return home. Although the French thought the Neapolitans' investigation rather strange treatment, they attributed it to the strict sanitary laws, and as they were seeking hospitality in a foreign land, they made no protest.

When all were ashore, they were crowded into one room that was so small there was not space for them to lie down at night. Despite objections at this point, they all—generals and sailors alike—remained in this unsanitary position for two days. While the French were in this unfortunate condition, all of their belongings were confiscated, including Dumas's two remaining Arabian horses, his pistols, and the sword that had been given to him by Bonaparte in Egypt. Then Dumas, Manscourt, and Dolomieu were removed and given their own private rooms to continue their quarantine. Shortly after settling into their new quarters, the French received an unexpected visit from the crown prince Francis, son of the king of Naples.

The prince was introduced, and he asked about the health of Generals Bonaparte and Berthier. He also inquired about the condition of the Army of Egypt. After Dumas and Manscourt had satisfied his curiosity, the prince abruptly departed without saying a word. Dumas and his friends became suspicious of this man. His language and manners were not those of an aristocrat. Both Dumas and Manscourt had been raised in aristocratic circles before the Revolution and were thus in a position to judge the behavior of European nobility, which was generally uniform throughout the Continent. Indeed, they were quite correct in their assessment. The man posing as Prince Francis was actually a Corsican adventurer, something of a vagabond, by the name of Corbara. With the assistance of local Neapolitans, Corbara and three of his companions had taken control of the local government in and about Taranto in the name of the Bourbons.[7] Of this pretender Dumas wrote:

> In the meantime, the pretending prince Francis assumed the role of dictator, cashiering magistrates, naming governors of towns, imposing taxes, and doing all of these things with perhaps more intelligence, and certainly with more boldness, than would have been carried out by the true heir to the throne.[8]

Just eight days after this strange visit, several members of the government presented themselves before Dumas and his companions and announced in the name of His Royal Highness that they were now prisoners of war. The French were informed that there existed a state of war between the Kingdom of Naples and the French Republic. At the same time, these government officials gave Dumas and Manscourt reason to believe that they could soon be freed. They were told that they could be exchanged for Neapolitan generals being held by the French in northern Italy and France. Furthermore, they were also assured that all of their possessions, which had been confiscated upon their arrival, would be returned to them. The Neapolitans even went so far as to require Dumas to pay for the keep of his two horses for several months after their landing. Thus, the prisoners believed that their stay in Taranto could be brief.

A little more than a month after his arrival in Italy, Dumas received a letter from Cardinal Fabrizio Ruffo, who at the time was the vice general of the Neapolitan army. This letter invited Dumas and Manscourt to write to the French generals who commanded the armies of Naples and Italy in order to negotiate an exchange of themselves for General Boccheciampe and other Neapolitan generals in French hands. The cardinal added that the king of Naples was particularly fond of Boccheciampe and desired his return. Dumas wrote the necessary letter and sent it to Cardinal Ruffo. Unfortunately for the prisoners, the Neapolitans were informed that Boccheciampe was not a prisoner of war but had been killed in battle. At that point, all negotiations for Dumas's exchange came to an end, and it would be two years before he would again see France.

Shortly after their hopes of being exchanged had been raised, Dumas and Manscourt received a visit from the governor of Taranto. He informed them that he had received orders to move the two generals to the castle in Taranto. Dolomieu remained behind and was later transferred to a dungeon in Naples. After two years of ill treatment, he was released and returned to France, where he died shortly thereafter as the result of his years in prison.[9] In their new quarters, Dumas and Manscourt each had a room of his own and a very small area in which they could spend time outdoors. Although they did have some contact with one another, it was limited and regulated.

At the time Dumas was moved to the castle, he had not yet been informed that the exchange for General Boccheciampe had failed. Thus, when the commander of the fortress came to see him, Dumas explained the situation. The commander invited him to write again to Cardinal Ruffo, which he did without delay. However, as the Neapolitans had lost interest in exchanging Dumas when they learned of the death of Boccheciampe, nothing resulted from the correspondence.

The day after Dumas had entered the castle, while he was lying on his bed, a parcel was thrown between the bars of the open window and landed in the middle of the room. Dumas opened the parcel and found that it contained two volumes by the author Tissot entitled *The Country Doctor*. There was a note between the first and second pages of one volume that read: "From the patriotic party of Calabria; look up the word *poison*."[10] When Dumas turned to the word "poison," he found that it had been doubly underlined. He realized that his life was in danger, and that he was being warned by an anti-Bourbon faction in Taranto. Fearing that he would not be allowed to keep the books, he hid them in his room, for he took this warning seriously. Dumas read and reread over the following days the section on poison until he had almost memorized the various symptoms and remedies by heart.

The living conditions at the castle were tolerable for the first week or so. Beside an adequate private room, Dumas and Manscourt were allowed to exercise in a large courtyard. But then the governor, under the pretext that the French had captured Naples, confined the prisoners to their respective rooms. New bolts were put on their doors, and their exercise area was reduced by a new wall to twelve by eight feet. During the next eight months, the prisoners were forced to pay all of their own expenses, and at prices that were twice their value. At the end of that period, as all their money had been spent, the king granted to Dumas and Manscourt ten *carlins* (equal to four francs ten sous) each per day with which they had to purchase all of their food and services. This provided the bare necessities for the prisoners.

One of the reasons Dumas had left Egypt was his poor health. Under the conditions of his imprisonment, his health became worse. Some time before he had been transferred to the castle, Dumas had suffered a paralyzing attack of the left cheek. With some difficulty, he was able to have a doctor sent to him who prescribed remedies that had no effect whatsoever. Then one morning several days after he had been moved to the castle (on June 16), this same doctor came to see him without Dumas having made any request. On this occasion, the doctor recommended a new remedy. He said that a biscuit soaked in wine would relieve the paralysis. Dumas agreed to try this remedy, and the doctor immediately sent biscuits and wine. Dumas followed the instructions, but by the middle of the afternoon he suffered violent pains in his stomach and vomiting. His condition worsened until he thought he was on the verge of dying. Realizing that he had been poisoned, Dumas decided to make use of the advice in *The Country Doctor*, which his unknown friends had thrown through his window. He asked for milk, and a goat he had brought from Egypt to provide nourishment during the sea voyage was brought to his room. This animal provided him with a bottle and a half of milk, which he quickly drank. He followed this with thirty to forty spoonfuls of cooking oil to which had been added some citrus juice.

When General Manscourt saw Dumas in this miserable condition, he informed the governor and requested that the doctor come as quickly as possible. The governor sent back word that the doctor had left town, but that as soon as he returned he would come to see Dumas. When Manscourt's demands took on a menacing tone, the governor himself came with the doctor that evening to see the patient. They were accompanied by a dozen army soldiers. Of this visit, Dumas writes: "Without doubt the doctor had need of this armed force to present himself before me; because when he entered my room he was as pale as a dead man."[11] Dumas questioned the doctor, who was extremely nervous. The man stammered so when answering that the general wrote, "It was easy for me to see that if he was not the author of the crime—and this was likely, for the man had no interest in my death—he was at least the instrument of it."[12] The only remedies that the doctor prescribed were that Dumas should drink ice water and suck on snow. The Neapolitans were so anxious for him to begin the treatment that he became suspicious. Nevertheless, he began drinking the ice water, and within half an hour his condition grew noticeably worse. He gave it up and went back to the oil and ceteras juice prescribed by *The Country Doctor*.

The following day Dumas found his goat dead, and two days later the doctor was also dead. Dumas speculated that as the doctor had not been successful in his mission of disposing of him, the authorities had removed him so that he would be unable to tell what he knew of the murderous plot. There was no doubt in Dumas's mind but that he had been poisoned, and the symptoms he suffered indicated that the poison used was arsenic.

But the authorities had not only poisoned Dumas, they had also tried to poison Manscourt. The doctor had gone uninvited to see General Manscourt on the day after he had seen Dumas for the first time. Manscourt was suffering from a scorbutic disorder, which was most likely the result of poor diet since leaving Egypt. The doctor prescribed a remedy for the general, but seeing what had just happened to Dumas after taking the biscuits, Manscourt did not dare to take the medicine. Dumas believed that by not following the remedy, Manscourt had saved his life, because the Neapolitans had also decided upon his death. Indeed, within a short period of time, Manscourt began to develop severe headaches and then fits of delirium, which Dumas attributed to a poisonous powder that was being added to Manscourt's pipe tobacco. He wrote that the powder was so strong that it caused corrosion on the bottom of the tobacco can. Once again they went to *The Country Doctor*, and this time it prescribed bleeding. Manscourt undertook to bleed himself at three different parts of his body. Dumas asserts that this remedy gave his friend relief.[13] Dumas, on the other hand, was not so fortunate.

Following the attempt upon his life, Dumas began to lose his hearing and complete sight in one eye, and the paralysis on the left side of his face grew worse. Thus, despite the very bad experience he had had with the first doctor who attended him, Dumas felt that his condition had degenerated to the point that he needed medical help. He asked the governor to send him a French doctor who had recently become a prisoner of war while on his way from Egypt back to France. This request was denied, but the castle doctor—the replacement for the one who had so recently died—was allowed to come and see the prisoner. This man's name was Carlin, and he was fluent in the

French language. However, Carlin overwhelmed Dumas with exaggerated assurances of his sympathy for the plight in which he found himself. Such overwrought devotion caused Dumas to be suspicious.

Carlin tried to ease the prisoner's mind in light of his previous experience with the last doctor. He then examined Dumas very carefully and announced that he suffered from an attack of "languor." After expressing total disapproval of the treatment prescribed by the previous doctor, whom he denounced as ignorant and incapable, he prescribed his own remedy, which was injections in the ears and a half ounce of cream of tartar every morning. However, after about a week, Dumas's hearing, which had been improving, took a turn for the worse, and his stomach became so irritated that he could no longer digest any food. Dumas remained suspicious of the doctor who came to see him regularly and continued to express great sympathy for the French.

Even though there was little improvement in his condition, it is possible that Carlin was indeed trying to help him. The science of medicine was still in a primitive state at the end of the eighteenth century. Eyes, ears, paralyses, and internal medicine were all a great mystery to the medical profession, and while the first doctor most likely did poison Dumas, Carlin may well have been doing his best to help him. That his remedies were not effective may say more for the state of medicine than the intentions of the doctor. Whatever the case, the governor soon forbade Carlin to see Dumas on the pretense that Carlin was helping the prisoner to maintain communication with the Italian patriotic party in Taranto.

In retrospect, Dumas thought that the governor prevented Carlin from coming to him in order to build up the prisoner's confidence in the doctor. At the time, Dumas pleaded for Carlin, as his condition did not improve. Finally, the governor sent a third doctor to see the prisoner. This one expressed his disapproval of the remedies prescribed by Carlin. He said that the injections in the ears would only make his deafness worse by irritating the delicate membrane—which was probably correct. This third doctor then prepared his own remedy from drugs that he had brought with him. Dumas took the preparation, and his condition began to improve. Unfortunately, he made his improvement known, and after this doctor's second visit, he was removed from the case. When Dumas asked again for him, he was told that the doctor refused to come to the castle to continue the treatment. Thus, the prisoner once again was forced to rely on *The Country Doctor* to treat himself.

Dumas's condition did not improve. His eyesight and his hearing both grew worse. Seeing this, Manscourt put forward a remedy for the eyes that he had seen used with success. He proposed that sugar candy be ground into a fine powder and blown into the eyes seven or eight times a day. Dumas, who was desperate to try anything that might help, agreed, and the procedure was begun. For whatever reason, Dumas writes that it produced such an improvement that by the time he was freed from prison in the spring of 1801, his vision was much better with only a slight glaucoma of the right eye. However, as his hearing grew worse, he again demanded to see Doctor Carlin.

When the governor at length agreed to allow Carlin to see the prisoner, it was on the condition that the doctor spoke no French and that the governor himself was present. Under these conditions, Carlin and the governor came to Dumas's room. But Carlin found the patient in such a poor condition that he declared a consultation with other doctors was necessary. After some discussion, the governor gave his approval. Carlin brought with him to Dumas's room a doctor from the town, the castle surgeon, and a French surgeon. The French surgeon was allowed to join in the consultation as the result of the direct intervention on the part of the Marquis de Valvo, a Neapolitan minister who was in Taranto at that time on a special mission. Hearing that the marquis was in the city, Dumas had sought his assistance, and he had taken pity on the prisoner. Before entering Dumas's room, the French surgeon was threatened with the loss of his life if he so much as uttered one word to the sick man.

The four medical men gathered around Dumas's bed, and Carlin explained the history of the case. This was followed by a discussion of the best treatment for the patient in which the French surgeon, because of his poor Italian and the threats made by the governor, took a minor part. In the end, it was decided that the original treatment prescribed by Carlin should be resumed with the addition of some pill. Dumas, out of desperation, accepted this treatment, and for the next month he followed the instructions given him by Carlin. However, not only did his condition not improve, but he also began to suffer from perpetual insomnia. Again he asked for the doctor. This time he explained to Carlin that there had been no improvement. Nevertheless, the doctor insisted that the prescribed treatment was the only way to save his life, and as Dumas had consumed all of the pills, he ordered some more.

Dumas said that he would continue the treatment and received the additional pills. But instead of taking them, he saved them for future analysis, as he was sure that they contained a poison and that the Neapolitans were again trying to kill him.[14] Eight days after this visit by Carlin, during which period Dumas had not taken any of the doctor's medicine, he was suddenly taken by an attack of apoplexy. Manscourt informed the governor and asked for a doctor. However, the governor simply sent back word that the doctor was in the country, and when he returned he would be sent to see the patient. Over the next four hours, Dumas regained partial consciousness and believed that he was in fact dying. He sent the elderly woman who prepared the meals for himself and the other prisoners in the castle to the governor demanding to see the castle doctor, whom he knew full well was not in the country. If the doctor did not arrive quickly, Dumas threatened to cry out the window of his cell that he was being poisoned.[15] This produced the desired result, and the doctor, who was supposed to be in the country, arrived at his door within five minutes.

Dumas had referred to *The Country Doctor*, and the remedy that it prescribed was bleeding. Therefore, when the doctor arrived, Dumas instructed him to begin that process. The doctor, with a fleam used to bleed horses, made three openings in Dumas's arm before he cut a vein and blood flowed freely. Despite this treatment, Dumas had a second attack of apoplexy just three days after the first. The doctor returned and again bled the patient. On this second occasion, the openings were made on the foot. So clumsy was the doctor—although Dumas suggests that it may have been intentional—that the sinew was injured.[16] This made it all but impossible for Dumas to walk. His foot would swell up after taking only a few steps. Considering the state of the art of medicine and the remedies that were being used on Dumas, it is not at all surprising that his condition did not improve.

News of Dumas's deteriorating condition and poor treatment by the governor reached the patriotic party in the city. In an attempt to help the unfortunate general, a stone wrapped in a piece of paper was thrown through his open window. The message on the paper read:

> They are trying to poison you, but you should have received a book [*The Country Doctor*] in which the word *poison* is underlined. If you have need of any remedy that you cannot obtain in prison, let down from your window a string and we will attach what it is that you request.[17]

In addition to the note, there was string and a hook wrapped around the rock thrown through the window. That night, Dumas let down the string with a request for quinine to be used as a remedy and chocolate to provide nourishment, which he felt was lacking in the food served to the prisoners. The following night when he again lowered his string, the requested items were attached, and he pulled them up to his room. With the quinine and the chocolate, Dumas actually began to improve and had no further attacks of apoplexy. "I remained, however, crippled in the right leg, deaf in the right ear, paralyzed in the left cheek, and with virtually no sight in the right eye. Furthermore, I continued to have violent headaches and a buzzing in my head."[18]

In his "Report Made to the French Government," General Dumas seems to maintain a sense of chronology but not of time. He writes, for example, that an event took place "after eight days," or that "at length" something happened, but without dates one does not know if the event took place in 1799, 1800, or 1801. This may well be because he had no calendar and thus did not know the dates, or perhaps that after one has been in prison a prolonged period, dates no longer have much meaning. Whatever was the situation, it is only known for sure the date he arrived in Italy and the date on which he wrote his report to the government after his release.

Sometime after Dumas had received the quinine and chocolate, the Neapolitans decided to move him and some of the other prisoners from Taranto to the castle at Brindisi. Dumas attributed this move to the fact that the patriotic party in Taranto, knowing of the mistreatment of the prisoners, was protesting and that the authorities had become concerned that the death of French generals would cause a scandal that they would like to avoid. In fact, the events in Italy had taken a turn in favor of the French, and the Neapolitans had very good reason to be concerned about their treatment of French prisoners of war.

General Bonaparte, after a hapless expedition into southern Syria, had returned to France in the late summer of 1799. The coup d'état of Brumaire (November 9-10, 1799) had overthrown the Directory and established the Consulate with Bonaparte as the First Consul. The new constitution gave to Bonaparte extraordinary powers to govern with little interference from the elected or appointed assemblies. At the head of an army,[19] he crossed the Alps into northern Italy and defeated the Austrian army commanded by General Michael Melas at Marengo (June 14, 1800), and the French were once again master of northern Italy. Negotiations between France and Austria dragged on for some months until the Treaty of Luneville was signed on February 9, 1801. By this treaty, France was again given a free hand in Italy, which meant that Bonaparte was free to deal with southern Italy. Although the king of Naples could count on some support from his English ally, there was little hope of prevailing against the French Army of Italy. Thus, despite the fact that the king and queen of Naples continued to hate the French, it became most prudent to begin to take better care of their French prisoners of war and to open negotiations with Bonaparte so as to obtain as favorable a peace treaty as possible. When Naples went to war with France in 1799, it was in a position of strength with England, Austria, the Ottoman Empire, and Russia by its side. But Russia had withdrawn from active participation in the war in January 1800, and Austria had been defeated and forced out of the struggle. Naples was left in a position of weakness.

Dumas, of course, had little knowledge of the events taking place outside of his prison walls and knew nothing of Bonaparte's return from Egypt, the coup d'état of Brumaire, the Marengo campaign, or the Peace of Luneville. It is thus understandable that he attributed the course of events to local conditions rather than the international changes of fortune.

It was most likely in March of 1801 that the Marquis de la Squiave led a squad of soldiers to Dumas's room at about eleven o'clock one night and announced that Dumas was to be transferred to the fortress at Brindisi on the east coast of the Italian peninsula. Dumas had been warned by the patriots of Taranto that he and his fellow prisoners were going to be moved. They also conveyed to him that he was to be murdered en route to Brindisi. Dumas had informed Manscourt of this warning, but after the generals had discussed the matter, they had concluded that it was probably only a rumor and not to be taken too seriously. However, when de la Squiave entered Dumas's room and informed him he was to be moved, Dumas quickly reasoned that if the patriots were correct on the one account, they were very likely right about the plan to murder him once out of the castle and on the road. He, therefore, declared that he would not leave his room, and when the marquis drew his sword and advanced on him, Dumas grabbed his cane, which had a heavy gold knob for a handle, and sprang into action.[20] He advanced on the marquis with such vigor and anger that de la Squiave dropped his sword and ran for the door. The soldiers accompanying him quickly decided that they did not wish to confront so powerful a man armed with a formidable weapon and immediately followed the example of their leader. Within a few seconds, the room was emptied except for the general. Dumas concludes his account of this affair with the following thoughts:

> I do not know, however, what would have happened to us as a result of this act of rebellion if the armistice concluded at Foligno[21] had not come to put an end to this long torture, for we would necessarily have succumbed in the end. But the Neapolitan government remained vile until the last moment, and did not tell us of the end of our captivity.[22]

It is most likely that the Marquis de la Squiave had been informed of the armistice signed between France and the Kingdom of Naples on February 18, 1801, and that the prisoners were being exchanged. Dumas seems to imply that de la Squiave learned of the armistice after the scene in his room.

Following the Austrian defeat at Marengo in June 1800, there was signed an armistice that put an end to the fighting in northern Italy and Germany. But as the Austrians were delaying the signing of a peace treaty, Bonaparte renewed the fighting in December. At that time, the Neapolitan army moved north in support of their hard-pressed ally. Austria could not hold its own against the French force, and after General Jean-Victor Moreau defeated the archduke John and General Paul Kray at Hohenlinden (December 3, 1800), a second armistice led directly to the Peace of Luneville. With the signing of the Peace of Luneville, Bonaparte ordered General Murat at the head of an army to march on Naples and force that kingdom out of the war. At Foligno, on February 18, 1801, the Chevalier de Micheroux, on behalf of the king of Naples, signed an armistice with the French in order to stop Murat's march south. This armistice was based upon a treaty to be signed that would require the king of Naples to close all of his ports to allied ships (both English and Turkish), the evacuation of the Papal States, complete amnesty for all political prisoners in the kingdom, and the immediate release of all French prisoners of war. However, in the interim between the signing of the truce and working out the final language of the treaty, Bonaparte added another demand: a French division would be allowed to occupy the Gulf of Taranto. It further provided that all Neapolitan troops would be removed from all fortresses on the gulf, leaving behind their artillery and military supplies.

When the government at Naples rejected this last demand, Murat renounced the armistice on March 10. He gathered his troops and renewed his march south. When a French force, five thousand men strong, captured Perouse, the Neapolitans again gave way. They had little hope of stopping a French invasion. On March 29, a peace treaty was signed at Florence that gave the French all they demanded.[23]

The news of the military events in central Italy, the armistices, and the negotiations between the king of Naples and the French that went on during

February and March must surely have been known in Taranto, if not in detail, at least in general terms. The Neapolitans in Taranto may not have known of the provision that would require them to turn over the fortress to French troops, as that aspect of the treaty was added after the first armistice. But the return of French prisoners of war had been agreed upon at Foligno in mid-February, six weeks before the presumed time of the scene in Dumas's room in the castle.

The day following the episode with the Marquis de la Squiave, he returned with sufficient force to convince Dumas that he should allow himself to be removed and taken, with the other French prisoners of war, to Brindisi. Needless to say, no attempt was made on the lives of any of the French. However, they were not told that they were being released and sent back to France until they were put aboard ship at Brindisi on April 5, 1801. One can only imagine their joy after two years of imprisonment and in light of the fact that only a few days earlier they believed that they were in danger of being murdered on the road from Taranto to Brindisi. Including Dumas, there were ninety-six French officers, soldiers, and sailors released at this time by the Neapolitans.

When Dumas was put aboard ship and told that he was being freed, he demanded that the Neapolitans return to him the possessions that had been taken upon his arrival at Taranto. He wanted in particular the sword given to him by Bonaparte while in Egypt, but also his pistols, two Arabian horses, and private papers. He was told that he would have to make that request directly to the king of Naples. It is sufficient to say that he never again saw any of his possessions. Dumas writes of his request:

> I have since learned that my request for the return of my belongings had been transmitted to King Ferdinand; but as he went hunting every day on my horses which rode very well and used my guns which fired quite well, he decided to keep them all.[24]

The French sailed north from Brindisi to Ancona on the Adriatic coast due east of Florence. They were fortunate in that they did not encounter English, Turkish, or Barbary pirate ships. Upon their arrival at Ancona on April 12, General François Watrin, who commanded the French garrison in the city, provided money from his own pocket when he saw the miserable condition of the ex-prisoners. Watrin's money enabled them to purchase clothing and pay the ship's captain, who had brought them from Brindisi for the sum of one hundred piastres. From Ancona, Dumas traveled to Murat's headquarters at Florence, where he rested and wrote his lengthy account of his captivity. He concluded this report on a bittersweet note:

> The above is an accurate account of my imprisonment during which there had been three attempts to poison me and one attempt at assassination.[25]

For the rest, now that my life will not last long, I am thankful to God that he has allowed me to live this long, because, dying as I am, I still have the strength left in me to denounce to the world the cruel treatment, which the people of the civilized world would blush to inflict upon their worst enemies.

Written at the general headquarters of the Army of Observation of the South, at Florence, the 15th germinal, the year 9 of the Republic [April 5, 1801].

[Signed] Alex. Dumas[26]

8

THE LAST YEARS

The day following General Dumas's arrival at Ancona he wrote to his wife informing her of his release and that he would soon return to France.[1] He had written many times to his wife while a prisoner, but as he had never received a letter from her, he quite correctly assumed that his correspondence had never reached Villers-Cotterêts. Marie-Louise Dumas had received a letter from her husband on May 13, 1799, which he had written shortly before he left Alexandria, informing her that he was preparing to return to France. When he did not arrive and there was no information about him, she wrote to the minister of the navy. However, there was no news about her husband. She then began to inquire as to his whereabouts from his friends. She sought the help of General Jean-Baptiste Jourdan, and he in turn wrote to the minister of war, General Jean-Baptiste Bernadotte, in July 1799:

> Madame Dumas, my dear General, the wife of citizen Dumas, general of division, who had gone to Egypt with General Buonaparté,[2] is inquiring of the whereabouts of her husband. She knows that he embarked to return to France and was taken prisoner in the Gulf of Taranto and taken to Messina [*sic*] during the month of germinal [February-March]. If you have any certain information of his whereabouts please let her know.[3]

Madame Dumas also wrote directly to the minister of war on July 22 and again on August 11. In her second letter, she informed him of what she knew: that he had left Egypt and that he was reported to have been taken prisoner and was at Mason. However, she had no confirmation of this news and asked the minister if he in fact knew for sure that this was true and, if so, what was the condition of her husband at that time.[4] General Bernadotte wrote back to Madame Dumas: "At this time I have received nothing official on him [General Dumas]. If I receive any news I will send it to you."[5]

It was not until October, five months after she had learned that Dumas was leaving Egypt, that she received unofficial information that he was most likely a prisoner of war in the Kingdom of Naples. It was not known just where in the kingdom that the general was being held; perhaps in Naples or in Sicily. Then in November, the French consul at Genoa confirmed the fact that General Dumas was indeed a prisoner of the Neapolitans and that there might be some communication with him through the Spanish ambassador. It may well be that it was at this time that the Neapolitans wanted to exchange Dumas for General Boccheciampe. The failure of this approach to communicate may be explained by the fact that the Neapolitans learned Boccheciampe was not a French prisoner; thus, there was never any communication to or from Dumas while he was a captive.[6]

A year after Madame Dumas had sought information about her husband, the wife of Chef de Bataillon Nicolas-Martin Barthelemi wrote to the minister of war. In a letter dated August 25, 1800, she explained that her husband commanded the 15th Regiment of dragoons in Egypt, and she asked if there was any recent definite information of General Alexandre Dumas.[7] The minister of war answered her letter on September 17:

> General Dumas, madame, of whom you asked news by your letter of the 25th of last month, is still a prisoner of war at Mason in Sicily, and as there does not exist between France and the Kingdom of Naples any means of exchanging prisoners of war, it is not possible to anticipate when that General would return to this country.[8]

A year and half after Dumas had been taken prisoner, the government in Paris did not know that he was in fact being held in Taranto, not in Sicily.

From Florence, after his release, Dumas wrote his second letter to Marie-Louise. In both this letter and his first, he expressed his love for his wife in a most tender language. He also sent his love to his daughter, his in-laws, and several close friends. Furthermore, in both letters, Dumas announced that he had taken up smoking, like his father-in-law, and requested that Monsieur Labouret buy a supply of wine, naming particular brands.[9]

Dumas remained in Florence for more than a month. The general and the other prisoners of war received medical care and began the long period of recuperation. More than half of the prisoners had been seriously wounded in Egypt—they were blind, lame, or maimed in some way—and had been on their way to France for medical care when they were captured and taken to southern Italy. When General Murat had provided for these men as best he could, he made arrangements to send them back to France. Dumas, as the senior officer of the returned prisoners, was placed in command of the detachment with instructions to conduct the men to the Hôtel des Invalides in Paris. He left Florence on May 14, 1801, and was in Lyon early in June, where he received the first letters from his wife in more than two years.[10]

The France to which General Dumas returned in the summer of 1801 was quite different from the one he left in the spring of 1798. Bonaparte, as First Consul, held such extraordinary power that he was virtually dictator of France. His popularity with the nation had soared to new heights as the result of new military victories, the restoration of peace in the Vendée, and a rapprochement begun with Rome and the Catholic church in France.

He had his enemies, to be sure: the Jacobin left and the royalist right. But both extremes had been discredited, and the overwhelming majority of Frenchmen were very satisfied with the new Bonaparte regime. It seemed to keep the best of the revolutionary reforms while at the same time it threw off the abuses and corruption of the previous republican regimes. This was certainly the perception, if not the reality, and the French people were pleased with their general-turned-statesman.

When Dumas arrived in Paris in mid-June 1801, his wife and daughter were there to greet him. It was a joyful reunion for the Dumas, who had not seen one another for more than three years. And for most of that period, they had all wondered whether the general would ever reach France alive.

Dumas spent several days at the Invalides attending to his affairs and recovering from the long journey from Florence. His health had still been poor when he left Italy, but after resting and receiving medical attention, he was given leave to go home with his family to Villers-Cotterêts for a prolonged recuperation.

With rest, good care, nourishing food, and the love of his family, Dumas's overall condition gradually improved. He regained most of his sight, and his foot healed. The headaches and most of the paralysis in his face went away. However, the problems with his stomach, while they improved from time to time, remained with him. As he became stronger, he took walks in the forest and began again to hunt with friends and neighbors. In 1802, there actually seemed to be the real possibility that Dumas would be physically able to rejoin the army on active duty.

After his health, the most pressing matter for Dumas was financial. He had learned while in Florence that the treaty signed by the king of Naples provided that he would pay the sum of five hundred thousand francs in compensation to the prisoners of war who had been held in his kingdom. Quite naturally, Dumas believed that he was entitled to a portion of that sum. The Neapolitans had taken from him two very valuable horses, his firearms, and his sword. More important, he had suffered great physical and mental harm. Surely, he felt, he would be compensated generously. However, upon inquiring about this indemnity when he reached Paris, he could not find anyone who knew of this clause of the treaty. In July 1801, he wrote from Villers-Cotterêts to Murat, who was still in Florence.

> I would very much like to know, my dear Murat, something positive about the five hundred thousand francs that you told me about that the Neapolitan government was forced to pay, as an indemnity, to those prisoners of war who have survived the stay in their prisons. I have inquired of many persons about this subject, but no one has been able to give me any information relating to this indemnity. . . .
>
> The first consul [Bonaparte] was indignant, I have been told, at the manner in which I was treated by the king of Naples, and has promised me the return of those objects that had been taken from me, and in

particular the saber that he had given to me in Alexandria, which is still in the hands of that miserable Cesare [*sic*].[11]

This letter is interesting because it is the first indication that Dumas was getting some kind of red-tape runaround from the bureaucracy in Paris. At the same time, it shows that he believed Bonaparte was his friend and that he could expect that the First Consul would treat him in a favorable manner. But in point of fact, Dumas never received a franc of this indemnity, nor did he ever see any of the objects taken from him when he had arrived at Taranto. Murat wrote back to Dumas telling him that he should contact the minister of foreign affairs, who was responsible for seeing that the treaty was carried out. After further inquiry, the frustrated general wrote directly to Bonaparte:

> General [Jean] Lannes has informed me that you are not able to give me any part of the indemnity until you have knowledge that General Murat has extracted that sum from the government of Naples. . . .
>
> General Murat has written to me that the minister of foreign affairs is charged with the distribution of the sum of five hundred thousand francs that the government of Naples must pay to the prisoners of war of that country who were the victims of its barbarism.
>
> I hope that you will take an interest in this just demand, by a man to whom you have so often given verbal and written assurances of your esteem and affection.[12]

Despite the fact that the First Consul did not answer Dumas's letter, Dumas continued to cling to the hope that he would be compensated for the two years he had spent in the Neapolitan prison.

In addition to the expectation of receiving a portion of the indemnity, Dumas was sure that he would receive two years of back pay for the time he was a prisoner of war, which amounted to a considerable sum. Without giving it a second thought, he applied to the minister of war for his back pay and waited to receive the money. Much to his surprise, General Berthier, the minister of war under the Consulate, informed him by a letter dated September 16, 1801, that he was being denied a large portion of what Dumas figured to be due him.[13] He was, in fact, denied 28,500 francs for a part of year VII and all of year VIII (1799–1800). This denial was based on an order signed by the First Consul to the effect that Dumas was only due "that which the law allowed, that is to say, two months of active duty pay."[14]

Believing that there must be some administrative confusion or bureaucratic mix-up, Dumas wrote directly to Bonaparte on September 29:

> I sincerely hope that you will do me the honor of remembering my back pay from February 18, 1799. A review of my service record has established the details of that which is due to me since that date. I have

been paid for the first three quarters of the year IX [September 1800–June 1801]. . . . [There follows Berthier's explanation.]

However, General Consul, you know the misfortune that I have experienced! You know how little wealth I have! You remember the treasure of Cairo![15]

I hope that I can count on your friendship to believe that you will give the order that I should be paid what is due me for the rest of the year VII and all of the year VIII. This is all that I ask. . . .

I hope, General Consul, that you will not allow the man who shared your work and your dangers to languish like a beggar when it is within your power to give him a testimony of the generosity of the nation for which you are responsible.[16]

Dumas was counting on the friendship of his former commander in chief without taking into consideration that Bonaparte might still be angry over the general's departure from Egypt three years earlier.

At the same time that he was seeking to recover his back pay, Dumas also wrote to the minister of war asking to be given employment with the army. On October 7, 1801, he wrote a long letter to Berthier in which, after acknowledging the minister's letter of September 16 and questioning his lack of pay while a prisoner of war, he reviewed his military career from private to general in command of armies. He reminded the minister that he was the senior general of division in the entire French army and that Berthier had told him he would be given a command as soon as he had recovered his health. Yet, he continued, he found himself in a state of virtual retirement. He concluded by coming very close to saying that France owed him employment.[17]

Despite the fact that he received no satisfaction, Dumas continued to write to the minister of war and to the First Consul. In February 1802, he wrote to Berthier and again reminded him of his promise to employ him as soon as his health would permit.[18] The minister answered his letter by saying, "You can be sure that I will do everything possible on your behalf, and that I will not let pass any favorable occasion to put before the eyes of the First Consul the fact that you merit his confidence and the goodwill of the government."[19] Dumas seemed to have forgotten that this minister of war was the same man who had been the army's chief of staff in January 1797, whom he had so crudely insulted by questioning his courage and using a most vulgar language. Berthier was well known for his long memory, and although his words may have given Dumas some comfort, his lack of action on the general's behalf surely spoke much louder and should have reminded Dumas that he had made an enemy of this man five years earlier.

In June of the same year, Dumas again wrote to Bonaparte. After reminding him once more of his past military record, he expressed the sincere hope that the First Consul would keep him in mind when making the appointments for the army for the coming year.[20]

It should not have been a surprise that Dumas's request was not honored. As was the case with a portion of the indemnity from Naples and back pay, his request to be placed back on active duty was never acted upon in a favorable manner. The final disappointment came when his name was struck off of the list of active army officers on September 13, 1802, and placed on the roll of the retired. Article 1 of the order reads, "General of division Alexandre Dumas is placed on the list of the retired"; Article 2, "He will no longer be carried on the lists of General of Divisions of the Republic"; and Article 3, "The minister of war is charged with the execution of this order."[21] He was informed of his retirement, not by Bonaparte or Berthier, but by an unfeeling and insensitive letter signed only with the initials "JNS." "I am sending to you, citizen General, a copy of the order of September 13 stating that you have been admitted to retirement pay and that you are no longer on the list of the generals of division of the General Staff of the army."[22]

Dumas's health had improved substantially by 1802, and he was bored with the lack of activities available at Villers-Cotterêts. It is true that he had family and friends in the small town, but Dumas, who was only forty years of age, was restless. He needed the active live of an army officer to give him a sense of usefulness. The military made him feel important, gave him a sense of accomplishment, a raison d'être. It had been his whole life for more than fifteen years.

There is little doubt but that First Consul Bonaparte was still angry with Dumas. He had tried everything to keep the general with him in Egypt. Dumas was one of the most senior officers with the army in Egypt, he had an outstanding reputation for bravery, and he was a good organizer and cavalry commander who was respected by officers and men alike. His departure served no purpose other than to undermine morale at a time when both officers and men wanted to return to France. It is understandable that General Bonaparte looked upon Dumas's departure with great displeasure. Although there is no record of Bonaparte ever saying so, it is also likely that he thought that Dumas's capture and imprisonment for two years was somehow poetic justice for his having deserted him in his time of need.

There was one event that did bring hope and joy into Dumas's life in these years: the birth of a son on July 24, 1802. Named Alexandre Dumas after his father, he would become known to the literary world as *the* Alexandre Dumas. When the author of *The Three Musketeers* and *The Count of Monte Cristo* had a son, who came to be known as Alexandre Dumas (*fils*), the general's son became Dumas (*père*). Although it is seldom used, the general could be referred to as Dumas (*grand-père*). The boy became his father's pride and joy. Deprived of his military career, Dumas turned much of his attention to his son. Although young Dumas was only four years of age when his father died, he had developed an attachment and an admiration that lasted all of his life. Evidence of this affection may be seen in the *Mémoires* Dumas (*père*) wrote some fifty years after his father's death.

The Dumas family had purchased a two-story house on the rue de Lormet (today it is the rue Alexandre Dumas), which was, in fact, one of the newer and nicer homes in Villers-Cotterêts. Despite the general's pleas of near poverty, he did receive about four thousand francs a year as a retired general of division.[23] This was not a large sum of money, but it did enable the Dumas family to live comfortably in the small town of Villers-Cotterêts. Dumas may well have felt poor compared to his fellow generals of division on active service, and certainly after the establishment of the empire in 1804, he had reason to think of himself as living in poverty compared to the newly created marshals of the empire. Napoleon had given to eighteen generals of division not only the title of marshal but also large amounts of money so that they could maintain lavish homes in Paris as well as country estates.[24] Dumas must have felt as entitled to a marshal's baton as less well-known men like Louis-N. Davout or Guillaume-Marie-A. Brune.

General Brune had been one of Dumas's closest friends in the army. The two men were the same age and had known one another since 1793. They had served together under Bonaparte in Italy in 1796–1797. Perhaps more important, both Brune and Dumas were sincere republicans and neither became true Bonapartists, although Brune would serve under the emperor Napoleon as a diplomat and soldier. In 1804, Napoleon named him a marshal of the empire and gave him the Grand Eagle of the Legion of Honor. However, as governor general of the Hanseatic towns, he signed a treaty with Sweden in which he made a reference to "the French army" rather than "the Army of His Imperial and Royal Majesty." It may have been just a republican slip, but it so infuriated Napoleon that he relieved Brune of his command and did not give him a position again until he returned from Elba in 1815.[25]

The day after the birth of his son, Dumas wrote to Brune, who was at that time in Paris, and asked him if he would be godfather for the infant Alexandre. Dumas was very insistent and urged Brune to come to Villers-Cotterêts as soon as possible. The baby's sister, Marie-Alexandrine-Aimée, would be the godmother.[26] However, Brune, after expressing deep affection for Dumas and his family, wrote:

> I have been a godfather five times, and my five goddaughters are all dead. After that, I promised myself that I would never again be a godfather. You may think that my prejudice is foolish, but I would be extremely unhappy if I should renounce it. . . . I must be very firm in my resolution to refuse to be the godfather for your charming son.[27]

Despite Brune's rather justifiable superstition, Dumas would not take no for an answer. He was insistent and pressed poor Brune until the two old friends arrived at a compromise. Brune would be the godfather of young Alexandre Dumas, but he would not come to Villers-Cotterêts and hold the child during the service. The boy's grandfather thus stood in for him.[28]

In 1802, Bonaparte was given the title of First Consul for life with the authority to appoint his successor. His popularity knew few limitations. He had defeated the Austrians again on his second Italian campaign in 1800 and forced that nation once again to sign a pro-French treaty. In 1801, he had made peace with the English at Amiens. Thus, for the first time in ten years, France was at peace with all of Europe. He had brought an end to the civil war in the Vendée and signed a concordat with Pope Pius VII in 1801. The end of the schism within the Roman Catholic church in France and the restoration of harmony between church and state was popular with most Frenchmen, albeit the old-line republican-anticlerics did not rejoice. The new constitution of the VIII (1799–1800) was also generally popular. It may have given all real power to the First Consul, but it was couched in democratic terms so as to give the impression of representative government and power in the people. Finally, while France had reverted to an authoritarian form of rule, Bonaparte provided good government. The fanaticism of the Republic (that is, the Reign of Terror) and the corruption and turmoil of the Directory were replaced by the stability and efficiency of the Consulate. It was then not surprising that in May 1804, Napoleon Bonaparte was named emperor of the French. The coronation took place in the cathedral of Notre Dame on December 2 of the same year.

Aside from the terminology, little changed under the empire. Napoleon already had the power of government. The new marshals of the empire became members of the newly created imperial court and the envy of the army. Most of them received titles over the next ten years. Two of them, Murat and Bernadotte, became kings and several others—Berthier, Davout, Masséna, and Michel Ney—became princes, while still others were named counts or dukes. It was just as well that Dumas did not live to see most of these men receive their honors and wealth; it would only have caused him more pain. Napoleon was determined to give him nothing. He was not even awarded the Eagle of the Legion of Honor, which Bonaparte had created on May 19, 1802, to be bestowed upon soldiers and civilians alike for service to France. Surely he was deserving, but the bitterness generated in Egypt stood between Dumas and any reward, no matter how justifiable, over which Bonaparte had control.

Dumas lived his last few years on the rue Lormet. He continued to hunt in the lush forests about the town and watched his son, upon whom he doted, grow from a baby into a child. Upon the renewal of the war with England in 1803, Dumas wrote three times to the First Consul offering his services. Desperate to rejoin the army, he anticipated that it would be increased in size and thus require additional experienced senior officers. In October of 1803, he made one last attempt to renew his military career:

> Since the beginning of the war I have had the honor of twice writing to you to offer to you my services. Painfully I once again offer to you that service. I am in good health and active. . . .

My only consolation, the only motive that keeps me from despair, is that I have served under your orders, that soon you will give me the means of happiness and esteem. This gives me confidence and courage. I hope that sooner or later you will address my situation.[29]

However, as with all of his previous appeals and pleas, Dumas waited in vain for that letter that would restore him to active duty.

The Dumas family was able to maintain the life-style of a retired general on his pension. The household included, in addition to the Dumas, a gardener by the name of Pierre, a cook named Marie, a general all-around handyman named Mocquet, and a valet for the general named Hipolyte. The younger Dumas believed that his father kept Hipolyte, who was black, out of charity rather than for his usefulness, because the man seemed to lack the ability to cope with the real world.[30] The Dumas were also able to afford the expense of sending their daughter to Paris to be educated. The family was neither wealthy nor poor. So long as the general lived, it was as comfortable as could be expected of a retired general of division.

Dumas's health varied during the last five years of his life. He would experience four to six months of reasonably good health and then suffer a setback for several months. However, by 1804, his condition was in a gradual state of decline. He was most likely dying slowly of stomach cancer, and the remedies, at best, may have made him more comfortable from time to time. At one point, it was thought that a change of air would help the ill man. In 1804, the family spent six months with friends at the Château des Fossés, which was located about fifteen to twenty miles east of Villers-Cotterêts just next to the small village of d'Haramont. The château was surrounded by water from a small stream that ran through the ground. The result was a near-perpetual damp condition that Marie-Louise came to believe only aggravated the rheumatism in the general's right leg. Therefore, in 1805, the family rented a house in Antilly.[31]

Despite the move and the loving care of his wife and servants, Dumas's condition took a turn for the worse in the fall of 1805. The family returned home to 46 rue de Lormet by the beginning of 1806, and General Alexandre Dumas died at 11:00 P.M. on February 27. He was buried in the Villers-Cotterêts cemetery on the south side of the town. Inscribed on the stone that covers him is

Family
Thomas Alexandre
Dumas
Davy de la Pailleterie
general of division
born at Jérémie
on the Island of St-Domingue

March 25, 1762
Died at Villers-Cotterêts
February 27, 1806.[32]

Marie-Louise Dumas then found herself with two children to be raised and educated on what she expected to be the pension of a widow of a general of division. Much to her dismay, however, even this was denied her. She sought the assistance of her husband's influential friends, and some of them tried to intercede on her behalf with the emperor. When General Brune brought up the question of Marie-Louise's pension, the emperor is reported to have said to Brune in an angry voice, "I have forbidden you to speak to me of that man!"[33]

Although she continued her husband's attempts to recover from the war office the 28,500 francs of back pay due to the family for the period the general was a prisoner of war, she received no more satisfaction than had her husband.[34] Napoleon would make no concessions to the Dumas family. When the general's son was ready to be educated, he was unable to secure a financial scholarship; neither was he admitted to the national military school, to which, as the son of a deceased general, he should have been given special consideration tantamount to acceptance. It is easy to understand the long-lasting hatred of Dumas (*père*) for Napoleon that comes through so clearly in his *Mémoires*.

Following the first abdication of the Emperor Napoleon (April 6, 1814), Madame Dumas made yet another attempt to recover her husband's back pay. With the restoration of the Bourbon monarchy, she hoped to receive a more just treatment than she had during the empire. Although the general had been an outspoken republican since 1792, he had also served Louis XVI faithfully from the time he had entered the army in 1786 until the king's removal from power in August 1792. To be sure, the royalists owed the Dumas family nothing, and in Marie-Louise's letter to the "Minister Secretary of State and of War," there was no mention of the nobility of the Davy de la Pailleterie family. Indeed, she signed herself simply "Madame Dumas."

> The death of General Alexandre Dumas has left his family without wealth and with no resources to support his widow except the pension assigned to widows of generals, and which by a most unjust exception she has been refused. Furthermore, she is to be paid a sum of 28,500 francs due to her husband for the remainder of his appointment in the army for the years VII and VIII. But . . . Bonaparte, who until now had appeared to have authorized that reimbursement, had at the same time given other orders to the Bureau of War, . . . so that no payments were ever made. This is easily verified.

> The brave General Dumas, who was respected by combat veterans, received no military decoration or recompense, and was a victim of the implacable hatred of Bonaparte. . . .

The justice of your administration, Monseigneur, has redressed the wrongs of the old government. The widow of General Dumas claims today with confidence, she requests of you, Monseigneur, to give her the pension due to the wife of a general, and to pay her at the same time, if not the principal, at least the interest on the 28,500 francs.[35]

There is no indication that the Dumas family ever received any part of the money to which it seems to have had a just claim.

9

CONCLUSION

The life of Alexandre Dumas is truly an extraordinary odyssey. This son of an African slave mother from the island of Saint Domingue rose to the highest rank in the French army. In his youth, he languished in that shadowy gray area between slavery and freedom. As a mulatto on his native island, he was a "man of color" and thus a second-class subject of the king of France. In France as a young man, his position improved greatly. He was the son of an aristocrat, and although still a mulatto, he had money and a place, at least, on the edge of "good" society. His entry into the army as a private was certainly not a promising move on Dumas's part. If the French Revolution had not occurred in timely fashion, Dumas, with a successful career, would most likely have risen only to the rank of sergeant major. His life would have been of little interest to future generations, and it is unlikely that a son of his would have become one of the greatest authors of the nineteenth century. But the Revolution did break on France and then Europe; and like Napoleon, Wellington, Blücher, Nelson, and so many other military men who would have had a rather ordinary military career, Dumas was in the right place at the right time to benefit from the extraordinary events and opportunities this great upheaval offered.

Dumas might be better compared to men like Michel Ney, Joachim Murat, or François-Joseph Lefebvre than to Wellington or Blücher. The latter two would have been important men in their own countries even without the Revolution. It was the Revolution that catapulted them to "greatness." But Dumas, Ney, Murat, and Lefebvre would have had no place in history without the Revolution. It was the fall of the monarchy, the establishment of the Republic, and the wars of the revolutionary years that provided the opportunities for men like Dumas to rise in the ranks of the army and enabled them to make a name for themselves and a place in history. Nevertheless, the rise of Dumas, like the others, was a combination of timing, luck, and talent. To have been born twenty-five years earlier or later would have made them too old or too young to have taken advantage of the opportunities presented by the Revolution and the wars that it spawned. The fact that Dumas was half black was instrumental in his astonishing rise from corporal to lieutenant colonel in a matter of a few weeks. Furthermore, he was promoted to general of division, not because of his past military record—he had never commanded or even taken part in a major battle—but primarily on the basis of his well-known political orientation. He was a true, sincere, and devoted republican at a time when this was the foremost qualification for promotion to high rank.

Dumas's military talents were brought out during the course of the revolutionary wars, and they served him well. His strength was renowned, even before the Revolution. His bravery as a common soldier brought him to the attention of Saint Georges and spurred his rapid promotion. As commander of the Army of the Alps, his ability as an organizer was established, while his capture of the great passes in the Alps was an achievement that displayed his ability at the head of an army. Few men in the French army were as talented as Dumas at the head of a cavalry attack. In the Tyrol and in Egypt, his fearlessness and feats of daring and bravery in the face of the enemy made him something close to a legend.

There is no indication that the fact that Alexandre Dumas was a mulatto had a negative effect upon his career. This is not to say that there were no prejudiced men in France in the second half of the eighteenth century. The incident at the theater when he was a young man, which was clearly an insult based on his color, was certainly an embarrassment and a humiliation for Dumas. Furthermore, although there is no documentary evidence, there must certainly had been other incidents, perhaps more subtle and less blatant, of a similar nature that caused him pain and reminded him of his color. Indeed, it is not known how many of the the numerous duels he fought as a dragoon might have been the result—at least in part—of his being a man of color. But the young Alexandre was able to cope one way or another with who he was. In fact, it was because he was black that he was promoted from lieutenant to lieutenant colonel in one step in the American Legion. As a general of division, coping must have been much easier, although he always remained a *nègre*. Nevertheless, there was prejudice in the French army to varying degrees, and Dumas must have felt the effects. Evidence of such prejudice is seen in the memories of Baron Paul-Charles Thiébault, who had served with Dumas in the Tyrol in 1797. After expressing sorrow upon receiving the news of Dumas's death, he added: "He is the only man of color whose skin I could pardon."[1]

The question of color did not seem to have diminished the career or the legacy of General Dumas's son. Alexandre Dumas (*père*) and his son, Alexandre Dumas (*fils*), moved quite well in the society of mid-nineteenth-century France. Perhaps this is because the author of *The Three Musketeers* and *The Count of Monte Cristo* was only one-quarter black. On the other hand, the marriage of the general's daughter may have been a different story. On June 2, 1813, Marie-Alexandrine-Aimée, using the last name of Dumas Davy de la Pailleterie, married Joseph-Marie-Victor Letellier. His family did not approve of the marriage and caused some delay in the union of the two young persons. In fact, no member of the Letellier family attended the marriage. Although there is no proof to corroborate the theory, it is implied that the Letelliers were most likely prejudiced and objected to the union because Alexandrine was one-quarter black.[2]

Dumas's color does not seem to have been a factor in his relationship with Napoleon, who was willing to accept a man on the basis of his usefulness. Bonaparte's attitude and actions with respect to slavery were governed by political practicality rather than racist motivations. The two men seemed to have gotten along very well until the incident at Mantua in January 1797 when Dumas unjustly insulted General Berthier and indirectly Bonaparte himself. Still, Dumas's sterling service during the campaign in the Tyrol, marked by the sympathetic reports of General Joubert, put him back into the good graces of his commanding general. Bonaparte not only gave Dumas commands in northern Italy after the campaign had been successfully completed but also invited Dumas to command the cavalry when he took an army to Egypt. He could have given that command to any one of a number of generals. His choice of Dumas clearly shows that he held him in high esteem at that time as a soldier.

It was in Egypt that the relationship between Dumas and Bonaparte went bad. Although Bonaparte would refer to him as "that *nègre*," his dislike of Dumas had nothing to do with the fact that he was a man of color[3] but rather because Dumas refused to remain in Egypt when Bonaparte strongly wished him to do so. On one level, Bonaparte felt deserted by Dumas and would never forgive him of that. On yet another level, Bonaparte realized that he would never be able to dominate the strong-willed Dumas, and while Dumas might serve under his command, he would never be attached to him personally. Back in France, the First Consul and later emperor never believed that Dumas would become a true, sincere Bonapartist. Dumas wished to return to active service in the army after his return from imprisonment in Italy, but in the Army of France, not in a Napoleonic army. Thus, from Dumas's departure from Egypt early in 1799 until his death in 1806, Napoleon would have nothing to do with him.

It has been argued that Napoleon disliked General Dumas because he was truly a republican and thus opposed to the creation of any type of authoritarian state, whether it was in the form of a consulate or an empire.[4] But this is contradicted by the fact that Napoleon supported, rewarded, and promoted to the marshalcy known sincere republicans like Brune, Lefebvre, Augereau, and Bernadotte. They all cooperated with Napoleon and his authoritarian regime despite the fact that some of them, Brune for certain, would have preferred a republic. Indeed, Dumas desired very much to serve in the army under the Consulate, and had he been named a marshal of the empire in 1804, there is no indication that he would have declined the honor, money, and prestige. He may well have remained a republican at heart, as did some Frenchmen, but could easily have rationalized that as a soldier he was serving France.

Bonaparte's dislike of General Dumas carried over to his widow and two children. Both Marie-Louise and Alexandre Dumas (*père*) believed that

Napoleon treated them unfairly as he had the general. In his *Mémoires*, Dumas (*père*) took every opportunity to vilify Napoleon and to blame him for the troubles of his family before and after the death of his father.[5]

If it is true that Bonaparte was responsible for the financial hardships of the Dumas family after the general's return from Italy, it must also be pointed out that Dumas contributed to his difficulties by word and action. He was quick to anger or to take offense, which may be seen in his numerous duels as a young dragoon, in his reaction to the official account of the battle before Mantua, in the affair in his tent at Damanhûr in Egypt, and many other similar episodes. He made enemies of men who would have served him well had they been friends. He certainly felt wronged in the case of Berthier, and with good reason, but he could have obtained satisfaction without having created a life-long enemy. In the case of Bonaparte, only his remaining in Egypt would have prevented the rupture in their relationship, and Dumas would not stay.

His relationship with General François Kellermann can be understood only in terms of misplaced pride combined perhaps with misguided arrogance and paranoia with respect to returning émigrés and priests. Nevertheless, there is no good excuse for the manner in which Dumas acted toward Kellermann. Kellermann was his commanding officer, and as such, Dumas owed him respect and obedience. Indeed, Dumas would accept nothing less from those who served under his command. His brief period with the Army of the Alps in 1796 were not the proudest of his military career.

This having been said, Dumas was a man of principles and convictions, and he stood by them even when it was unpopular or dangerous. Destroying the guillotine and sparing the lives of the men about to be executed when he took command of the Army of the Alps early in 1794 was not popular. In fact, it made enemies of the powerful Jacobin society, which could have cost him his command or even his life. Yet he believed the punishment was excessive and took action to prevent it from being carried out. His republicanism was not merely a convenience during the years of the Terror and the Directory. Dumas believed in liberty, equality, and democracy, not only when it was politically correct but also under the Bonaparte regime, when equality and democracy were no longer in vogue. He strove to be both honest and just, and if he occasionally came up wanting, he certainly believed in his heart that his actions were justifiable.

NOTES

BIBLIOGRAPHY

INDEX

NOTES

1. The Early Years

1. The best study of the Davy de la Pailleterie family is Robert Landru's *A propos d'Alexandre Dumas: Les aïeux, le Général, le bailli, premiers amis.*

2. Landru, *A propos d'Alexandre Dumas*, p. 31.

3. On Charles Davy, see Landru, *A propos d'Alexandre Dumas*, pp. 31–52.

4. Pierre de Vaissière, *Saint-Domingue (1629–1789): La Société et la vie créoles sous l'Ancien Régime*, p. 45.

5. On the French slave trade, see Robert Louis Stein, *The French Slave Trade in the Eighteenth Century: An Old Regime Business.*

6. See Alexandre Dumas (*père*), *Mes Mémoires*, vol. 1, pp. 2–4. Hereafter referred to as *Mémoires.*

7. Ernest d'Hauterive, *Un soldat de la Révolution: Le Général Alexandre Dumas (1762–1806)*, p. 12.

8. For a good discussion of the questions of marriage and mistresses on Saint Domingue in the eighteenth century, see Vaissière, *Saint Domingue*, pp. 73–76; and T. Lothrop Stoddard, *The French Revolution in San Domingo*, pp. 41–43.

9. Stoddard, *The French Revolution in San Domingo*, p. 42.

10. Stoddard, *The French Revolution in San Domingo*, p. 45.

11. Dumas (*père*), *Mémoires*, vol. 1, pp. 2–3.

12. See Landru, *A propos d'Alexandre Dumas*, pp. 61–63; Victor Emmanuel Roberto Wilson, *Le Général Alexandre Dumas: Soldat de la Liberté*, pp. 38–40, and 55–56; and d'Hauterive, *Un soldat de la Révolution*, pp. 12–13.

13. Landru suggests that Thomas-Alexandre may have arrived at l'Havre on August 30, 1776, listed as the slave Alexandre of one Lieutenant Jacques-Louis Roussel. However, he acknowledges that there is no way of being sure that this really was Thomas-Alexandre Davy. See Landru, *A propos d'Alexandre Dumas*, p. 65.

14. On race conditions in France on the eve of the Revolution, see Anna Julia Cooper, *Slavery and the French Revolutionists 1788–1805*; Charles Oscar Hardy, *The Negro Question in the French Revolution*; Philip D. Curtin, *The Atlantic Slave Trade: A Census*; and David B. Davis, *The Problem of Slavery in the Age of Revolution 1770–1823.*

15. As quoted in Landru, *A propos d'Alexandre Dumas*, pp. 68–69.

16. Dumas (*père*), *Mémoires*, vol. 1, pp. 18–21.

17. Dumas (*père*), *Mémoires*, vol. 1, pp. 19–20.

18. Landru, *A propos d'Alexandre Dumas*, p. 78. Landru writes that he was quoting from "the text (with its errors) of the enrollment on 2 June, 1786 written on the registre de contrôle of troops" (p. 77).

19. On the pre-revolutionary army, see Robert S. Quimby, *The Background of Napoleonic Warfare: The Theory of Military Tactics in Eighteenth-Century France*; Samual F. Scott, *The Response of the Royal Army to the French Revolution: The Role and Development of the Line Army*; Jean Paul Bertaud, *The Army of the French Revolution: From Citizen-Soldiers to Instrument of Power*; and John A. Lynn, *The Bayonets of the Republic: Motivation and Tactics in the Army of Revolutionary France*.

20. See d'Hauterive, *Un soldat de la Révolution*, p. 18. Stories of Dumas's strength have also been passed on without documentation.

2. The Republican General

1. Bertaud, *The Army of the French Revolution*, p. 20.

2. Bertaud, *The Army of the French Revolution*, p. 34.

3. On the opening weeks of the war, see Romsay W. Phipps, *The Armies of the First French Republic and the Rise of the Marshals of Napoleon I*, vol. 1, pp. 62–83.

4. See Richard Hayes, *Biographical Dictionary of Irishmen in France*, pp. 68–70.

5. Phipps, *The Armies of the First French Republic*, vol. 1, p. 82.

6. Dumas (*père*) gives a lengthy, highly romanticized account of this affair with too much detail to repeat as being creditable. See Dumas (*père*), *Mémoires*, vol. 1, p. 30.

7. On the various legions formed in 1792, see "Corps francs: légions des armées," Service Historique de l'Etat-Major de l'Armée (hereafter referred to as the Archive de la Guerre, i.e., "Arch. Guerre"), X^k 9.

8. On the formation of the legion, see "Formation du Régiment d'hussards américains et du Midi, d'après le décrêe du septembre, 1792," Arch. Guerre, X^k 9; Edouard Desbrière and Maurice Sautai, *La Cavalerie pendant la Révolution: Du 14 juillet 1789 au 26 juin 1794*, pp. 140–42; and Charles Rouel, "Historique du 13e Régiment de Chasseur à cheval," unpublished manuscript, Arch. Guerre.

9. Desbrière and Sautai, *La Cavalerie pendant la Révolution*, p. 123.

10. On Saint Georges and his role in the formation of the Black Legion, see "Formation du Régiment d'hussards américains et du Midi, d'après le décrêe du septembre, 1792," Arch. Guerre, X^k 9; *and Grand Dictionnaire Universel du XIXe Siècle*, vol. 14, pp. 67–68. On Saint Georges in England, see Marcel Dogue, *The Black Presence in the French Revolution*.

11. See "Certificate de Services," November 6, 1848, Arch. Guerre, Dossier Dumas, GD 91.

12. François-Jacque La Roche is listed along with Dumas as lieutenant colonel on the early lists of officers of the legion. See "Légion Franche de Cavalerie

des américain et du Midi: Etat major," September 15, 1792, Arch. Guerre, X^k 9.

13. See Wilson, *Le Général Alexandre Dumas*, p. 90.

14. On the Labouret family, see Landru, *A propos d'Alexandre Dumas*, pp. 82–83.

15. See the brief history of Saint Nicolas de Villers-Cotterêts posted on the wall in the back of the church.

16. See the marriage certificate at the Musée Alexandre Dumas, 24 rue Démoustier, Villers-Cotterêts.

17. See the baptismal certificate of Alexandre Dumas (*père*) in the Alexandre Dumas Musée in Villers-Cotterêts.

18. This document is dated December 15 in the first year of the Republic (1792) and signed by six members of the city council (Arch. Guerre, Dossier Dumas, GD 91). In the summer of 1793, the government abolished the Gregorian calendar and proclaimed a new revolutionary means for keeping time. The first day of the new calendar was the first day of the French Republic—September 22, 1792. Year II (usually in roman numerals) began 365 days after. The twelve-month year, with thirty days in each month, had five (and in leap year six) complementary days at the end. The months were named with respect to the seasons. This calendar was used from 1793 to the end of 1805, at which time Napoleon put France back on the Gregorian calendar.

19. See Rouel, "Historique du 13e Régiment de Chasseur à cheval," unpublished manuscript, Arch. Guerre, p. 6.

20. "Le Maréchal de Camp Bécourt Commandant à Lille au Citoyen [name not legible] adjoint à la 5e Division du Ministre de la Guerre," February 25, 1793, Arch. Guerre, X^k 9.

21. As quoted in Desbrière and Sautai, *La Cavalerie pendant la Révolution*, p. 141.

22. There is a thin folder in the X^k 9 carton (Arch. Guerre) entitled "Légion du Midi, appelée aussi Légion franche des Américains. Devenue 13e chasseurs," which contains documents on the officers of the legion.

23. On Dumouriez's defection, see Phipps, *The Armies of the First French Republic*, vol. 1, pp. 154–62. On Dumas's role in this affair, see d'Hauterive, *Un soldat de la Révolution*, pp. 27–32. On Davout's near capture of Dumouriez, see John G. Gallaher, *The Iron Marshal: A Biography of Louis N. Davout*, pp. 19–20.

24. Lieutenant Colonel La Roche was still being carried on the lists of officers of the regiment. However, there is no indication in the documents that he was actually with the legion in the fall of 1792 or the 13th Regiment in 1793. See the documents in X^k 9, Arch. Guerre.

25. See Desbrière and Sautai, *La Cavalerie pendant la Révolution*, pp. 141–42.

26. The author has relied entirely upon d'Hauterive's account of this affair without being able to verify it with primary material. See d'Hauterive, *Un soldat de la Révolution*, pp. 32–33.

27. Dumas (*père*), *Mémoires*, vol. 1, pp. 32–35.

28. See "Certificate de Service: Dumas Davy de la Pailleterie (Thomas-Alexandre)," dated November 6, 1848, Arch. Guerre, Dossier Dumas, GD 91.

29. "Certificate de Service: Dumas Davy de la Pailleterie (Thomas-Alexandre)," November 6, 1793, Arch. Guerre, Dossier Dumas, GD 91. See also the letter of appointment from the minister of war to Dumas quoted in Dumas (*père*), *Memoires*, vol. 1, p. 35.

30. Dumas to minister of war, September 15, 1793, Arch. Guerre, Dossier Dumas, GD 91.

31. William Doyle, *The Oxford History of the French Revolution*, p. 252.

32. On the Reign of Terror, see Doyle, *The Oxford History of the French Revolution*, pp. 247–71; and Georges Lefebvre, *The French Revolution from 1793 to 1799*, pp. 39–136.

33. On the appointment of General d'Elbhecq's replacement, see George Six, *Les Généraux de la Révolution et de l'Empire*, p. 110.

34. Dumas, (*père*), *Mémoires*, vol. 1, pp. 39–49.

35. See letter from the Committee of Public Safety to representatives of the people with the Army of the West Pyrenees, signed by Robespierre, Carnot, Bouchotte, et al., 10 frimaire, an II [November 30, 1793], as quoted in Dumas (*père*), *Mémoires*, vol 1, p. 41.

36. "Décret de la Convention Nationale," signed Paré and countersigned Gohier, December 22, 1793, Arch. Guerre, Dossier Dumas, GD 91.

3. Commander of the Army of the Alps

1. See Dumas to minister of war, January 21, 1794, Arch Guerre, B³ 9.

2. As quoted in Phipps, *The Armies of the First French Republic*, vol. 3, p. 74.

3. As quoted in Phipps, *The Armies of the First French Republic*, vol. 3, p. 84.

4. On the Army of the Alps in 1793, see Phipps, *The Armies of the First French Republic*, vol. 3.

5. See Dumas to minister of war, January 21, 1794, Arch. Guerre, B³ 9.

6. Dumas (*père*), *Mémoires*, vol. 1, pp. 53–54.

7. See Dumas to the representatives of the people at Lyon, January 23, 1794, Arch. Guerre, B³ 9.

8. See Dumas to "Citizen Colleagues," February 27, 1794, Arch. Guerre, B³ 9.

9. On the general conditions of the French army during the early years of the revolutionary wars, see Bertaud, *The Army of the French Revolution*; Scott, *The Response of the Royal Army of the French Revolution*; and Lynn, *The Bayonets of the Republic*.

10. See Dumas's correspondence from February and March 1794, Arch. Guerre, B³ 9, 106. More specifically, see Dumas to his colleagues, February 27, 1794, Arch. Guerre, B³ 9.

11. "Extract of the Register of the Committee of Public Safety of the National Convention," signed Carnot, B. [Bertrand] Barere, and [Jacques-Nicolas] Billaud Varenne to Dumas, January 25, 1794, Arch. Guerre, B³ 9; and minister of war to Dumas, January 27, 1794, Arch. Guerre, B³ 9.

12. Extract of the "Register of the Committee of Public Safety . . ." to Dumas,

January 25, 1794, Arch. Guerre, B³ 9.

13. Dumas to minister of war, February 3, 1794, Arch. Guerre, B³ 9.

14. See Dumas's correspondence dated January 28–29, 1794, Arch. Guerre, B³ 9.

15. "Order of the Day," signed Dumas, January 29, 1974, Arch. Guerre, B³ 9.

16. Dours to Dumas, January 30, 1794, Arch. Guerre, B³ 9.

17. Dumas to minister of war, January 30, 1794, Arch. Guerre, B³ 9.

18. Dumas to minister of war, February 3, 1794, Arch. Guerre, B³ 9.

19. See minister of war to representatives of the people, February 7, 1794, Arch. Guerre, B³ 9.

20. Minister of war to Dumas, February 8, 1794, Arch. Guerre, B³ 9.

21. Minister of war to Dumas, February 27, 1794, Arch. Guerre, B³ 9.

22. See "Extrait de l'Arrêté pris en conseil de guerre tenu à Chambery le 8 ventôse de l'an 2 de la république [February 26, 1794]," signed Alex Dumas, Gaston, Basdelaune, Rival, and Sarret, Arch. Guerre, B³ 9.

23. See "Extrait de l'Arrêté pris en conseil de guerre tenu à Chambery . . . [February 26, 1794]," Arch. Guerre, B³ 9.

24. Dumas to "Citoyens Collègues," February 27, 1794, Arch. Guerre, B³ 9.

25. See "Mémoire de la renseignement que peut donner le capitaine Ratel sur l'Armée des Alpes dans le Departement du Mont Blanc," February 28, 1794, Arch. Guerre, B³ 9.

26. Dumas to minister of war, March 1, 1794, Arch. Guerre, B³ 10; and Dumas to Committee of Public Safety, "Correspondance du Général Alexandre Dumas," March 1, 1794, Arch. Guerre, B³ 108.

27. Gaston to his colleagues of the Committee of Public Safety, March 2, 1794, Arch. Guerre, B³ 10.

28. Gaston to his colleagues of the Committee of Public Safty, March 2, 1794, Arch. Guerre, B³ 10.

29. Dumas to the Committee of Public Safety, March 16, 1794, Arch. Guerre, B³ 10.

30. On Savoy in 1793–1794, see Lefebvre, *The French Revolution: From Its Origins to 1793*, vol. 1, pp. 273–76.

31. See Dumas to the Committee of Public Safety dated March 14, 1794, and Dumas to the residents of France in Vallois, March 14, 1794, "Correspondance du Général Alexandre Dumas," Arch. Guerre, B³ 108. See also Dumas to the Committee of Public Safety, March 16, 1794, Arch. Guerre, B³ 10.

32. On the problems of the returning emigrants, see Dumas to the residents of France in Vallois, March 14, 1794, and Dumas to the representatives of the people with the Army of the Alps, April 15, 1794, "Correspondance du Général Alexandre Dumas . . . ," Arch. Guerre, B³ 108; Dumas to minister of war, March 8 and 15, 1794, Arch. Guerre, B³ 9.

33. See minister of war to Dumas, April 12, 1794, Arch. Guerre, B³ 10.

34. See Dumas to the Committee of Public Safety, March 21, 1794, Arch. Guerre, B³ 10; and Dumas to the representatives of the people with the Army of the Alps, March 22, 1794, Arch. Guerre, B³ 10.

35. See a letter from Dumas to a recipient whose name is not legible, March 20, 1794, and Dumas to the Committee of Public Safety, March 13, 1794, Arch. Guerre, B³ 10.

36. See Dumas to the Committee of Public Safety, April 2, 1794, Arch. Guerre, B³ 108.

37. See Dumas to the Committee of Public Safety, April 1, 1794, Arch. Guerre, B³ 108.

38. On the problems of supplying the army, see Dumas's correspondence, Arch. Guerre, B³ 10 and B³ 108.

39. Dumas to General (Jean-Mathieu) Sérurier, commander of the Army of Italy, March 8, 1794, Arch. Guerre, B³ 108.

40. See d'Hauterive, *Un soldat de la Révolution*, p. 45.

41. See Gaston to the Committee of Public Safety, March 2, April 2, and April 11, 1794, Arch. Guerre, B³ 10.

42. See d'Hauterive, *Un soldat de la Révolution*, pp. 46–47.

43. See Dumas to minister of war, March 30, 1794, Arch. Guerre, B³ 10.

44. Dumas to the Popular Society of Chambéry, March 8, 1794, Arch. Guerre, B³ 10.

45. "Extrait des Registres. Au Nom du Peuple Français. Le Représentant du Peuple près l'Armée des Alpes," signed Gaston, March 13, 1794, Arch. Guerre, B³ 10.

46. Minister of war to Dumas, March 12, 1794, Arch. Guerre, B³ 10.

47. On the formation of new battalions, see Gaston to minister of war, April 2, 1794, Arch. Guerre, B³ 10.

48. See Dumas to minister of war, April 4, 1794, Arch. Guerre, B³ 10.

49. See Dumas to minister of war, March 21, 1794, Arch. Guerre, B³ 10.

50. See Dumas to minister of war, March 22, 1794, Arch. Guerre, B³ 10.

51. See Dumas to minister of war, March 21, 1794, Arch. Guerre, B³ 10.

52. See Dumas to Committee of Public Safety, March 24, 1794, Arch. Guerre, B³ 10.

53. A copy of the six-page report is attached to Dumas's letter to the Committee of Public Safety, April 1, 1794, Arch. Guerre, B³ 10.

54. See "Copie de l'instruction et de l'ordre donné par le Général de Brigade Sarret Commandant en maurienne pour l'attaque du Mount Cènis," April 7, 1794, Arch. Guerre, B³ 10.

55. "Copie du Rapport du Général de Brigade Gouvion sur l'attaque du Mount Cènis," signed Gouvion, and verified by the signature of General Dumas, April 7, 1794, Arch. Guerre, B³ 10.

56. See "Copie du Rapport du Général de Brigade Gouvion sur l'attaque du Mount Cènis," signed Gouvion, April 7, 1794, Arch. Guerre, B³ 10.

57. On the actions taken by General Dumas when he heard of the failure of the attacks, see his letter to the Committee of Public Safety, April 11, 1794, Arch. Guerre, B³ 10.

58. Dumas to the Committee of Public Safety, April 11, 1794, Arch. Guerre, B³ 10.

59. Dumas to the Committee of Public Safety, April 11, 1794, Arch. Guerre, B³ 10.

60. Dumas to the Committee of Public Safety, April 16, 1794, Arch. Guerre, B³ 108.

61. Dumas to minister of war, April 19, 1794, Arch. Guerre, B³ 10.

62. Dumas to the Committee of Public Safety, April 11, 1794, Arch. Guerre, B³ 10.

63. Gaston to the Committee of Public Safety, April 11, 1794, Arch. Guerre, B³ 10.

64. Gaston to the Committee of Public Safety, April 11, 1794, Arch. Guerre, B³ 10.

65. Gaston to the Committee of Public Safety, April 11, 1794, Arch. Guerre, B³ 10.

66. See Dumas's correspondence to the Committee of Public Safety dated April 11 and 15, 1794, Arch. Guerre, B³ 10, and April 16, 1794, Arch. Guerre, B³ 108; to the minister of war dated April 12 and 19, 1794, Arch. Guerre, B³ 10; and to the representatives of the people with the Army of the Alps, April 15, 1794, Arch. Guerre, B³ 10.

67. Dumas to the Committee of Public Safety, April 24, 1794, Arch. Guerre, B³ 10.

68. On Dumas, Espagne, and Laffont accompanying the advance units, see Gaston to the Committee of Public Safety, April 24, 1794, Arch. Guerre, B³ 10.

69. Dumas to the Committee of Public Safety, April 24, 1794, Arch. Guerre, B³ 10.

70. See Dumas to the Committee of Public Safety, April 24, 1794, Arch. Guerre, B³ 10; and Basdelaune to Dumas, April 24, 1794, Arch. Guerre, B³ 10.

71. Dumas to the Committee of Public Safety, April 24, 1794, Arch. Guerre, B³ 10.

72. Gaston to the Committee of Public Safety, April 24, 1794, Arch. Guerre, B³ 10.

73. Gaston to the Committee of Public Safety, April 24, 1794, Arch. Guerre, B³ 10.

74. Carnot to the representatives of the people with the Army of the Alps, May 8, 1794, Arch. Guerre, B³ 10.

75. See Dumas to Gouvion, April 25, 1794, Arch. Guerre, B3 10; and Dumas to the Committee of Public Safety, May 2, 1794, Arch. Guerre, B³ 10.

76. See Dumas to Basdelaune, May 3, 7, and 8, 1794, Arch. Guerre, B³ 10.

77. See Dumas to General Jean-Louis Pellapra (commander of the 4th Division of the Army of the Alps), May 10, 1794, and two letters dated May 11, 1794, Arch. Guerre, B³ 10; and Dumas to the Committee of Public Safety, May 6, 1794, Arch. Guerre, B³ 10.

78. For a detailed account of this operation, see Dumas to the Committee of Public Safety, May 14, 1794, Arch. Guerre, B³ 10. There is also a copy of this letter in "Correspondance du Alexandre Dumas," pp. 24–26, Arch. Guerre, B³ 108.

79. On the capture of the Sardinian positions at Mount Cenis, see Dumas's

report to the Committee of Public Safety, May 13, 1794, Arch Guerre, B³ 10; and Basdelaune's report to Dumas, May 13, 1794, Arch. Guerre, B³ 10.

80. See Basdelaune to Dumas, May 13, 1794, Arch. Guerre, B³ 10.

81. Carnot to the representatives of the people with the Army of the Alps, May 22, 1794, Arch. Guerre, B³ 10.

82. See Dumas to the Committee of Public Safety, May 26 and 29, 1794, Arch. Guerre, B³ 10; and June 12, 1794, Arch. Guerre, B³ 11.

83. See Dumas to the Committee of Public Safety, May 26, 1794, Arch. Guerre, B³ 108.

84. See Dumas to the Committee of Public Safety, May 30, 1794, Arch. Guerre, B³ 108.

85. See Dumas to the Committee of Public Safety, June 11, 1794, Arch. Guerre, B³ 108.

86. See Dumas to Committee of Public Safety, June 21 and 24, 1794, Arch. Guerre, B³ 11.

87. "Extrait des Registres du Comité de Salut Public de la Convention Nationale," dated June 24 and published June 26, 1794, Arch. Guerre, GD 91.

88. See Dumas to General Pierre-Jadart Dumerbion (commander in chief of the Army of Italy), July 4, 1794, Arch. Guerre, B³ 11.

89. See Dumas to the Committee of Public Safety, July 4, 1794, Arch. Guerre, B³ 11.

90. See the extensive correspondence in the War Archives at the Château de Vincennes, in particular Dumas's correspondence, B³ 108, and the correspondence of the Army of the Alps and the Army of Italy from January to July 1794, B³ 8 to B³ 11.

4. Under Kellermann with the Army of the Alps

1. See Dumas (*père*), *Mémoires*, vol. 1, pp. 14–15.

2. See "Extrait des Registres du Comité de Salut Public de la Convention Nationale," signed by several members of the committee including Carnot, August 2, 1794, Arch. Guerre, GD 91.

3. See Dumas to the Commission of Organization of the Army of the Land, August 5, 1794, Arch. Guerre, GD 91.

4. See the list of Dumas's commands and their dates in Arch. Guerre, GD 91. There is a lack of documents for the period of Dumas's career from his departure from the Army of the Alps in July 1794 until the summer of 1795, when he was called to Paris from his home at Villers-Cotterêts. Dumas (*père*) dismisses this year in one paragraph in his *Mémoires* (see vol. 1, p. 57).

5. On the war in the Vendée, see Phipps, *The Armies of the First French Republic*, vol. 3, pp. 32–37.

6. Alexandre Dumas (*père*) places this letter in year II of the revolutionary calendar, which would be early October 1793. However, General Dumas did not arrive in the Vendée from the south of France until early December 1793. Furthermore, he was never "commanding general" of any army in the West in the fall

of 1793, whereas in 1794 he was unquestionably the commander of the army and had the time to gain a knowledge of the situation before writing the letter. Finally, in October 1793 Dumas was a brand-new general—he had been a lieutenant colonel three months earlier, without any experience in the command of an army. It is unlikely, though not impossible in light of Dumas's personality, that he would have written such a letter to Paris during the Reign of Terror. On the other hand, in the fall of 1794, the Terror had ended, and Dumas was an experienced and successful army commander and was much more likely to write this letter. For these reasons, I believe that this letter was written in the fall of 1794 and not, as his son indicates, 1793.

7. As quoted in Dumas (*père*), *Mémoires*, vol. 1, pp. 42–45.

8. See "Certificate of Service: Dumas Davy de la Pailleterie (Thomas-Alexandre)," dated November 6, 1848, and a second copy of the same document dated February 3, 1962. There is also a second document, without a date, that gives Dumas's commands for the years 1793–1794 only, which indicates that he left the Army of the West on October 23 to join an army, the name of which is not legible (presumed to be the Army of Brest), Arch. Guerre, GD 91. Also see Phipps, *The Armies of the First French Republic*, vol. 3, pp. 36–37.

9. See "Ampliation d'un Arrêté du Comité de Salut Public," signed by Carnot and five other members of the committee, dated 17 frimaire, year III (December 7, 1794), Arch. Guerre, GD 91.

10. As quoted in Dumas (*père*), *Mémoires*, vol. 1, p. 57.

11. As quoted in Dumas (*père*), *Mémoires*, vol. 1, p. 58. The other signatures were from General Jean-Baptiste Huché, Captain Th. Artel, General Nicolas Bertin, General Pierre-Mathieu Parein (du Mesnil), and Commissioner Roinay.

12. As quoted in Dumas (*père*), *Mémoires*, vol. 1, p. 59. General Bonaparte had not yet changed the Italian spelling of his name.

13. See "Report Presented to the Minister of War," November 16, 1795, Arch. Guerre, GD 91. See also an undated memorandum from the minister of war to Dumas, Arch. Guerre, GD 91.

14. See "Report Presented to the Minister of War," November 16, 1795, Arch. Guerre, GD 91.

15. See memorandum "Directoire Executif" dated November 14, 1795, Arch. Guerre, GD 91; and "Lettre de Service," dated brumaire, year IV (October/November 1795), Arch. Guerre, GD 91.

16. Dumas to minister of war, November 25, 1795, Arch. Guerre, GD 91.

17. Dumas to minister of war, December 4, 1795, Arch. Guerre, GD 91.

18. See d'Hauterive, *Un soldat de la Révolution*, p. 78.

19. See the internal memo of the war offices entitled "Rapport," December 23, 1795, Arch. Guerre, GD 91.

20. See the long note in the margin of the "Rapport," December 23, 1795, Arch. Guerre, GD 91. See also two letters that do not have dates. The first is General Jean-Baptiste Jourdan to Dumas, Arch. Guerre, GD 91; and the second is a memorandum to the commander in chief of the Army of the Rhine and Moselle, Arch. Guerre, GD 91.

21. Dumas to minister of war, January 19, 1796, Arch. Guerre, GD 91.

22. Dumas acknowledged his new appointment in a letter to the minister of war, February 7, 1796, Arch. Guerre, GD 91. See also Dumas to minister of war, February 2, 1796, Arch. Guerre, GD 91.

23. See Dumas to minister of war, February 11, 1796, Arch. Guerre, GD 91.

24. See the postscript at the end of the letter Dumas wrote to the Directors, April 23, 1796, Arch. Guerre, GD 91.

25. See Dumas to the members of the Executive Directory, May 30, 1796, Arch. Guerre, GD 91.

26. "Report Presented to the Minister of War," June 25, 1796, Arch. Guerre, GD 91.

27. "Order of the Day" by the chief of staff of the Army of the Alps, August 23, 1796, Arch. Guerre, B³ 28. On August 26, Dumas wrote to Kellermann that he had arrived at Saint Jean. See Dumas to Kellermann, August 26, 1796, Arch Guerre, B³ 28.

28. See Dumas to "the Local Municipal Administration" (of Saint Jean), September 1, 1796, Arch. Guerre, B³ 29.

29. Dumas to Kellermann, September 5, 1795, Arch. Guerre, B³ 29.

30. Dumas to the Executive Directory, September 6, 1796, Arch. Guerre, B³ 29.

31. Dumas to the Directors, September 9, 1796, Arch. Guerre, B³ 29.

32. Kellermann to the Executive Directory, Arch. Guerre, B³ 30.

33. Kellermann to the Executive Directory, Arch. Guerre, B³ 30. Kellermann then added a postscript to this letter in which he told the Directory that the Swiss border provided a greater problem than did the Sardinian border and that it was from Switzerland that the greatest number of illegal refugees were reentering France.

34. Kellermann to Dumas, September 30, 1796, Arch. Guerre, GD 91.

35. Dumas to Kellermann, October 1, 1796, Arch. Guerre, GD 91.

36. Dumas to Kellermann, October 1, 1796, Arch. Guerre, GD 91.

37. Dumas to Kellermann, October 4, 1796, Arch. Guerre, B³ 91.

38. Kellermann to Dumas, October 4, 1796, Arch. Guerre, GD 91.

39. Kellermann to minister of war, October 5, 1796, Arch. Guerre, GD 91.

40. Kellermann to minister of war, October 5, 1796, Arch. Guerre, GD 91.

41. John G. Stoessinger, *Why Nations Go to War*, p. 141.

42. Minister of war to Dumas, October 13, 1796, Arch. Guerre, B³ 31.

43. Dumas's correspondence continued in a normal manner through October 15 and then abruptly ended (see Arch. Guerre, B³ 31). His orders, which were written on the 13th, must have taken several days to reach Grenoble and then his headquarters at Saint Jean.

44. See Dumas to Kellermann, October 21, 1796, Arch. Guerre, B³ 118.

45. See Dumas to Kellermann, October 22, 1796, Arch. Guerre, B³ 118.

46. Minister of war to Kellermann, October 13, 1796, Arch. Guerre, GD 91.

47. See minister of war to the Directors, October 13, 1796, Arch. Guerre, GD 91.

5. With Bonaparte in Italy

1. Bonaparte had married Marie-Joseph-Rose Tascher de la Pagerie, who had been the mistress of the Director Paul-François Barras. The rumor in the army was that Barras had given Bonaparte command of the Army of Italy because he had taken Josephine off of his hands. It was said that she had wanted a husband but that Barras was not interested in marriage.

2. In his *Mémoires*, Dumas (*père*) wrote incorrectly, "My father arrived at Milan on October 19, 1796" (vol. 1, p. 69). But General Dumas was still writing letters to General Kellermann from his headquarters at Saint Jean de Maurienne on October 21 and 22 (see chapter 4, notes 44 and 45). Dumas (*père*) also wrote that when his father arrived at Milan, he was "very well received by Bonaparte as well as by Josephine" (vol. 1, p. 69). However, according to Louis Garros's itinerary of Napoleon Bonaparte (*Quel roman que ma vie! Itinéraire du Napoléon Bonaparte: 1769–1821*, pp. 103–05), Bonaparte left Milan on October 12 and did not return to that city until November 27. Furthermore, when he did return on the 27th, Josephine was not at Milan. (See the entry for November 27, 1796, p. 105.)

3. On the movements of Bonaparte and Josephine, see Garros, *Quel roman que ma vie!*, pp. 103–06.

4. On the siege of Mantua, see Phipps, *The Armies of the First French Republic*, vol. 4, pp. 125–57.

5. On the general military situation in mid-December, see Phipps, *The Armies of the First French Republic*, vol. 4, pp. 88–158; David G. Chandler, *The Campaigns of Napoleon*, pp. 88–116; and Vincent J. Esposito and John R. Elting, *A Military History and Atlas of the Napoleonic Wars*, pp. 20–26.

6. See Dumas's correspondence in December 1796, Arch. Guerre, B³ 118.

7. Dumas to Bonaparte, December 25, 1976, Arch. Guerre, B³ 118.

8. See the letter from Alvintzy to Würmser, quoted in Dumas (*père*), *Mémoires*, vol. 1, p. 76.

9. Dumas (*père*) uses the word *cire*, which could also mean covered with oilskin. See *Mémoires*, vol. 1, p. 74.

10. See Dumas to Bonaparte, December 25, 1796, Arch. Guerre, B³ 118.

11. This letter from the Emperor Francis II to General Würmser is quoted in Dumas (*père*), *Mémoires*, vol. 1, pp. 75–76. Dumas (*père*) wrote of it: "I am transcribing this letter from a copy of it in my father's handwriting. The original, as I have already mentioned, was sent to Bonaparte" (p. 76).

12. Alvintzy to Würmser, no date, as quoted in Dumas (*père*), *Mémoires*, vol. 1, p. 76.

13. See Dumas (*père*), *Mémoires*, vol 1, pp. 74–76.

14. See Bonaparte to the Executive Directory, December 28, 1796, *Correspondance de Napoléon Iʳᵉ*, vol. 2, no. 1319, pp. 259–60.

15. On Sérurier's return to Mantua, see Bonaparte to Berthier, December 21 and 25, 1796, *Correspondance de Napoléon Iʳᵉ*, vol. 2, nos. 1306 and 1314,

pp. 247, 256.

16. See Dumas's correspondence beginning with December 29, 1796, Arch. Guerre, B³ 118.

17. See Dumas to Bonaparte, January 2, 1797, Arch. Guerre, B³ 118.

18. See Dumas to Bonaparte, January 3, 1797, Arch. Guerre, B³ 118.

19. Dumas to Bonaparte, January 3, 1797, Arch. Guerre, B³ 118.

20. Esposito and Elting write that one of Provera's aides was able to enter the city and tell Würmser of his presence and his plans (*A Military History and Atlas of the Napoleonic Wars*, p. 29). However, Phipps says that he signaled with drums (*The Armies of the First French Republic*, vol. 4, p. 137).

21. As quoted in Dumas (*père*), *Mémoires*, vol. 1, p. 83. Sérurier's first letter is also quoted in Dumas (*père*), *Mémoires*, vol. 1, p. 83.

22. See d'Hauterive, *Un soldat de la Révolution*, p. 91; and Phipps, *The Armies of the First French Revolution*, vol. 4, p. 142.

23. See Phipps, *The Armies of the First French Republic*, vol. 4, p. 142.

24. Their regimental histories in the War Archives at the Château de Vincennes give a vivid account of their triumphs and hardships during those crucial days.

25. On the action at St. Antonio, see Dumas to Bonaparte, January 17, 1797, Arch. Guerre, B³ 118; Phipps, *The Armies of the First French Republic*, vol. 4, pp. 138–42; and d'Hauterive, *Un soldat de la Révolution*, pp. 92–99.

26. On the Mantua phase of this Italian campaign, see Phipps, *The Armies of the First French Republic*, vol. 4, pp. 35–41; Chandler, *The Campaigns of Napoleon*, pp. 120–21; and Esposito and Elting, *A Military History and Atlas of the Napoleonic Wars*, p. 29.

27. Bonaparte also wrote a long letter to the Directory the day following the combat at Mantua in which he said: "Würmser wanted to make a sortie [from Mantua] in order to attack the left wing of our army, but it was received in the usual way and obliged to withdraw." Bonaparte to Executive Directory, January 17, 1797, *Correspondance Napoléon Iʳᵉ*, vol. 2, no. 1394, p. 319.

28. From the original handwritten copy of the report (which was written by Alexandre Berthier) on the battle of Rivoli and the fighting before Mantua, which is usually referred to as the battle of La Favorita (Arch. Guerre, B³ 37).

29. The date is given in the revolutionary calendar: 27 nivôse, year V.

30. As quoted in Dumas (*père*), *Mémoires*, vol. 1, p. 96.

31. The document is entitled "Relation des Batailles et affaires décisives qui on eû lieu entre l'Armée de la République Française et cell de l'Empereur and Roi, depuis le 19 nivôse jusqu'au 27 du même mois l'an 5ᵐᵉ," by General of Division Berthier, chief of staff of the Army of Italy, no date, Arch. Guerre, B³ 37.

32. As quoted in Dumas (*père*), *Mémoires*, vol. 1, p. 96.

33. See Berthier's correspondence in Arch. Guerre, B³ 37. There is also a summary of the reorganization in *Correspondance de Napoléon Iʳᵉ*, vol. 2, nos. 1396 and 1397, pp. 321–25.

34. Dumas to Bonaparte, January 17, 1797, Arch. Guerre, B³ 118.

35. Bonaparte to the Executive Directory, *Correspondance de Napoléon Iʳᵉ*,

January 18, 1797, vol. 2, no. 1399, pp. 326–31.

36. See d'Hauterive, *Un soldat de la Révolution*, pp. 106–11.

37. Esposito and Elting give the field army at forty thousand (*A Military History and Atlas of the Napoleonic Wars*, p. 30); Phipps puts the total figure of the Army of Italy at fifty-eight thousand (*The Armies of the First French Republic*, vol. 4, pp. 162–63); and Chandler gives the army at sixty thousand men (*The Campaigns of Napoleon*, p. 122).

38. See "Order of the General in Chief," *Correspondance de Napoléon Ire*, presumed March 6, 1797, vol. 2, no. 1548, pp. 479–81.

39. On General Baraguey d'Hilliers, see Georges Six, *Dictionnaire biographique des généraux et amiraux Français de la Révolution et de l'Empire (1792–1814)*, vol. 1, pp. 48–49. See also Joubert, "Order," March 19, 1797, Arch. Guerre, B³ 211.

40. Dumas (*père*) says that Joubert actually gave Dumas joint command of his corps (*Mémoires*, vol. 1, p. 101). However, this is most unlikely. Joubert had no authority to do that without explicit orders from Bonaparte, and no such order was given.

41. See Bonaparte to Berthier, *Correspondance de Napoléon Ire*, March 17, 1797, vol. 2, no. 1593, p. 514.

42. See Joubert to Dumas, March 20, 1797, and to Baraguey d'Hilliers, March 19, 1797, "Correspondance Joubert," Arch. Guerre, B³ 211.

43. See Dumas (*père*), *Mémoires*, vol. 1, p. 111. Jean Mabire's article on Dumas in Historama (pp. 32–37) is entitled "Dumas Grand-Père, Le Diable Noir."

44. Joubert to Bonaparte, March 22, 1797, "Correspondance Joubert," Arch. Guerre, B³ 211.

45. On the affair at Klausen, see Dermoncourt's account as quoted in Dumas (*père*), *Mémoires*, vol. 1, pp. 112–14.

46. See Dermoncourt's account as quoted in Dumas (*père*), *Mémoires*, vol. 1, pp. 113–14.

47. Joubert to Bonaparte, March 24, 1797, "Correspondance Joubert," Arch. Guerre, B³ 211.

48. Joubert to Bonaparte, March 26, 1797, "Correspondance Joubert," Arch. Guerre, B³ 211.

49. Bonaparte to the Executive Directory, April 1, 1797, *Correspondance de Napoléon Ire*, vol. 2, no. 1666, p. 575.

50. On Joubert's campaign into the Tyrol, see Joubert to Bonaparte, April 8, 1797, "Correspondance Joubert," Arch. Guerre, B³ 211; and Phipps, *The Armies of the First French Republic*, vol. 4, pp. 174–78.

51. See Dumas (*père*), *Mémoires*, vol. 1, pp. 115–16; and Phipps, *The Armies of the First French Republic*, vol. 4, pp. 174–75.

52. As quoted in Phipps, *The Armies of the First French Republic*, vol. 4, p. 175.

53. On communications between Joubert and Bonaparte, see Phipps, *The Armies of the First French Republic*, vol. 4, pp. 175–76.

54. See [Berthier], "By order of the Commander in Chief" to Joubert,

Correspondance de Napoléon Ire, April 3, 1797, vol. 2, no. 1681, pp. 586–88.

55. "By order of the General in Chief [Berthier]", to Joubert, *Correspondance de Napoléon Ire*, April 3, 1797, vol. 2, no. 1681, p. 587.

56. See Dumas to his wife as quoted in d'Hauterive, *Un soldat de la Révolution*, pp. 146–48.

57. As quoted in d'Hauterive, *Un soldat de la Révolution*, p. 150. While this letter is addressed "*A ses meilleurs amis*," in it Dumas asked his "dear Manette" to console his wife.

58. See d'Hauterive, *Un soldat de la Révolution*, p. 148.

59. Bonaparte to Joubert, *Correspondance de Napoléon Ire*, vol. 2, no. 1706, p. 611.

60. As quoted in Dumas (*père*), *Mémoires*, vol. 1, p. 127.

61. This legendary hero of ancient Rome, with only two companions, held back the entire Etruscan army at a bridge over the Tiber while the Romans destroyed the other end of the bridge. He then dove into the river and swam to safety. Another version of the legend has Horatius Cocles defending the bridge alone and then drowning in the Tiber. See "Horatius Cocles," *Encyclopedia Britannica*, 1943 ed., vol. 11, p. 743.

62. On the reorganization of the army, see Bonaparte's correspondence in mid-April, *Correspondance de Napoléon Ire*, April 13–17, 1797, vol. 2, nos. 1719–40, pp. 624–45.

63. See Bonaparte to Dumas, *Correspondance de Napoléon Ire*, May 6, 1797, vol. 3, no. 1779, p. 38.

64. See Bonaparte to Dumas, *Correspondance de Napoléon Ire*, May 6, 1797, vol. 3, no. 1779, p. 38.

65. See Dumas to Bonaparte, "Correspondance Dumas," May 19, 1797, Arch. Guerre, B³ 118.

66. See Dumas to Bonaparte, "Correspondance Dumas," May 26, 1797, Arch. Guerre, B³ 118.

67. Dumas (*père*) stresses his father's enlightened republicanism that won the deep gratitude of the Italian people over whom he governed. He gives several explicit examples and says that when his father left Treviso, the citizens held six days of festivals and gave him a fine carriage with four horses to make the journey to his new command. See Dumas (*père*), *Mémoires*, vol. 1, pp. 127–31.

68. See Dumas to Bonaparte, "Correspondance Dumas," May 19, 1797, Arch. Guerre, B³ 118; and Bonaparte to Dumas, *Correspondance de Napoléon Ire*, May 6, 1797, vol. 3, nos. 1797 and 1779, p. 38.

69. Dumas to Berthier, "Correspondance Dumas," May 19, 1797, Arch. Guerre, B³ 118.

70. Dumas to Bonaparte, "Correspondance Dumas," May 24, 1797, Arch. Guerre, B³ 118.

71. See Bonaparte to Berthier, *Correspondance de Napoléon Ire*, June 16, 1797, vol. 3, no. 1928, p. 173.

72. See Dumas (*père*), *Mémoires*, vol. 1, pp. 133–34.

6. The Egyptian Campaign

1. Bonaparte to the Executive Directory, *Correspondance de Napoléon Ire*, August 16, 1798, vol. 3, no. 2103, p. 235.

2. See "Note au Directoire Exécutif," signed Bonaparte, March 5, 1798, *Correspondance de Napoléon Ire*, vol. 4, no. 2426, pp. 1–3.

3. See "Tableau des corps de Troupes rassemblés à Toulon, Marseille, Genes et Cività-Vecchia," signed [Barthelémy-Louis-J.] Scherer, Minister of War, April 14, 1798. *Correspondance de Napoléon Ire*, vol. 4, no. 2508, pp. 83–84.

4. "General Order," *Correspondance de Napoléon Ire*, June 23, 1798, vol. 4, no. 2706, pp. 252–53.

5. On the French capture of Malta, see J. Christopher Herold, *Bonaparte in Egypt*, pp. 40–50.

6. As quoted in d'Hauterive, *Un soldat de la Révolution*, pp. 173–74.

7. Caffarelli du Falga would be struck in the arm by a cannonball at the siege of Acre on April 9, 1799. Despite the best efforts of Dr. Dominique-Jean Larrey, who amputated the shattered arm, he died of the wound.

8. Herold, *Bonaparte in Egypt*, p. 61. d'Hauterive states that Dumas put himself at the head of a company of grenadiers of the 4th Light Infantry Regiment for the march to Alexandria (*Un soldat de la Révolution*, p. 176).

9. In a letter to the Directory, Bonaparte gives thirty to forty men killed and eighty to a hundred men wounded (*Correspondance de Napoléon Ire*, July 6, 1798, vol. 4, no. 2765, p. 308). Chandler gives French casualties at three hundred men (*The Campaigns of Napoleon*, p. 220).

10. Dumas (*père*), *Mémoires*, vol. 1, p. 141.

11. This quotation is taken from A. F. Davidson's English translation of Dumas (*père*), *The Memoirs of Alexander Dumas (Père)*, vol. 1, pp. 40–41.

12. Bonaparte to Desaix, *Correspondance de Napoléon Ire*, July 2, 1798, vol. 4, no. 2722, p. 269, and July 3, 1798, vol. 4, no. 2724, pp. 272–73.

13. In his memoirs, Bonaparte gives the figure at only three hundred horses. See "Campagnes d'Egypte et de Syrie," *Correspondance de Napoléon Ire*, vol. 29, p. 436.

14. "Ordre du Jour," *Correspondance de Napoléon Ire*, June 29, 1798, vol. 4, no. 2717, p. 266.

15. On the conditions of the army on the march to Damanhür, see Herold, *Bonaparte in Egypt*, pp. 66–84.

16. As quoted in the English edition of Dumas (*père*), *Memoirs*, vol. 1, p. 41.

17. Bonaparte to Berthier, *Correspondance de Napoléon Ire*, July 4, 1798, vol. 4, no. 2744, p. 288.

18. Bonaparte to Desaix, *Correspondance de Napoléon Ire*, July 4, 1798, vol. 4, no. 2746, p. 288. In point of fact, Leclerc did not leave on July 4 and was of no use to Desaix.

19. See Bonaparte, "Au Directoire Exécutif," *Correspondance de Napoléon Ire*, July 6, 1798, vol. 4, no. 2765, p. 307.

20. See Bonaparte to "Sous-chef de l'état-major," *Correspondance de Napoléon I*ʳᵉ, July 7, 1798, vol. 4, no. 2782, pp. 321–22.

21. "Campagnes d'Egypte et de Syrie," *Correspondance de Napoléon I*ʳᵉ, vol. 29, p. 534.

22. As quoted in d'Hauterive, *Un soldat de la Révolution*, p. 179.

23. See Dumas (*père*), *Mémoires*, vol. 1, pp. 145.

24. It is possible that someone outside of the tent or an orderly or an aide-de-camp could have overheard the conversations. However, officers of a lesser rank would have had great difficulty gaining access to the commander in chief of the army. Thus, it is reasonable to believe that it was one of the generals who informed Bonaparte of the affair.

25. The size of the army under Ibrahim is estimated at about one hundred thousand men. It had been assembled in great haste in the days just preceding the French arrival at Cairo, and it began to disintegrate the day after the battle of the Pyramids (July 21).

26. The author has no documentation to verify the exact whereabouts of General Dumas during the battle. But if Murat was with Dugua, it most likely that Dumas was with Desaix.

27. This is a reference to the fact that several hundred Mameluke and a large number of the fellahin were drowned trying to escape the French by attempting to cross the river.

28. Dumas to Kléber, July 27, 1798, as quoted in Dumas (*père*), *Mémoires*, vol. 1, p. 148.

29. Dumas to Kléber, July 27, 1798, as quoted in Dumas (*père*), *Mémoires*, vol. 1, p. 148.

30. In reference to General Dupuy as Governor of Cairo, Dumas (*père*) quotes from Miguel de Cervantes Saavedra's *Don Quixote de la Mancha*: "'Without doubt a governor is a great person, said Sancho; but, rather than being governor of Barataria, I would prefer to remain in my village and guard my goats'" (*Mémoires*, vol. 1, p. 151).

31. Dupuy to Carlo, as quoted in Dumas (*père*), *Mémoires*, vol. 1, p. 150.

32. Emmanuel, Comte de Las Cases, *Le Mémorial de Saint Hélène*, vol. 1, p. 156.

33. Baron Gaspard Gourgaud, *Journal de Sainte Hélène, 1815–1818*, vol. 1, p. 244. Dumas (*père*) writes at great length about the affair in his father's tent and the scene with Bonaparte. He even gives two full pages of quoted dialogue between his father and Bonaparte. The problem with this account is that it sounds more like a few pages out of *The Three Musketeers* than a historical account. However, Dumas (*père*) swears that the entire conversation between his father and Bonaparte was told to him by General Dumas's aide-de-camp, Captain Paul-Ferdinand Dermoncourt, who heard it from the general himself just half an hour after the conversation had taken place. See Dumas (*père*), *Mémoires*, vol. 1, pp. 155–57.

34. Dumas (*père*), *Mémoires*, vol. 1, pp. 155–57.

35. Dumas (*père*), *Mémoires*, vol 1, p. 157.

36. Bonaparte to Berthier, *Correspondance de Napoléon Ire*, November 23, 1798, vol. 5, no. 3662, pp. 202–03.

37. See Bonaparte to Desaix, *Correspondance de Napoléon Ire*, December 5, 1798, vol. 5, no. 3715, pp. 237–38; and Gallaher, *The Iron Marshal*, pp. 48–49.

38. Bonaparte to Berthier, *Correspondance de Napoléon Ire*, October 16, 1798, vol. 5, no. 3485, p. 86.

39. Nicolas was born at Der-el-Kamar in the Druzes Mountains of Syria in 1763. His ancestors were Greek from Constantinople. Nicolas was a poet who was held in high esteem at the court of Emir Bechir, the prince of Druzes. When the French landed in Egypt, the emir sent him to the Nile to report firsthand his observations on just what was taking place. See Mou' Allem Nicolas El Turki, *Expédition Française en Egypte*, pp. 1–2.

40. Nicolas El Turki, *Expédition Française en Egypte*, p. 20.

41. Shortly before the Cairo insurrection, there had been an uprising in the lower delta that had culminated in the massacre at Mansure of 130 French soldiers and a large number of Christians. General Bonaparte's first orders were to execute all of the inhabitants of Mansure, but he was persuaded to spare them after the town paid the sum of two hundred thousand *thalaris*. On this revolt see Nicolas El Turki, *Expédition Française en Egypte*, pp. 15–16, 18.

42. Abdurrahman Gabarti was born in Cairo in 1756. The son of Sheik Hassan, he received an excellent education at the mosque of Azhar. When the French arrived in Egypt, he retired to Ebiar where he had property, but he was named a member of the divan and took an active part in the administration during the occupation. See Abdurrahman Gabarti, *Journal d'Abdurrahman Gabarti, pendant l'Occupation Française en Egypte*, pp. 1–2.

43. See Gabarti, *Journal d'Abdurrahman Gabarti*, pp. 44–46. Other reasons most often cited are destruction of houses and a mosque that were too close to the ramparts of the Citadel and the removal of the gates that had separated different sections of the city. For a good general discussion of the causes of the revolt, see Herold, *Bonaparte in Egypt*, pp. 191–92, which is also based on the writings of Gabarti and Nicolas the Turk; and Jean Thiry, *Bonaparte en Egypte*, pp. 250–51.

44. Nicolas El Turki, *Expédition Française en Egypte*, p. 18.

45. On the death of General Dupuy, see Gabarti, *Journal d'Abdurrahman Gabarti*, pp. 46–47; and Nicolas El Turki, *Expédition Française en Egypte*, p. 19.

46. On Bonaparte's movements on the morning of October 21, see *Correspondance de Napoléon Ire*, "Campagnes d'Egypte et de Syrie," vol. 29, pp. 597–98.

47. See Dumas (*père*), *Mémoires*, vol. 1, pp. 162–63.

48. The stone referred to here is the one that is found in every mosque to indicate the direction to Mecca so that the faithful will know which way to face when praying.

49. Dumas (*père*), *Mémoires*, vol. 1, p. 164.

50. Dumas (*père*), *Mémoires*, vol. 1, p. 165.

51. As quoted in Dumas (*père*), *Mémoires*, vol. 1, pp. 160–61.

52. On Dumas's last months in Egypt, see Dumas (*père*), *Mémoires*, vol. 1, pp. 165–66.

7. The Prisoner of War

1. On the formation of the Second Coalition, see Alexander Bankier Rodger, *The War of the Second Coalition, 1798–1801: A Strategic Commentary.*

2. Following the battle of Aboukir (August 1, 1798), Nelson was given a hero's welcome in Naples and appeared on the royal balcony and was cheered by the people below—all in the presence of the French ambassador.

3. On the military operations in southern Italy in late 1798 and early 1799, see Phipps, *The Armies of the First French Republic*, vol. 5, pp. 239–54.

4. As quoted in Phipps, *The Armies of the First French Republic*, vol. 5, p. 246.

5. This report is quoted in its entirety in Dumas (*père*), *Mémoires*, vol. 1, pp. 170–89. In the "selected" English translation of the Memoirs, Davidson gives most of the report but chose to omit some sections (see *Memoirs*, vol. 1, pp. 54–72). It should be noted that the author has himself translated from the French edition all quotations from this report.

6. Dumas, "Report Made to the French Government," in Dumas (*père*), *Mémoires*, vol. 1, p. 171.

7. The other three men who were a part of this deception were Colonna, who impersonated the High Constable of the monarchy (actually an adventurer like his good friend Corbara); Boccheciampe, who said he was the brother of the king of Spain (an artilleryman who was also a deserter); and De Cesare, said to be the duke of Saxony (a former livery servant). See Dumas, "Report Made to the French Government," in Dumas (*père*), *Mémoires*, vol. 1, p. 173.

8. Dumas, "Report Made to the French Government," in Dumas (*père*), *Mémoires*, vol. 1, pp. 173–74.

9. On Dolomieu, see Dumas (*père*), *Mémoires*, vol. 1, p. 176, footnote.

10. Dumas, "Report Made to the French Government," in Dumas (*père*), *Mémoires*, vol. 1, p. 176.

11. Dumas, "Report Made to the French Government," in Dumas (*père*), *Mémoires*, vol. 1, p. 179.

12. Dumas, "Report Made to the French Government," in Dumas (*père*), *Mémoires*, vol. 1, p. 179.

13. On the poisoning of Manscourt, see Dumas, "Report Made to the French Government," in Dumas (*père*), *Mémoires*, vol. 1, p. 180.

14. The author has been unable to find any indication that these pills were ever analyzed after Dumas was released from prison. Thus, there is no "smoking gun," so to speak, that proves beyond a doubt that the Neapolitans were trying to murder Dumas by using poison.

15. In his report, Dumas added that this "news [that someone in the castle was being poisoned], . . . would certainly not astonish anyone, but would at least expose to the light of day his infamous treatment" (Dumas, "Report Made to the French Government," in Dumas (*père*), *Mémoires*, vol. 1, p. 184).

16. See Dumas, "Report Made to the French Government," in Dumas (*père*), *Mémoires*, vol. 1, p. 185.

17. Dumas, "Report Made to the French Government," in Dumas (*père*), *Mémoires*, vol. 1, p. 185.

18. Dumas, "Report Made to the French Government," in Dumas (*père*), *Mémoires*, vol. 1, p. 186.

19. According to the constitution, the First Consul could not command an army. Thus, General Berthier commanded on paper while Bonaparte commanded in fact.

20. Dumas writes that he had been allowed to keep the walking stick because his captors believed that the knob was brass, not gold. See Dumas, "Report Made to the French Government," in Dumas (*père*), *Mémoires*, vol. 1, p. 187.

21. See pp. 130–31 on the armistice of Foligno.

22. Dumas, "Report Made to the French Government," in Dumas (*père*), *Mémoires*, vol. 1, p. 187.

23. On the French advance into southern Italy and the negotiations with the Kingdom of Naples, see Marcel Dupont, *Murat; Cavalier, Maréchal de France, Prince, et Roi*, pp. 119–23.

24. Dumas, "Report Made to the French Government," in Dumas (*père*), *Mémoires*, vol. 1, p. 188.

25. Dumas seems to be exaggerating here a bit, although it is most likely true that the Neapolitans were attempting to poison him.

26. The date of April 5, 1801, which Dumas penned to his report to the French government, is the date that his captivity ended and he went aboard ship at Brindisi. He actually wrote the document several weeks later in Florence. Dumas, "Report Made to the French Government," in Dumas (*père*), *Mémoires*, vol. 1, pp. 188–89.

8. The Last Years

1. Dumas (*père*) writes that his father was being exchanged for the Austrian general Karl Mack von Leiberich, of the battle of Ulm (1805) fame, whom the emperor had sent to Naples to bolster his ally's weak military position. See Dumas (*père*), *Mémoires*, vol. 1, p. 189. However, as the truce of Foligno provided for the release of all French prisoners of war, and the treaty signed at Florence shortly after ended the war, both Dumas and Mack were released without reference to one another.

2. Jourdan was still using the Italian spelling of Napoleon Bonaparte's name. Bonaparte himself had changed the spelling several years earlier. However, Jourdan had not served with him, and it was possible that he was not aware of the change. But it is more likely that Jourdan spelled the name the way he did intentionally, as he was not an admirer of the popular general.

3. Jourdan to minister of war, July 25, 1799, Arch. Guerre, GD 91.

4. See Madame Dumas to minister of war, August 11, 1799, Arch. Guerre, GD 91.

5. Minister of war to Madame Dumas, August 25, 1799, Arch. Guerre, GD 91.

6. On the knowledge that Dumas was a prisoner of war and on the attempts to communicate through the Spanish, see d'Hauterive, *Un soldat de la Révolution*, pp. 233–34.

7. See Madame Barthelemi to minister of war, August 25, 1800, Arch. Guerre, GD 91.

8. Minister of war to Madame Barthelemi, September 17, 1800, Arch. Guerre, GD 91. The reference to the "25th of last month" is a date in the revolutionary calendar.

9. Dumas to Marie-Louise Dumas, dated April 13, 1801, as quoted in d'Hauterive, *Un soldat de la Révolution*, pp. 236–38.

10. See Dumas to his wife, May 10 and June 7, 1801, as quoted in d'Hauterive, *Un soldat de la Révolution*, pp. 238–40, 241–44.

11. Dumas to Murat, July 1801, as quoted in Dumas (*père*), *Mémoires*, vol. 1, p. 191.

12. Dumas to Bonaparte, no date (presumed late summer or early fall of 1801), as quoted in Dumas (*père*), *Mémoires*, vol. 1, p. 192.

13. See d'Hauterive, *Un soldat de la Révolution*, p. 245.

14. See Madame Dumas to minister of war, October 2, 1814, Arch. Guerre, GD 91.

15. This is a reference to the large amount of wealth that Dumas had found in the house he had occupied in Cairo in 1798 and which he turned over to General Bonaparte.

16. Dumas to Bonaparte, September 29, 1801, as quoted in Dumas (*père*), *Mémoires*, vol. 1, pp. 193–94.

17. See Dumas to minister of war, October 7, 1801, as quoted in Dumas (*père*), *Mémoires*, vol. 1, pp. 194–95.

18. Dumas to Berthier, February 23, 1802, Arch. Guerre, GD 91.

19. Berthier to Dumas, March 3, 1802, Arch. Guerre, GD 91.

20. Dumas to Bonaparte, June 27, 1802, Arch. Guerre, GD 91.

21. "Département de la Guerre; Ampliation; Au nom du Peuple Français," September 13, 1802, Arch. Guerre, GD 91.

22. JNS to Dumas, September 17, 1802, Arch. Guerre, GD 91.

23. The figure of four thousand francs a year is given by d'Hauterive, *Un soldat de la Révolution*, p. 248.

24. For a complete list of the marshals of the empire and the dates on which they received their batons, see Chandler, *Napoleon's Marshals*, pp. 535–36.

25. The unfortunate Brune, who hated to see the return of the Bourbon monarchy in 1814, reconciled his differences with Napoleon during the Hundred Days and was named governor of Toulon. After Napoleon's defeat at Waterloo and his second abdication, Brune was murdered by a royalist mob at Avignon and his body thrown into the Rhône river. For a brief account of Brune's life, see Alan Shepperd's chapter in Chandler, *Napoleon's Marshals*, pp. 79–92.

26. See Dumas to Brune, July 25, 1802, as quoted in Dumas (*père*), *Mémoires*,

vol. 1, pp. 196–97.

27. Brune to Dumas, July 29, 1802, as quoted in Dumas (*père*), *Mémoires*, vol. 1, pp. 197–98.

28. In his *Mémoires*, Dumas (*père*) tells a charming story of a meeting of General Dumas and General Bonaparte and his wife, Josephine, in the couple's bedroom at Toulon just before the men sailed for Egypt. According to the author, Bonaparte agreed that he and Josephine would be the godparents for the son whom Dumas would have upon their return from the Egyptian campaign. Furthermore, Dumas and his wife would be godparents for the son Bonaparte hoped to have upon his return to France (see *Mémoires*, vol. 1, pp. 137–39). However, the Bonapartes did not have any children, and the First Consul was not on speaking terms with Dumas in the summer of 1802.

29. Dumas to Bonaparte, October 17, 1803, Arch. Guerre, GD 91.

30. Dumas (*père*) refers to Hipolyte as an *"espèce de Jocrisse*, whose naivete was proverbial" (*Mémoires*, vol. 1, p. 199).

31. See Landru, *A propos d'Alexandre Dumas*, p. 103; and Wilson, *Le Général Alexandre Dumas*, p. 256.

32. The author copied this quote from the tomb of General Alexandre Dumas in the cemetery of Villers-Cotterêts in the summer of 1990.

33. As quoted in Wilson, *Le Général Alexandre Dumas*, p. 268. (He cites this quote as Placide David, *Sur les rives du passé—choses de Saint-Dominque* [Paris: La Caravelle, 1947].)

34. See the "Report to the Emperor," no signature, November 11, 1807, Arch. Guerre, GD 91.

35. Madame Dumas to minister secretary of state and of war, October 2, 1814, Arch. Guerre, GD 91.

9. Conclusion

1. As quoted in Wilson, *Le Général Alexandre Dumas*, p. 268.

2. Landru, who relates the account of the marriage of Alexandrine Dumas, gives greater details. See *A propos d'Alexandre Dumas*, pp. 105–06.

3. See Valerie Parks Brown, "Napoleon and General Dumas," pp. 188–99. Brown makes this point in a most convincing manner.

4. See Brown, "Napoleon and General Dumas," pp. 188–99.

5. See the numerous anti-Bonaparte statements throughout the first volumn of Dumas (*père*), *Mémoires*.

BIBLIOGRAPHY

The principal archival sources for this study were found in the archives of the French Ministry of War, that is, the Service Historique de l'Etat-Major de l'Armée, which are stored at the Château de Vincennes. The Dossier Dumas, GD 91, contains a substantial amount of correspondence, reports, and orders written by General Dumas. Carton B³ 118, entitled "Général A. Dumas—Correspondance," covers the years 1794 to 1797. Material on the Légion franche des Américains (13th Chasseurs) is found in X^k 9, "Corps francs: légions des armées." The material on Dumas as commander of the Army of the Alps and when he served under Kellermann, as well as when he served under Bonaparte in Italy, is found in the B³ series. In this series, one finds the general correspondence of "Armées des Alpes et d'Italie" (cartons numbered 3 to 48) with General Dumas' correspondence in carton number 108. Numerous other cartons were used from the War Archives, and they are duly noted in the footnotes. The author also made use of the documents in the Dumas Museum in Villers-Cotterêts and the archives of the Department of Aisne at Leon.

Bertaud, Jean Paul. *The Army of the French Revolution: From Citizen-Soldiers to Instrument of Power.* Translated by R. R. Palmer. Princeton: Princeton University Press, 1988.

Binoche, Jacques. "Les Deputes d'outre-mer pendant la Révolution Française (1789–99)." *Annales historiques de la Révolution Française* 50.1 (1978): pp. 45–80.

Boissonnade, P. *Santo Domingo on the Eve of the Revolution and the Question of Representation in the Estates General.* Paris, 1906.

Bourrienne, Louis Antoine Fauvelet de. *Memoirs of Napoleon Bonaparte.* 4 vols. Boston: The Napoleon Society, 1895.

Brown, Valerie Parks. "Napoleon and General Dumas," *Journal of Negro History* 61.2 (1976): pp. 188–99.

Brutus, Edner. *Révolution dans Saint-Dominque.* 2 vols. Paris: Edition du Pantheon, n.d.

Chandler, David G. *The Campaigns of Napoleon.* New York: Macmillian Co., 1966.

————. *Napoleon's Marshals.* New York: Macmillan Co., 1987.

Cooper, Anna Julia. *Slavery and the French Revolutionists 1788–1805.* Translated by Frances Richardson Keller. Lewiston, NY: Edwin Mellen Press, 1988.

Copies of Original Letters from the Army of General Buonaparte in Egypt, Intercepted by the Fleet under the Command of Admiral Lord Nelson. London, 1798.

Curtin, Philip D. *The Atlantic Slave Trade: A Census.* Madison: University of Wisconsin Press, 1969.

Davis, David B. *The Problem of Slavery in the Age of Revolution 1770–1823.* Ithaca: Cornell University Press, 1975.

Desbrière, Edouard, and Maurice Sautai. *La Cavalerie pendant la Révolution: Du 14 juillet 1789 au 26 juin 1794.* Paris: Berger-Levrault et Cie., 1907.

Desvernois, Nicolas Philibert, Baron. *Mémoires du Général Baron Desvernois.* Paris: Plon Nourrit, 1898.

Dogue, Marcel. *The Black Presence in the French Revolution.* Washington, DC: Martin Luther King Memorial Library, 1989.

Doyle, William. *The Oxford History of the French Revolution.* Oxford: Clarendon Press, 1989.

Dumas, Alexandre (père). *The Memoirs of Alexandre Dumas (Père).* Selected and translasted by A. F. Davidson. Vol. 1. London: W. H. Allen and Co. Limited, 1891.

————. *Mes Mémoires.* 5 vols. Paris: Michel Levy Freres, 1865.

Dupont, Marcel. *Murat; Cavalier, Maréchal de France, Prince, et Roi.* Paris: Copernic, 1980.

Elting, John R. *Swords Around a Throne: Napoleon's Grande Armée.* New York: Free Press, 1988.

Esposito, Vincent J., and John R. Elting. *A Military History and Atlas of the Napoleonic Wars.* New York: Praeger, 1965.

Fieffé, Eugene. *Histoire des troupes étrangeres au service de France.* 2 vols. Paris: Dumaine, 1854.

Foner, Laura. "The Free People of Color in Louisiana and Saint-Domingue." *Journal of Social History* 3 (1970): pp. 406–30.

Frossard, Marcel. "La Baron Dermoncourt aide de camp du Général Dumas." *Bulletin de la Fédération de Société d'Histoire et d'Archéologie de l'Aisne* 25 (1980): pp. 162–78.

Gabarti, Abdurrahman. *Journal d'Abdurrahman Gabarti, pendant l'Occupation Française en Egypte.* Paris: Chez l'Editeur, 1838.

Gallaher, John G. *The Iron Marshal: A Biography of Louis N. Davout.* Carbondale: Southern Illinois University Press, 1976.

Garrett, Mitchell Bennett. *The French Colonial Question: 1789–1791.* New York, 1916.

Garrigus, John. "Between Servitude and Citizenship: Free Coloreds in Pre-Revolutionary Saint Domingue." Ph.D. diss. Johns Hopkins University, 1988.

Garros, Louis. *Quel roman que ma vie! Itinéraire du Napoléon Bonaparte: 1769–1821.* Paris: Les Editions de l'Encyclopédie Française, 1947.

Geggus, David. "Racial Equality, Slavery, and Colonial Seccession During the

Constituent Assembly." *American Historial Review* 94.5 (December 1989): pp. 1290–1308.

———. *Slavery, War and Revolution*. Oxford: 1982.

Gorman, H. *The Incredible Marquis, Alexandre Dumas*. Murray Hill, NY: Farrar and Rinehart, Inc., 1929.

Gourgaud, Baron Gaspard. *Journal de Sainte Hélène, 1815–1818*. Vol. 1. Paris: Flammarion, n. d.

Grand Dictionnaire Universel du XIXe Siècle. 17 vols. Paris: Administration du Grand Dictionnaire Universel, 1874.

Hardy, Charles Oscar. *The Negro Question in the French Revolution*. Menasha, WI: George Banta Publishing Co., 1919.

Hauterive, Ernest d'. *Un soldat de la Révolution: le Général Alexandre Dumas (1762–1806)*. 2d ed. Paris: P. Ollendorff, 1897.

Hayes, Richard. *Biographical Dictionary of Irishmen in France*. Dublin: M. G. Gill and Son, Ltd., 1949.

Herold, J. Christopher. *Bonaparte in Egypt*. New York: Harper and Row, 1962.

Homan, Gerlof D. "Jean François Reubell à l'Assemblée Nationale Constituante." *Annales Historiques de la Révolution Française* 44.1 (1972): pp. 28–42.

James, Cyril Lionel Robert. *The Black Jacobins: Toussaint L'Ouverature and the San Domingo Revolution*. New York: Vintage Books, 1963.

Keller, Frances Richardson. "The Perspective of a Black American on Slavery and the French Revolution: Anna Julia Cooper." *Proceedings of the Annual Meeting of the Western Society for French History*. 3 (1975): pp. 165–76.

Kerbs, Léonce, and Henri Moris. *Campagnes dans les Alpes pendant la Révolution d'après les Archives des Etats-Majors: 1794, 1795, 1796*. Paris: E. Plon, Nourrit et Cie, 1895.

Lachouque, Henry. *Napoleon's Battles: A History of His Campaigns*. Translated by Roy Monkcom. New York: Dutton, 1967.

Lacroix, François Joseph. *Mémoires pour Servir à l'Historique, de la Révolution de Saint-Dominque*. 2 vols. Paris: Pillet, 1820.

La Jonquière, Clément Etienne Lucien Marie de Taffanel, marquis de. *L'Expédition d'Egypte, 1789–1801*. 5 vols. Paris: Charles-Lavauzelle, [1899–1907].

Landru, Robert. *A propos d'Alexandre Dumas: Les aïeux, le Général, le bailli, premiers amis*. Vincennes, 1977.

Las Cases, Emmanuel, Comte de. *Le Mémorial de Saint Hélène*. Vol. 1. Paris: Flammarion, n. d.

Leclerc, Général Charles Victor E. *Histoire de la catastrophe de St. Dominque, avec correspondance des Général Leclerc*. 1824.

Lefebvre, Georges. *The French Revolution*. Translated by John Hall Stewart and James Friguglietti. 2 vol. New York: Columbia University Press, 1964.

———. *Napoleon*. Vol. 1, *From 18 Brumaire to Tilsit 1799–1807*. Translated by Henry F. Stockhold. New York: Columbia University Press, 1964.

Lenmonier-Delafosse, Jean Baptiste. *Seconde Campaigne de Saint-Dominque*. Havre, 1853.

Leucas-Dubreton, J. *Alexandre Dumas, Père*. Paris: Librarie Gaillinard, 1928.

Louverture, Toussaint. *Mémoires de Général Toussaint Louverture.* Paris: Pagnere, 1853.

Lynn, John A. *The Bayonets of the Republic: Motivation and Tactics in the Army of Revolutionary France.* Urbana: University of Illinois Press, 1984.

Mabire, Jean. "Dumas Grand-Père, Le Diable Noir." *Historama* 5 (1984): pp. 32–37.

Massio, R. "Lettres de Bigourdans de Saint-Domingue." *Revue d'Histoire de l'Amerique Française* 11.2 (1957): pp. 277–83.

Maurel, Blanche. "Un Depute de Saint-Dominque à la Constituante: J. B. Gerard." *Revue d'histoire moderne* 9 (1934): pp. 227–52.

Maurois, Andre. *Les Trois Dumas.* Paris: Hachette, 1957.

Napoleon I. *Correspondance de Napoléon Ire.* 32 vols. Paris: Imprimerie Impériale, 1857–1870.

Nemours, Alfred. "Bonaparte et St. Dominque." *Revue des études napoleoniennes* 31 (1930): pp. 156–60.

Nemours, August. *Histoire militaire de la Guerre de l'Independance de Saint-Dominque.* 2 vols. Paris: Berger-Levrault, 1925, 1928.

Nemours, Luc. "Julien Raimond, le chef des gens de couleur et sa famille." *Annales historiques de la Révolution française* 23 (1951): pp. 257–62.

Nicolas El Turki, Mou' Allem. *Expédition Française en Egypte.* Paris: Chez l'Editeur, 1838.

Ott, Thomas. *The Haitian Revolution, 1789–1804.* Knoxville: University of Tennessee Press, 1973.

Phipps, Romsay W. *The Armies of the First French Republic and the Rise of the Marshals of Napoleon I.* 5 vols. Oxford: Oxford University Press, 1926–1939.

Poyen-Bellisle, Isidore Henry de. *Histoire militaire de la Révolution de St. Dominque.* Paris: Berger-Levrault, 1899.

Quimby, Robert S. *The Background of Napoleonic Warfare: The Theory of Military Tactics in Eighteenth-Century France.* New York: Columbia University Press, 1952.

Quinney, Valerie. "The Problem of Civil Rights for Free Men of Color in the Early French Revolution." *French Historical Studies* 7.4 (1972): pp. 544–57.

Rodger, Alexander Bankier. *The War of the Second Coalition, 1798–1801: A Strategic Commentary.* Oxford: Clarendon Press, 1964.

Rogers, Hugh C. B. *Napoleon's Army.* New York: Hippocrene Books, Inc., 1974.

Ross, Steven T. *French Military History, 1661–1790: A Guide to the Literature.* New York: Garland, 1984.

———. *Quest for Victory: French Military Strategy, 1792–1799.* South Brunswick, NJ, 1973.

Rouel, Charles, "Historique du 13e Régiment de Chasseur à cheval." Paris, July 25, 1872. Service Historique de l'Etat-Major de l'Armée, regimental histories.

Roussier, Paul, ed. *Lettres du Général Leclerc.* Paris: Société de l'histoire des colonies françaises, 1938.

Scott, Samuel F. *The Response of the Royal Army to the French Revolution: The Role and Development of the Line Army.* Oxford: Oxford University Press, 1978.

Six, Georges. *Dictionnaire biographique des généraux et amiraux Français de la Révolution et de l'Empire (1792–1814)*. 2 vols. Paris: G. Saffroy, 1934.

———. *Les Généraux de la Révolution et de l'Empire*. Paris: Bordas, 1947.

Stein, Robert Louis. *The French Slave Trade in the Eighteenth Century: An Old Regime Business*. Madison: University of Wisconsin Press, 1979.

Stoddard, Theodore Lothrop. *The French Revolution in San Domingo*. New York: Houghton Mifflin Co., 1914.

Stoessinger, John G. *Why Nations Go to War*. New York: St. Martin's Press, 1985.

Susane, Louis. *Histoire d'Artillerie française*, Paris: Hetzel, 1874.

———. *Histoire de la Cavaliere française*. 4th ed. 3 vols. Paris: Hetzel, 1874.

———. *Histoire de l'infanterie française*. 5 vols. Paris: Hetzel, 1876–1877.

Tarrade, Jean. *La commerce colonial de la France à la fin de l'ancien régime: L'évolution du régime de "l'Exclusif" de 1762 à 1789*. 2 vols. Paris: Presses Universitaires de France, 1972.

Thiry, Jean. *Bonaparte en Egypte*. Paris: Berger-Levrault, 1973.

———. *Bonaparte en Italie*. Paris: Berger-Levrault, 1973.

Vaissière, Pierre de. *Saint-Domingue (1629–1789): La Société et la vie créoles sous l'Ancien Régime*. Paris: Librairie Académique Perrin et Cie., 1908.

Vertray, M. *L'armée française en Egypte*. Paris: G. Charpentier, 1883.

Vidal, Joseph. *Histoire et Statistique de l'Insoumission*. Paris: M. Giard et Briene, 1913.

Wilkinson, Spencer. *The French Army Before Napoleon*. Oxford: Oxford University Press, 1915.

Wilson, Victor Emmanuel Roberto. *Le Général Alexandre Dumas: Soldat de la Liberté*. Quebec: Les Editions Quisqueya-Québec, 1977.

INDEX

JOHN G. GALLAHER received a B.A. from Washington University and an M.A. and Ph.D. from St. Louis University. He also studied at the Sorbonne and the University of Grenoble and spent a third year in France as a Fulbright scholar at the University of Poitiers. He is a professor emeritus of history at Southern Illinois University at Edwardsville and the author of *The Iron Marshal: A Biography of Louis N. Davout, The Students of Paris and the Revolution of 1848,* and *Napoleon's Irish Legion.*